Trade and shipping
Lord Inchcape 1852-1932

Business and Society

General editor   **Alex J. Robertson**

Other books in the series

Ferranti and the British electrical industry, 1864-1930
J. F. Wilson

Trade and shipping
Lord Inchcape 1852-1932

STEPHANIE JONES

Manchester University Press
Manchester and New York

Distributed exclusively in the USA and Canada by St. Martin's Press

Copyright © Inchcape Family Investments Ltd, 1989

Published by Manchester University Press
Oxford Road, Manchester M13 9PL, UK
and Room 400, 175 Fifth Avenue,
New York, NY 10010, USA

Distributed exclusively in the USA and Canada
by St Martin's Press, Inc.,
175 Fifth Avenue, New York, NY 10010, USA

British Library cataloguing in publication data
Jones, Stephanie, *1957–*
    Trade and shipping: Lord Inchcape 1852–1932.–
    (Business and society).
    1. Shipping. Inchcape, James Lyle Mackay, Earl, 1852–
    1932
    I. Title II. Series
    387′.0092′4

Library of Congress cataloging in publication data

Jones, Stephanie (Stephanie Karen)
    Trade and shipping: Lord Inchcape/Stephanie Jones.
        p.   cm — (Business and society)
    Bibliography: p.
    Includes index,
    ISBN 0–7190–2351–3
    1. Inchcape, Lord, 1852–1932. 2. Merchant marine—Great Britain–
Biography. 3. Businessmen—Great Britain—Biography. 4. Shipping–
Great Britain—History. I. Title. II. Series: Business and
society (Manchester, England)
HE569.16J65   1989
387.5′092′4—dc19
[B]   89-2807

ISBN 0 7190 2351 3 *hardback*

Typeset in Great Britain
by Witwell Ltd, Southport

Printed in Great Britain
by Anchor Press Ltd, Tiptree, Essex

Contents

General introduction *A. J. Robertson*   vii

Author's preface   xi

1 Contacts and connections: early life in Arbroath and London, 1852–1874   1

2 The merchant's apprentice: business life in India, 1874–1894   11

3 Commercial spokesman and viceregal adviser: public life in India, 1874–1894   31

4 Shipowner and empire builder: business life, 1894–1914   49

5 Plenipotentiary and government watchdog: public life, 1894–1914   73

6 'Let us go on with the war': business and public life, 1914–1918   89

7 'Let us get on with our business': 1918–1932   121

8 Retrenchment and disillusionment: public life, 1918–1932   155

9 Conclusion   185

Appendix 1   202

Appendix 2   203

A note on sources   205

Guide to further reading   209

Index   211

To my sister and my brother-in-law, Lesley and Ian Bebbington,
with love

General Introduction

To most professional historians, and indeed most students of history at any level, business history is something of a mystery, both in the sense of being unfamiliar territory and in the sense of being regarded as the virtually exclusive preserve of a particular type of technical specialist. Over the eighty years or so of its recognisable existence, the field of business history has given rise to a fairly extensive body of literature, but only occasionally (in Britain at least) has any of it made much of a general impression. This is unfortunate, because the subject seriously merits more widespread notice among those who seek through history to understand how modern societies were formed. For the decisions made by businessmen and the activities of business corporations have had far-reaching consequences in forming the tastes, living standards, social *mores* and economic security of communities throughout the developed and under-developed worlds alike. We may argue about the nature of their influence, but there is not much room for doubt that it has been, for good or ill or some combination of both, as significant in its way as the influence of monarchs, statesmen, generals and politicians, whose prominence in the historical landscape has generally been more obvious.

The series of studies in which the present book appears, published under the collective title of *Business and Society*, is intended to help generate a greater recognition of the importance of business history by making the subject as accessible as possible to a wide readership. We hope, of course, that the series will be of interest to those with a professional commitment to business history, to whom it may be of particular use for the purpose of undergraduate teaching. But our particular aim is to reach those people with a general interest in modern history and the forces that shaped it, but who may lack any substantial previous acquaintance with business history. Accordingly, authors have been enjoined to avoid producing studies of business activity narrowly defined – for example, with a focus primarily on the internal workings of the enterprise. Such matters clearly have their place, but the books in the series are intended to accord at least as much attention to broader perspectives on business activity and its significance as an influence on public policy and taste and on patterns of economic and social life in general. In this way, we trust, the right of the individual businessman or the corporation to be considered on a par with more generally recognised arbiters of modern social development may be established.

There are several possible approaches to the fulfilment of this objective, and one would not have to agree entirely with Ralph Waldo Emerson's dictum, 'There is properly no history, only biography', to accept nevertheless that the biographical approach is one of the most useful. This may be particularly true in the British context, where business was traditionally a highly individualistic affair conducted commonly within family concerns with patriarchal structures of control. Several of the earliest volumes to appear in the series adopt the biographical approach: the present study of Lord Inchcape follows John Wilson's already published work on S. Z. de Ferranti and the early electrical industry. They will soon be followed by books on Sir Eric Geddes (who figures, indeed, with Inchcape in formulating the public expenditure cuts of 1922, popularly described as the 'Geddes Axe') and Sir Montague Burton. But later books will adopt different approaches, and will include studies of the interrelationship between particular industries and society as well as studies of prominent local business communities and their role in the life of their localities. While most of the books will focus on Britain, studies relating to other societies will be commissioned. All are intended to be brief, to eschew technical jargon, and to combine a readable style with sound, indeed expert, scholarship.

There can be no question about Dr Stephanie Jones's expertise on the subject of James Lyle Mackay, first Earl Inchcape. Having worked for four years as Archivist to the Inchcape Group, she has been in an unrivalled position to construct her account of his life and activities through an intimate knowledge of both the group's and the family's archives. The career that emerges is in many ways a remarkable one, spanning over half a century and at least two continents.

Inchcape's eminence in the business world during the fifty years that straddled the First World War is quite obvious. One has only to consider that, of the 12½ million or so gross tons of merchant shipping under the British flag in 1914 – some two-thirds of the entire world's sea-going tonnage – the combined fleet of the P&O and British India lines then under Inchcape's control accounted for fully one-eighth. If Britannia ruled the mercantile waves in 1914, then Inchcape was her merchant prince. That alone gave him a position of enormous influence in the affairs of both Britain and India, linked together by his ships, most especially in wartime.

But Inchcape's influence and significance were not confined to the sphere of merchant shipping, far less to the inner councils of the companies whose fortunes he controlled. As Dr Jones demonstrates, his public service extended over a wide range of affairs in both Britain and India, to such effect indeed that he entertained not unreasonable but ultimately frustrated hopes of becoming Viceroy. He was particularly influential, perhaps, in the financial and monetary affairs of both countries, and especially in determining for both the scale and distribution of public expenditure in the period following the end of the Great War. The 'Geddes axe', in which Inchcape had a hand, had an exact counterpart in the recommendations of the Inchcape Committee (1922–23) for India's public finances.

Dr Jones also makes clear Lord Inchcape's limitations. He was clearly out of his depth with currency matters, as his participation in both the pre-war Indian Currency Inquiry and the post-war Cunliffe inquiry into Britain's currency amply demonstrated. And for a man of such wide-ranging activities, he could be surprisingly narrow-minded – as witness his views on social welfare in general and education in particular. In a small-town shopkeeper, attitudes like Inchcape's might be of no account. But in a man of his standing and influence, they could and did have dire repercussions. However, he could also exhibit remarkable enlightenment for a man of his time and his class. He appears, for instance, to have had a real sympathy for the Indian people he came into contact with, to the extent that he learned Hindi and took part with enthusiasm in local festivals. More significantly, he was a powerful force in the 'Indianisation' of the British Raj during the 1920s.

Dr Jones clearly believes that luck played, in Inchcape's rise to fame and fortune, at least as important a part as any innate

qualities of character he may have had. The importance of luck
perhaps manifested itself most clearly in the early years of his
working life. It was in a sense responsible for taking him to India in
the first place, and it evidently combined with a strong constitution
to ensure that he survived and prospered there. Perhaps nationality
had something to do with his success as well. Certainly, Dr Jones's
book several times calls to mind J. M. Barrie's observation that
'There are few more impressive sights in the world than a Scotsman
on the make.'

A. J. Robertson
(General Editor)
Manchester
December 1988

Author's preface

In the context of this series, Lord Inchcape is seen above all as a doyen among shipowners, the man who personified the British shipping industry of the First World War and the 1920s. This was indeed the case; so much so that the connection between Inchcape's name and the P&O is still so strong that it is erroneously but commonly believed that the Inchcape group today owns, or is itself part of, the P&O.

But Inchcape's eighteen-year chairmanship of the P&O is less than half of the story. Before that, as narrated in the first three chapters, he was making a name for himself, first in Scotland and then in India: his breathless, youthful enthusiasm makes this a particularly colourful part of his story. As he became older, he was untiringly active in Government circles and in the media, constantly appearing on a plethora of Government committees and in contributing to newspapers and journals, and by no means only on the subject of shipping. Simultaneously, he was building up a vast commercial empire in India and beyond, whose origins and growth are described in the history of the Inchcape Group, *Two Centuries of Overseas Trading*, (Jones, 1986).

Inchcape's diversity does not detract from his suitability for this series; indeed, he was very much a businessman in society, who never saw his business interests in isolation, but in the larger context of British shipping and trading, within the British economy and the British Empire as a whole. Although his business and public careers constantly interacted, for the sake of clarity they have been separated in the text which follows. While not forgetting the close relationship between both aspects of his work, this study considers Inchcape's life partly chronologically and partly thematically.

This biography seeks to examine not only the role of a businessman in society, his impact on policy and the way he responded to economic change, but also many wider issues. Why did Scots such as Inchcape so dominate British enterprise overseas in the nineteenth century? Were Inchcape's activities beneficial or harmful in the context of British political, economic and social overlordship in India? Does Inchcape's story shed any light on the reasons why British shipping was all-powerful before the First World War, and why it rapidly stagnated and declined? What was the role of Inchcape and other businessmen in the national retrenchment of the 1920s? How did British commerce cope with aggressive nationalism in Australia and India? What changes took place in the business structure and organisation in the immediate post-Inchcape era of the early 1930s, in the wake of the Royal Mail scandal?

In writing this book, I have been privileged to meet a surprising number of people who knew and distinctly remember Lord Inchcape. Members of his family – Captain Nigel Bailey, the Hon. Alan Mackay, Sir Hugh Mackay Tallack and the present Lord Inchcape – spoke of a kindly family man who delighted in country pursuits typical of a Scottish laird. Those who knew him at work – including Sachin Chaudhury and Wilfrid Mizen – saw him as knowledgeable and professional, but tough and ruthless. Interpreting their insights, together with hundreds of letters (both personal and to the press, speeches, committee questions and answers, reports, memos and diary entries which Inchcape left, has been complex but stimulating.

Many have been subjected to parts of the Lord Inchcape story in various stages of its preparation: my own students at LSE and SOAS, and members of audiences at the universities of Glasgow, Exeter, Leicester, Manchester, Bristol and St Andrews and conferences in Japan, Poland, Berne in Switzerland, Perth in Western Australia and Charleston, USA. Comments and suggestions received were invariably constructive; I would particularly like to thank Professor Bernard Alford, Dr Frank Broeze, Dr Peter Davies, Dr Stephen Fisher, Dr James Foreman-Peck, Dr J. Forbes Munro, Professor Keiichiro Nakagawa, Mr Alex Robertson, and Professor Anthony Slaven.

Mr David M. Williams of the University of Leicester read and commented minutely upon the whole text twice; mere thanks here seem so inadequate. Colonel Andrew Harfield applied military precision to the manuscript beyond the call of friendship and duty; the book is sharper and more comprehensible as a result.

This study would not have been written but for the constant support and lively interest of the third Earl of Inchcape, who always made time to argue about his grandfather's investments, character, views, family relationships and business methods. His help in providing sources of information, especially in opening doors in India, emphasised the lasting prestige of the Inchcape name.

Stephanie Jones
The London School of Economics
January 1988

A contemporary cartoon of Lord Inchcape
(Inchcape family collection: by courtesy of the third Earl of Inchape)

1

Contracts and connections
Early life in Arbroath and London, 1952–1874

James Lyle Mackay was seen by most contemporaries, and certainly saw himself, as a self-made man. His later achievements – his earldom and his business empire – were held up as striking examples of individual enterprise unaided by privilege. Yet, in looking at his early life, we find that his family background was advantageous to his future; by the age of twenty-two, on the threshold of his great business adventure, he had behind him generations of Scottish commercial talent, a small private income, and several years' mercantile experience to draw upon. No one could ever say that he started with nothing.

What advantages was he born with and what advantages did he acquire in this period? That he was born in Scotland, at Arbroath on 11 September 1852, was to be of crucial importance to his subsequent career in India. The enormous preponderance of Scots among foreign merchants in the Indian sub-continent from the early years of the nineteenth century has frequently been pointed out, but rarely quantified or explained. A glance at the first Bombay Chamber of Commerce proceedings of 1836 shows that an overwhelming nine out of eleven of the founding trading houses were Scottish. Of the pioneering merchants whose companies make up the present Inchcape group, two-thirds hailed from Scotland. In analysing why this is the case, perhaps it is wrong to see Scotland as just a particular region of Britain. A recent study of the Mackinnon 'investment group' (Munro, 1985) for whom Mackay was to work and eventually succeed to the leadership of the business, suggested that:

With its own legal and banking arrangements, a distinctive education system supplying the talents required by its professional and business classes, and import-export trades across the North Sea and the Atlantic conducted independently of ports to the south, Scotland was well-placed in the years before the First World War to retain a high degree of autonomy in its economic growth and its relationship with the rest of the world. Industrialisation, more especially the rapid rise of Clydeside, created new needs for internal markets and sources of raw materials, and was accompanied by a major outflow of Scottish emigrants, capital and expertise.

There were negative as well as positive reasons why Scots looked to foreign lands to make their fortunes rather than in England: the nonconformism practised by many – although not by Mackay – inevitably precluded them from many opportunities, and their isolated background would prevent them fitting in easily with London society and the City. Exploring new commercial opportunities without needing to fit in with English rules was undoubtedly attractive. Despite the business possibilities brought by the advent of the steamship and growth of heavy industry, Scotland itself was too limited for its inhabitants. As Mackay himself emphasised in later life in a speech at his old school, 'Let me recommend you not to be afraid to go out into the world. There is no scope in Scotland for the energy, the brains, the initiative and the ambition of all the youth in the country ... if there is no prospect for you here, the sooner you get away the better'.

Certainly, Scots overseas, particularly in India, were proud of their reputation for dominating commercial and even political affairs. Lord Lansdowne, the Viceroy during much of Mackay's stay in India, proudly asserted that 'the affairs of the world would have come to a stop long ago but for the part taken in their management by my fellow-countrymen'. In this environment, business contacts were made more easily, especially by succeeding generations of Scots, who either joined existing firms known through the family, friendship or neighbourhood links, or made contact with them soon after arrival. Mackinnon himself, venturing out in 1847, had first worked at a sugar refinery in Cossipore, but quickly joined a fellow Campbeltown man, Robert Mackenzie, who already managed a general mercantile business.

James Lyle Mackay had all these advantages, but he was no ordinary Scot, from the point of view of the background of both his parents. Their marriage, in 1844, took place in Nova Scotia: Mackay's mother was Deborah Lyle, the daughter of Alexander Lyle, a famous shipbuilder of Dartmouth, N.S. The Lyles first came to North America from Glasgow, where Mackay's great-great-grandfather, born about 1720, had been a tanner. Settling in New York, they had been prominent United Empire Loyalists, maintaining their allegiance to Britain against the rebellion and declaration of independence of the majority of American colonists. Under threat of persecution, the Lyles fled to Canada, where they were given a grant of underdeveloped land. They were known as hardy pioneers, of Protestant background and of strong independent spirit.

The second generation of Canadian Lyles – both of whom had fought at the Battle of Bunker Hill – first settled on 200 acres at Shelburne, N.S., before moving to the nearby Clyde River where they established the oldest shipyard in this area. Mackay's grandfather, the third generation of Lyles, opened his own shipyard at Dartmouth in the 1820s. In the next decades, he built three steam ferries for the port authorities, and several sailing ships for Edward Cunard of Halifax, father of Samuel Cunard who pioneered steamshipping across the North Atlantic. A branch of the Lyle family had remained in Scotland and set up a shipowning business in Greenock; their fleet of small schooners and brigs, named after capes, were well known in Nova Scotia, and frequently traded to Arbroath. Alexander Lyle came to Scotland in 1850, to visit the Greenock business and his daughter and son-in-law.

Mackay's father, Captain James Mackay, was recorded on his marriage as also hailing from the Clyde River, where he was well established in shipbuilding, but reference was made to his status as a prosperous shipowner and shipmaster of Arbroath. In 1844 he was apparently in command of the mail packet *Velocity*, of which no details have been traced; other sources mention his command of the *Barbara*, built by Alexander Lyle. This would explain their acquaintance.

James Lyle Mackay's father's predecessors are more mysterious, but no less remarkable. His great-uncle, Captain William Mackay, achieved posthumous fame when his account of the wreck of the *Juno* in 1795 inspired the shipwreck scene in the second canto of Lord Byron's *Don Juan*. William Mackay had been second mate of the *Juno*, wrecked off the Arakan coast south of Chittagong. His survival was against all the odds, for the ancient and dilapidated 450-ton ship had drifted 250 miles for twenty-three days as a complete waterlogged wreck before sinking. Nearly all the crew of seventy-two, mostly Lascars, perished. Sailing from Rangoon to Madras with teak, she had struck a sandbank but her timber cargo kept her afloat. The remaining crew survived on distilled seawater and four old coconuts, and frequently contemplated cannibalism. After further voyages on behalf of the East India Company, and on board a troop ship within a military expedition to the French and Spanish West Indies and Egypt, Captain William Mackay died at Calcutta in 1804, aged only thirty-three, from a liver complaint resulting from his sufferings on the *Juno*.

The family of Mackay was well known in Shelburne N.S., and included Donald Mackay, born in 1810, who moved to Massachusetts and opened a major shipyard. James Lyle, brother of Deborah, worked there as a young man. Donald Mackay's fast sailing clippers were regarded as the *crème de la crème* of the golden age of American sail in the middle decades of the nineteenth century. His *Flying Cloud* could make San Francisco from New York in eighty-nine days; the *Sovereign of the Seas* made Honolulu to New Bedford in 103 days and created lasting speed records on the Liverpool to Australia run. Captain James Mackay may have been connected with this family; we do not know when he was born, but the fact that he came from Nova Scotia and was already an established shipbuilder, shipowner and master both in Canada and Arbroath by the time of his marriage conflicts with local evidence that his father was works manager of the small Brothock Mill.

Instead, a more convincing explanation has been put forward by a prominent genealogist, to the effect that Captain James Mackay's father – and James Lyle Mackay's grandfather – was a well-known laird from a distinguished Scottish noble family, with strong connections with India. This explanation puts a new perspective on Mackay's start in life. Although there is no evidence that his aristocratic relatives subsequently supported their illegitimate offspring, they did apparently help to set up James Mackay's business in Arbroath and in Nova Scotia. Captain James Mackay's mother, Christina Mackay, may well have been related to the Mackays of Shelburne. Her illegitimate son was probably born about 1816, making him at most aged twenty-eight at the time of his marriage.

Nothing that James Lyle Mackay ever recorded suggests that he grew up in the atmosphere of tales about his noble relatives, their deeds as imperial pro-consuls in India or their achievements in commerce and public life. His aristocratic connections were apparently quite well known in Arbroath, although not widely publicised. Illegitimacy still carried a certain stigma, of course, and Mackay was certainly rather embarrassed about his unmarried grandmother in Arbroath. On the other hand, his distinguished forebears were not to be ignored altogether.

Captain James Mackay and his wife Deborah Lyle settled in Arbroath. The Lyles meanwhile had their shipyard in Greenock, and were closely connected with the Chapel family, with whom Alexander Lyle ran his shipyard in Dartmouth.

Arbroath was a fine place for a boy to acquire an enthusiasm for shipping and trading. It was to breed and nurture several famous men besides James Lyle Mackay; the noble house of Dalhousie (with a distinguished record of public service in Canada, India and other parts of the Empire) the original Buick of Buick automobiles in the USA, the founder of Burmah Oil and the inventor of the postage stamp, James Chalmers, all hailed from the locality. By the 1850s, more than a hundred ships were owned at Arbroath. From the Baltic ports, Russian flax had been imported in large quantities for the local linen industry since medieval times. There was a regular coastal service of small smacks and schooners to Leith, Glasgow, Newcastle and London. Local coasting firms included D. Corsar's Flying Horse Line, whose names were taken from Sir Walter Scott's *The Antiquary* – set in Arbroath and powerfully conveying its atmosphere – during James Lyle Mackay's early childhood. It was a thriving, prosperous town, exporting bale goods, grain, salt and fish and its imports – besides flax – included coal, iron and chemicals. Local industries were fishing, boatbuilding, tanning, shoemaking and silversmithing, clockmaking, handspinning and weaving, and the most prominent local firms were the engineers Douglas Fraser & Sons and Alexander Shanks & Sons.

Shanks's iron works, founded in 1830, were famous throughout Britain for pioneering the development of lawnmowers, producing the first effective model in 1842. Arbroath 'grassies' were to become a familiar sight on the courts of Wimbledon and on the best lawns in the land. By 1854, just after James Lyle Mackay's birth, the firm expanded to larger premises at 'the Dens' where they diversified into constructing conservatories and agricultural implements, supplying Bell's reaping machines and rollers, and manufacturing cranes, pumps, locomotives and even small iron tugs and ships' gear.

As equals in commercial status the Mackays were close friends of the Shanks's, and the young James grew up with their children. He won the friendship of Jeannie, Jane Paterson Shanks, although the Shanks had reservations about their subsequent marriage, because of Christina Mackay and the illegitmacy of the young James' father. On the early death of his parents – of which more later – James was cared for by a relative of the Shanks's, one Margaret Ambrose, unaccountably known as 'Aunt Higgins'.

Captain James Mackay's mercantile interersts expanded rapidly in the 1860s and his two sons, William Aberdeen and James Lyle were to become closely and enthusiastically involved in the family business. Mackay senior had been impressed by the opening up of trade with Australia during the Gold Rush, when such famous shipping companies as the Black Ball Line advertised passages to Melbourne in sixty-three days for sixteen guineas. In command of the *El Dorado*, Captain Mackay had offered the first service from Dundee to Melbourne and Port Adelaide in September 1852, the month of James' birth. Built in Dundee, she was registered in Arbroath in November 1852 as majority owned by William Mackay, merchant, with William Garland and James Muir, also merchants. The first named was a half-brother of Captain Mackay – another son of Christina – and the others were fellow Arbroath merchants. James Muir was subsequently to act as the young James Lyle Mackay's guardian.

The *El Dorado* was followed by a series of investments in vessels and trading ventures. Apart from the *Velocity* and the *Barbara*, we know nothing of Captain Mackay's earlier commands and we have no direct evidence that his activities enjoyed the support of his aristocratic relations. But by whatever means, he was now a wealthy man. One of his most successful vessels was the 308-ton barque *Asia*. Built at the Cochar yard in Montrose in 1859, the *Asia* was half owned by Mackay. Muir held the bulk of the remainder of the shares, by that date referring to himself on the register as 'banker'.

By 1859 James Lyle Mackay was seven, and pestering his father to be allowed to accompany him and his older brother to sea. His first voyage was very nearly his last. From Montrose to Archangel and back to Kirkcaldy, it was a long voyage, taking more than a week to transit the Pentland Firth. At Archangel, young James fell overboard twice into the Dwina River, to be rescued first by a brave Russian boy and then by the ship's cook. After several other voyages (without young James) the *Asia* was sold to Tasmanian owners and hulked in Australia in 1917 after fifty-eight years' service.

In 1861, Captain Mackay acquired a controlling interest in the 616-ton *Seafield*. On her maiden voyage to Bombay, he was tragically swept overboard off the Arakan coast, not far from the wreck of the *Juno*. The *Seafield* was taken over by Captain Mackay's executors; Muir and an accountant, John Sim, whose family was to become connected to the Mackays by marriage. Muir, who was to become the provost of Arbroath, took over Captain Mackay's interests in the *Asia* and the *Seafield*. Mackay had also invested in the 272-ton barque *Witch of the Wave* and the 247-ton barque *Clansman*; on his death, they were sold locally, remaining on the Arbroath register. The proceeds of the sale of these ships then became young James Lyle Mackay's inheritance.

James Lyle Mackay's elder brother William, four years his senior, obtained his masters' certificate at Dundee in 1871, aged only twenty-three, and in the same year acquired a certificate of competence as a steamship master. He took over the command of the *Seafield* until 1876, voyaging to the Cape Colonies, Ascension, St Helena, India, Burma, Mauritius and the Red Sea. He then became master of the *Elliot* of 1,117 tons, purchased by James Muir from the proceeds of the sale of the *Seafield* and the rest of the family business. An iron-built barque, she traded to India and the East until 1887 when William appears to have left the sea. Far too large to enter her home port of Arbroath, the *Elliot* achieved fame in 1882 as the only jute-laden sailing ship to dock at Dundee twice in one calendar year having made a remarkable two round trips to India during that period.

So young James grew up in an adventurous maritime tradition, but from the start favoured the land-based organisation of shipping rather than seafaring itself. His mother died shortly after her husband and, with his brother away at sea most of the time, he had to fend for himself. But Muir took him under his wing, and provided him with an income of £100 per year by investing his patrimony – his inheritance – of £2,000 in the *Elliot* and other ventures. This was a great deal of money in the late 1860s. For instance, a typical Arbroath dwelling – such as one advertised for sale in Croal's yard – consisting of house, backyard, coal cellars and garrets with an adjoining office and garden, could be acquired for £90. The entire George Inn with several rooms, stables, offices and shops, went for £500.

Young James' father had found difficulty in keeping the boy at school: even at the age of six he frequently played truant from the schoolrooms in the abbey ruins, mixing with seamen and merchants down in the harbour, and he was not afraid to stand up against teachers. His father must have believed he had potential – or perhaps felt that his lucky escapes on the *Asia* meant he was destined for higher things – so he sent James to Arbroath Academy. He was again fiercely independent, standing out among other lads also brought up in a tradition of single-mindedness and courage.

A few surviving letters to his schoolfellows showed that he adapted well to staying with his foster mother, 'Aunt Higgins' and visiting Provost Muir, his guardian at weekends, and that he was always game for anything. He went horse riding 'and not being accustomed to it I could hardly walk when I came off, and today at School the boys had a good laugh at me.' He looked forward to the deep winter despite the cold because of the chance to go skating. The letters reveal that he also had difficulty spelling: he was much more interested in a practical rather than academic education, despite the fact that in 1863, his mother, shortly before she died, had sent him to the prestigious Elgin Academy. Mackay's classics master at Elgin remembered only that he had boxed his ears for his rather free translations from Latin. He never did learn to spell perfectly – although he wrote with a fair hand – preferring to spend his time in illegal salmon fishing in the nearby Lossie and the Spey, and making friends with engine drivers on the Great North of Scotland Railway.

After a short and unremarkable scholastic career, young James was helped by Muir to find his first job, as a scrivener in an Arbroath lawyers' office. At least he could put his handwriting talents to good use, but he was frustrated by office work and left within a year to become a clerk with local rope and canvas maker Francis Webster. He liked it little better, but at least he respected the authority of his employer, who described Mackay as a 'forward sort of boy ... extremely naughty ... who would never come to any good'. From the outset, he was taught obedience and respect for authority, and keeping the firm's inner workings secret: 'Now Jeemie, you are to do as you are bidden and not a word must go out of the office, either black or white'. He was to set great store by this advice in the management of his own businesses in the future.

Mackay's pay was minimal: £5 for the first year, £10 for the second and £15 for the third, but this could be used as pocket money whilst the income from his patrimony mounted up. He put in long hours at Webster's and learnt the meaning of hard work. His employer finally admitted: 'Jeemie is no' a bad laddie, but he's a damned sicht ower-ambitious'. He was right.

By 1872, aged twenty, he could suffer Webster's and Arbroath no more, and scanned the newspapers for an opportunity in London. Muir, his guardian, helped him find a post with the prestigious Gellatly, Hankey, Sewell & Company. Founded by Duncan Dunbar in Limehouse in 1796 to deal in wines and spirits, the business had diversified into brewing, exporting India Pale Ale during the Napoleonic Wars. By 1862 the firm specialised in the buying and selling of merchant ships, managed a fleet of over seventy sailing vessels, owned shipyards and teak forests, and traded to the Sudan and the Middle East. They were Lloyd's agents in Hamburg, Marseilles and all over the Middle East. Then run by a senior employee, Edward Gellatly, the firm became leading cargo-loading brokers in London for many major shipping lines, including the mighty British India Steam Navigation Company (BI), an association it maintained for over a century.

When Mackay joined the Company as a trainee shipping clerk at the Leadenhall Street offices, with a salary of £50 per year, he found himself in the thick of the shipping industry: Gellatly's handled passenger bookings and cargo for such famous vessels as the *Cutty Sark*. A colleague related that after several months at the Bill of Lading desk, Mackay was appointed clerk of the Customs Department, transacting all the business relating to HM Customs. It was his work to clear through customs all goods consigned to the firm at Leadenhall Street, and all the goods shipped by them, paying all the Port and Trinity Light dues. Mackay had to provide vessels with documents for clearance not just in the Thames but in foreign ports of call. He had to accompany all outward bound vessels to Gravesend, where he met many of the captains who were later to become his associates in India.

Gellatly's were now developing new routes, operating sailing ships and only adapting to steam when forced to by the opening of the Suez Canal. In association with Thomas Wilson, Sons & Company, Gellatly's tried to rival the P&O in their service from London to Bombay, Colombo, Madras and Calcutta. They were to compete with Donald Currie's Union Castle Line on the South African run, and ultimately strained their relationship with the BI after forming their own Mogul Steamship Company in the pilgrim trade.

Thus, on his arrival on Mackinnon Mackenzie's doorstep in Calcutta in 1874, James Lyle Mackay was a young man to be reckoned with. His predecessors included the famous North American shipbuilders, Alexander Lyle and Donald Mackay, the hardy Captain William Mackay of the *Juno* and (if rather indirectly) a great Scottish noble family of considerable standing among the British in India: although his new employers were not aware of this.

Although Mackay was inexperienced in the ways of Indian commerce, by 1874 he already knew much of seafaring, shipowning and trading for someone so young. He was practical, strong, determined and independent, and in India his talents were given free rein.

2

The merchant's apprentice
Business life in India, 1874–1894

In twenty busy years, Mackay's abilities were stretched to their utmost, his early ambitions were formulated and largely achieved, and he absorbed influences which shaped his future outlook. The young shipping clerk of 1874 – fired with enthusiasm after landing an enviable and prestigious appointment, with a measure of confidence from his experience in London, and cushioned financially by the private income from his patrimony – was transformed. By the early 1890s he had acquired a degree of recognition and influence which he was to extend and draw upon for the rest of his life.

This period set the course for his commercial, public and private life, a course from which he was to make but few deviations. Firstly, he rose to prominence in the firm of Mackinnon Mackenzie and dedicated himself to leading the expansion and consolidation of the old Mackinnon Eastern shipping and trading empire into new geographical and commercial fields. Secondly, as discussed in Chapter Three, he established himself as an active spokesman of the mercantile community in India, both British and native, gaining the attention of political authorities in India and Britain through the influential platforms of the Bengal Chamber of Commerce and the Viceroy's Legislative Council. Thirdly, he achieved a personal happiness and security in his private life which underlay and encouraged his commercial and public achievements.

Mackay's business achievements were the result of both luck and judgement, and both favourable circumstances and the creation of opportunities. He was especially fortunate in his firm. Working for Mackinnon Mackenzie in Calcutta virtually guaranteed his prominence in British India. During Mackay's stay in India and for many years afterwards, it was undoubtedly the greatest shipping agency and managing agency firm in the mercantile world. With its associated tea, jute, coal and river steamers business through Macneill & Co., (see Jones, 1986 for further detail). Mackinnon Mackenzie was the leading trading and industrial pioneer in India and the hub of a network of enterprises at the heart of India's economic infrastructure. A position with them was the commercial equivalent of a place at Oxford or Cambridge.

Surviving evidence suggests that luck, more than outstanding personal credentials, played an important part in this appointment. Mackay was one of many young shipping clerks and assistants hankering for romance and a fortune in the East. Competition for overseas postings was intense. Sir William Mackinnon, founder of Mackinnon Mackenzie and the BI, who was to be Mackay's greatest patron, was inundated with requests to find positions in India. At least a quarter of his personal correspondence at this time dealt with pleas on behalf of the sons of the Scottish gentry, all of whom were receiving expensive public school education and able to pick and choose from a variety of openings, and yet were attracted to working for Mackinnon. Mackinnon, however, favoured self-motivated, experienced shipping clerks to work for his firm. Mackay's middle-class Scottish background stood him in good stead, and he had performed sufficiently well and gained enough experience with Gellatly's to be included with other candidates for a post in India, appointment to which was handled on Mackinnon's behalf by the firm of Gray, Dawes and Co. in London.

Gray Dawes had been founded in 1865 by Mackinnon to provide business opportunities for his nephew Archibald Gray, and Edwyn Sandys Dawes, a favoured young P&O officer. Both knew the Indian commercial scene well but had been forced home through family responsibilities and ill health, and both subsequently came to know and work with Mackay. Gray Dawes acted as Mackinnon Mackenzie's London agent and frequently came into contact with Gellatly through the latter's cargo and shipbroking work for the British India Steam Navigation Company (BI).

An anecdote of unknown origin confirms that Mackay was one of a crowd of hopefuls, and that he was by no means the most outstanding. The first and second candidates chosen by Gray Dawes had hesitated; the former wanted to go on his long-awaited summer holidays, and the latter felt obliged to seek parental permission. Mackay – typically – expressed unbounded eagerness and said he could sail that night, if necessary. There could be advantages in being an orphan.

There is no evidence that Mackay was subjected to a medical examination before his departure, but memoirs of his contemporaries show that this was usually the case, and that it could be rigorous. Mackay would find no problem here. His robust good health, encouraged by his healthy outdoor life in Scotland, was to be crucial in his performance and survival in India.

Edwyn Sandys Dawes, on the other hand, never took to the Indian climate, and the high death rate of Europeans after only a short sojourn in the subcontinent is clear from the tombstones in Calcutta's Park Street Cemetery – many wives and children died within a few months of arrival. For example, the children of Major General Nott, the 'hero of Ghazni', were all buried in 1812, and the well-known socialite Lady Anne Monson, a great-granddaughter of Charles II, fell victim to the climate in her first season.

Such stories would be known to Mackay, but did not deter him. Unlike most other Mackinnon Mackenzie employees, who quickly became 'seedy', Mackay was to thrive in unwholesome Calcutta and Bombay. Even in 1892, after eighteen years in India, he wrote that 'my health is standing out so well that I hope to be able to be in Calcutta for more of the hot weather than I contemplated when I proposed the Simla arrangement (staying up in the hills with his family) a year ago'.

The attraction of working for Mackinnon Mackenzie far outweighed any worries of danger or disease, even if Mackay was only aware of its association with the British India Line. Every fifth ship entering Calcutta by the mid-1870s was a BI steamer, in a trade dominated by British tonnage, with only the occasional visit of vessels under the Italian, Norwegian, French or German flags. The British India Company, originally the Calcutta and Burmah Steam Navigation Company, had been floated in 1856 with a paid-up capital of £39,800. Its early success with the contract to carry mail from Calcutta and the Burmese ports enabled Mackinnon to raise a total of £342,685 by 1865. The funding for the BI and all his associated ventures had been initially provided from Britain. It was supplemented from subsequent profits and from local, Indian capital raised under the managing agency system; this was the means whereby British firms acted as managers for a variety of small British and Indian businesses, assisting in their development and growth.

When Mackay was appointed, Mackinnon Mackenzie – according to a ledger dating back to 1849 – had long been thriving. Allowed a continual supply of credit from the City of Glasgow Bank of up to £15,000, net profits averaged Rs 16,171 or nearly £1,300 per year in the 1850s, providing Mackinnon and his two partners, Robert Mackenzie and James McAlister Hall, with over £400 each, compared with an annual salary of only £75 paid to Mackinnon's young nephew Peter in 1851. By 1853, the firm's assets had risen to Rs 744,402 or £57,250. Half way through Mackay's time in India, Mackinnon Mackenzie was to remit annually to Britain over £32,000, based on sterling funds of only £180,000 and a small working capital, representing a return of over twenty per cent. Yearly net profits for distribution at home were to rise to over £½m before Mackay left. He was to play a crucial part in this remarkable performance, and rapidly became indispensable to his firm.

Mackay's notes of his three-month voyage to India in 1874, at the age of twenty two, provide insights into several facets of his character, not least his great enthusiasm for understanding the technical aspects of steamshipping and navigation and, incidentally, the attitudes of his contemporaries:

I was on the Bridge with the Skipper when he was looking out for the light at sea. He could not sight it. The fact was, we were too far out. After having starboarded for a short time, we sighted the light and he exclaimed, 'There it is, the blackguards have just lighted it. Why do the British Government allow the Portuguese to hold that place?'

Such knowledge and keenness, which prevented him from remaining a passive passenger (later during the voyage the captain wakened him at a moment of particular crisis as they approached Calcutta!) must have been simultaneously impressive and irritating to crew and fellow passengers. Although he may not have intended to appear so, he must have seemed a know-all. His remark that 'we called at thirty-two ports on the way round and I can remember them all in sequence to this day' suggests pedantry and a boyish train-spotting mentality – both remained prominent personality traits throughout his life. He certainly concurred with the captain's views, and always held an unquestioning conviction of Britain's right to rule India.

The leisurely voyage gave him the opportunity to make friends and join in communal pranks, such as an incident on the overland journey between Alexandria and Suez before mail steamers used the canal. All the passengers detrained for refreshments and paid for full meals but consumed only the first mouthful of their soup. The imminent departure of the train was then announced, a ploy on the part of the shrewd Indian authorities to make money on the catering without actually providing it. A seasoned fellow-passenger suggested that as the train was solely for them and thus would hardly leave empty, everyone should stay and raid the store room:

'We did this and we rifled it of bread, butter, cheese, tins of all kinds, bottles of wine and beer, and everything we could lay our hands on. We then made for the train amidst the shouts and threats of the people who owned the refreshment room.'

Mackay's unabashed enjoyment of light-hearted and schoolboyish fun was to endear him particularly to Indian staff, and toned down the rough edges of a harsh and intolerant side of his personality which featured more prominently in his later life. That his enthusiasm and optimism during this early voyage was not dampened by sharing a cabin with seven other occupants, with only two small hand wash-basins and no fan, in the treacherous heat of the Red Sea, showed a pride in physical hardship that was to earn incredulity and grudging respect from his contemporaries.

That Mackay was originally detailed to Calcutta, and not to an obscure backwater, was another example of his early good luck. In 1874, Calcutta was a thriving port and major city with a population of nearly half a million. The business community's offices were centred around Burmah Bazaar and Waterloo Street, and they lived in Park Street and Chowringhee, following 'the practice of European people to reproduce as far as possible in the settlements and colonies . . . the characteristic social features of their national lives'.

The wealthy merchants lived in two storeyed 'pukka' houses and palatial mansions. Chowringhee was the least densely populated part of the city, with only 23–30 people per acre, and it was the first locality with public streetlighting. According to a contemporary guide, Calcutta had 2,720 gas lamps, 131½ miles of (mostly) stone roads, a new and 'first class' market for the European quarter and over 3,500 hackney carriages. The Bengal Club organised balls and sweepstakes, making Calcutta an exciting Eastern metropolis.

The poverty and overcrowding of the native areas would have struck Mackay as much as the comparative splendour of the European sector. Besides 7,500 Europeans, over 274,000 'Hindoos' and over 110,000 'Mahomedans' with a scattering of Chinese were crowded into the city centre. The floating population numbered several hundreds of thousands, and many more lived in ancient, fire-prone thatched huts, banned since 1837, in areas packed with over 700 persons per acre. As the census enumerator recorded:

In the European quarter perhaps little now remains to be done; this portion of Calcutta indeed may fitly compare with any other city in the world; but the native town is still far from being in that state in which one would desire to see it ... vast areas of solid filth and numberless collections of liquid sewage remain untouched, except for baneful use by the people themselves.

Commercial opportunities in the second city of the British Empire were practically unlimited. Nearly 900 vessels of almost a million gross tons entered the harbour each year. In 1874-5, imports were valued at forty-eight crores (a crore was 10m rupees) equal to £40m, excluding specie, or gold bullion and coins, and exports at over £45m including specie. The Port Commissioners, whom Mackay was to join ten years later, were supervising the building of additional jetties, wharves and harbour accommodation, vital with the rapidly increasing tonnage of steamers passing through the Suez Canal and arriving at the port. In 1870-1, steamships totalling 80,000 tons entered Calcutta; by 1876-7, arrivals totalled over 400,000 tons, each ship nearly double the average size of five years before. The Chamber of Commerce, founded in 1853, and later of great significance in Mackay's career, had eighty-six members by 1874, with over thirty Scottish firms including – besides Mackinnon Mackenzie and Macneill – Begg Dunlop, Finlay Muir, Jardine Skinner and Mackenzie Lyall, together with other British houses, Italian, German, Greek and American businesses and eight banks; but only seven native Indian merchants.

On arriving in Calcutta Mackay was, in his own words

cordially received by the senior partner, Mr Duncan Mackinnon [Sir William's nephew] and his charming wife, and after staying with them a few days, I transferred myself to a boarding house at No.10 Middleton Row, where I made the aquaintance of many youngsters like myself – assistants in mercantile firms.

What impression did Mackay make when he arrived? To Duncan Mackinnon, T.M. Russell, W.P. Alexander and E.D. Wylie (who had worked for Mackinnon Mackenzie since 1860, 1861 and 1871 respectively) he was fresh, enthusiastic and hardworking. The senior partners laboured under constant criticism from their superiors in Glasgow, who wrote between themselves of the ineptness and laziness of their colleagues in India; Mackay surprised them by throwing himself into this work with great dedication, as he had done for Gellatly's, immensely proud of the prestige of working for India's premier managing agency house and shipping line. In describing his first few years in Calcutta he wrote: 'I was installed in the office in a very minor capacity but, by degrees, more responsibility was given to me and I did my best to work for the firm and the British India Company.' He found himself involved in a plethora of local and international issues, many of which feature in the minutes of the Bengal Chamber of Commerce, providing an insight into Mackay's concerns during his first years in India.

Mackinnon Mackenzie, represented in the Chamber by W.P. Alexander, joined in the clamour for revising customs tariffs, producing accurate returns of imports and exports to argue their case: lobbied for new jute warehouses; pressed for a survey of the River Hooghly together with a new bridge over it; called for a telegraph service between Calcutta and Rangoon; and complained vociferously of the P&O's poor handling of the Indian mails and the long delays at Suez. Mackinnon Mackenzie were also involved in the compilation of a new tonnage schedule by the Chamber, and the establishment of a new system of testing and verifying weights and measures. They were particularly interested in the new prospects for trade between Burma and West China, and encouraging the 'country produce' trade of the Indian interior.

Mackinnon Mackenzie's importance in the Chamber is indicated by the fact that after a discussion of a bill to increase the accommodation allowance for native passengers on steamers, the chairman passed the whole matter over to them to resolve. The Government of India's generous allowance of nine square feet per person between the decks with six square feet on deck for exercise was criticised by W.P. Alexander, who pointed out that 'what may be necessary for a pilgrim steamer going to Jeddah, where a peculiar class of passenger is on board for twenty days, is not necessary for a coasting steamer where the passengers may be on board but ... a few hours'. These objections received due attention and the bill was dropped. The firm's significance is also revealed by a Chamber survey of firms requiring special export passes. Mackinnon

Mackenzie needed 214 separate export passes compared with only
ten for Finlay Muir & Co., and handled eight out of the total of
fifteen ships cleared with dutiable cargoes in the period of the survey.

Particularly controversial issues considered by the Chamber at this
time included the devaluation of silver and the possibility of India
adopting the gold standard; and the protection of infant Indian
industries versus the advocacy of completely free trade. His firm's
involvement in these questions was a window on to another world
for Mackay.

His experiences were further widened by travel. In 1877 alone,
Mackay was sent on lengthy expeditions along the firm's trade
routes, to Karachi, Gwadur, Muscat, Lingah, Bahrain, Kuwait,
Abadan and Basra. Aged only twenty-five and after just three years
in Calcutta, this was indicative of the trust placed in him by his
superiors.

A network of services by British India Steamers had been
established in the Persian Gulf since 1862, and by the time of
Mackay's visits it dominated the major Gulf ports and monopolised
the trade of the smaller and more remote outposts. Contemporary
notebooks and ledgers kept by Mackinnon Mackenzie and their Gulf
agents, Gray Mackenzie & Co. and Gray Paul & Co., reveal a
growing business in exporting dates, Arab horses, pearls, cane oil
and wheat, and importing tobacco, wool, coal and British and Indian
cotton piece goods. Mackay's attitude to his work shows his great
enthusiasm, energy and attention to detail:

I visited the steamers early in the morning, got to know the captains, the
officers and the engineers, as well as the native serangs, and I picked up
Hindoostani as quickly as I could. I found all the native establishment in the
office extremely agreeable and intelligent and we pulled together.

This view of the Indian labour force, although now possibly
appearing patronising, was undoubtedly sincere, and there is no
evidence that other partners and assistants took as much trouble as
Mackay did in learning their language and acknowledging their
customs. Perhaps the explanation lies in the fact that contact with
Indians coincided with Mackay's first experience of leadership. He
also found it easier to make friends in the smaller, more closely knit
European community of Calcutta than he had done in London,
thanks to his increased prestige. Furthermore, he was now enjoying
greater wealth:

I found my salary of Rs300 [about £25] a month for the first year, Rs 350 [£29] for the second and Rs 400 [£33] for the third, quite sufficient for my requirements and I lived well within it and did not require to draw on the income from my patrimony which was accumulating at home.

£25 a month was riches after £5 a year in his first job, and was considerably more than he could have earned in a comparable position at home. Long experience in handling his own finances, a careful Scottish upbringing and microscopic scrutiny of all items of expenditure were second nature to Mackay. During his time in India, he never drew on his patrimony at home. There were many opportunities for extravagance and financial profligacy in Calcutta, and several assistants quickly found themselves in debt. Mackay was to argue in later attacks on the high level of income tax in India that it was more expensive to live there than in Britain.

His careful financial management was among the qualities which most impressed the 'Seniors', as the senior partners were known. A cable from Calcutta to Gray Dawes in London in 1878 requested them to 'send us another assistant like Mackay', and communications were frequently sent from the Calcutta office to Mackay on his Gulf visits, asking him to return to deal with impending crises.

Mackay achieved such recognition so early not only because of his talents. His rise to prominence coincided with a time when the Seniors in Calcutta were ageing and tiring of the East: Russell and Alexander had done eighteen and seventeen years respectively, Wylie did not appear to have particular promise, and the young William Currie (uncle of the future chairman of P&O) was yet to appear on the scene. At the same time, developments on the East African coast were becoming increasingly attractive to the chairman and occupying much of his attention. Mackay's serious, dedicated and conscientious attitude and experience of dealing with captains and engineers – who respected his genuine knowledge of shipping matters – made him reliable and trustworthy. In a large London office full of thrusting, ambitious young managers and clerks, Mackay would not necessarily have seemed so exceptional, but in the context of Calcutta, where heat, discomfort and a plethora of servants encouraged inactivity, and where incompetent or unruly clerks and assistants could not be sacked and replaced in an instant, he was outstanding.

The reputation he had established in Calcutta made possible the

second breakthrough in Mackay's career. In 1878, partly as a result
of the collapse of the City of Glasgow Bank, the BI's Bombay agents
Nichol & Co. went bankrupt. As stated earlier, this bank had been of
crucial importance to Mackinnon Mackenzie in its early days, and
Mackinnon himself had been appointed a director in 1858.
Distrusting his fellow directors, he had resigned in 1870. By the time
of the collapse, Mackinnon had sufficiently distanced himself from
its affairs so that an attempt by the liquidators to sue him for alleged
malpractice during his directorship was dismissed in the Edinburgh
Court of Session in December 1881. By 1878, Mackinnon Mackenzie
were already remote enough from the Bank to be able to take over
Nichol & Co.'s affairs. Mackay was the obvious choice to take
charge, any possible hesitation on the part of his employers swept
away by his characteristic enthusiasm. According to notes made in
later life, Mackay departed Bombay within hours and 'found the
work quite interesting and had no trouble ... within a few weeks I
had surrounded myself with an efficient European and Indian staff'.

To Mackay, Bombay had all the attractions of Calcutta and more,
with the added advantage that his seniors were safely at arm's length
and he had considerable scope to run the business on his own lines.
According to a census of 1881, Bombay had nearly twice the
population of Calcutta (nearly 750,000 compared with just over
400,000), and had a thriving social life which Mackay felt freer to
enjoy than in Calcutta. An income of approximately Rs 400 or £40
per month enabled him to play a full part in society activities
including the famous Byculla Club, the Royal Bombay Yacht Club,
and the Bombay Hunt for which horses and hounds were brought
out every season from home. Mackay acquired a weekend hunting
lodge cum bungalow in Bandra, handy for the hunting country. His
love of this sport, which combined a somewhat contradictory
attachment to his horse and dog with an enthusiasm for killing
jackals, hyenas and any other prey available, stayed with him for his
entire life.

Besides its clubs and hotels, Bombay had five restaurants, four
theatres and a host of department stores and shops, including an
Italian confectioners, established since 1835, which advertised 'three
kinds of ices daily. Fresh pastry. Refreshments. Orders for ice cream
and ice puddings executed at the shortest notice, from 9 am to 11 am
daily'. Whisky, popular with the Scottish community and regarded
as a universal panacea for the ills of the East, cost Rs 27, or just over

£2 per dozen bottles of imported Teacher's. Beer was Rs 21 for six dozen pints.

Yet Mackay did not allow these distractions to tempt him from his responsibilities, working a twelve-hour day, doing a large amount of the necessary canvassing work personally and accompanying native clerks to the bazaars to book pilgrims for BI ships. The BI enjoyed a large passenger trade at Bombay, despite the competition from other European lines and local companies such as the Bombay Steam Navigation Co. and the Indus Flotilla Co. By 1877–8, customs receipts on imports totalling Rs 738,000 (nearly £70,000) were earned by the port on general merchandise, spirits and tobacco. The opium trade, which Mackay was to strongly defend against morally-inspired attacks from Britain, was thriving. Just over 40,000 cases were handled by the port of Bombay in 1871–2, which remained constant throughout the 1870s and 1880s, providing much work for BI steamers, although the P&O monopolised the lucrative China trade. Altogether, with nearly one and a half million tons of steamers entering Bombay each year, Mackay's shipping agency business flourished. By 1884–5, its receipts exceeded those of Calcutta and accounted for more than half of the Mackinnon Mackenzie's total remit that year. Equivalent to over £32,000, they reflect Mackay's achievement in building up this business.

Mackay's activities in Bombay extended beyond day-to-day concerns and embraced wider commercial and imperial issues. In 1882 he had written asking the authorities if the rumours he heard about abolishing or reducing the duty on Persian opium, if transhipped at Indian ports, were true. If so, should not some concession be secured from the Persian government in return, he argued, such as the opening of the Karun River to free navigation? The Shah was strongly opposed to the suggestion, but the Foreign Department of the Government of India did try out Mackay's idea. Output of opium from Persia was increasing rapidly, and was dominated by the BI and other British shipping lines, so Britain had considerable leverage. The idea behind reduced duty payable for Persian opium at Indian ports was to attract opium cargoes to Bombay. Mackay was supported by George S. Mackenzie of Gray Dawes in London, who had previously run their businesses in Persia. This ultimately led to the full opening of the Karun in 1885, another source of profit for the Mackinnon group. Gray Dawes had first suggested the idea to the Foreign Office in 1876, to open up trade between Mohammerah (now Khorramshah) and Isfahan, but it took Mackay's intervention to bring the project to fruition.

A rare insight into Mackay's early working life in India is provided by a letter he wrote towards the end of his work in Bombay to the BI secretary in London. His conscientiousness is revealed in his reference to the heartbreaking matter of cargo shortage. Pilferage was one of the greatest problems – it was almost impossible to provide security at every stage of loading and discharge, but *Nerbudda* on her last voyage – 'Calcutta to Bombay and back coasting – showed almost a clean page in shortages – fourteen rupees [just over £1 sterling] I think will cover her claims.' Mackay was already getting used to managing staff:

The clerk ... you sent us some time ago is an excellent man and to him much is due for this satisfactory result [the reduction of shortages]. I rewarded him by giving him spontaneously an increase in pay. This is the second clerk I have thus dealt with in the last four months and I believe the effect has been good.

Mackinnon Mackenzie struggled to pay their way before their business took off in the late 1880s and 1890s. The debit balance of August 1884 was Rs 8000, about £700, which rose to Rs 18,000, over £1,500 the following month. Mackay worried that because of 'unscrupulous shippers we deal with' Mackinnon Mackenzie were not always receiving the freight due to them for carrying the goods on the BI steamers. 'If any receipts show a less measurement, a remeasurement clause is inserted in the Bill of Lading, and as this means a certain delay in the delivery, shippers are thereby deterred from trying to put through smaller measurements.' This was a shrewd observation on Mackay's part; over the previous decade he had learned the deceptiveness and cunning of the typical Indian merchant.

Other matters with which Mackay was concerned, on instruction from the BI secretary in London, included the need to reduce crews as much as possible when vessels were laid up for repairs. He found this difficult, because 'our European staff except in cases of long lay-up we can never dispense with because they can't be paid off and allowed to go to their homes here as in England'. The native crews had to be kept on, 'because they are cheaper than daily labour would be and more efficient for the purposes of lifting out machinery, setting up rigging, scaling and painting etc'. The BI secretary in London also tried to reduce the number of engineers on the smaller steamers to three. But all the staff in India were against this. 'In the case of the *Pachumba* on the Kurachee line this was managed because there happened to be a very workable willing old Chief in her named Jupe, but we can't manage it as a rule.'

Sir William Mackinnon back at home was trying to negotiate an increased Government subsidy for the Calcutta and Bombay services offered by the BI, and had asked Mackay to put pressure on Government officials on the spot. He was greatly trusted by Mackinnon already, and had sufficient contacts with Government officials to represent the BI case to them. But Mackay did not always go along with his chairman.

I question if we will be able to get a remuneration worth the Company's while to come under any strict contract. The longer we work without a contract, the greater do the advantages of being free appear to be – only of course, there is always the consideration that the round sum from the Government at the end of the year is a desirable addition to earnings. The Post Office seem quite callous on the subject.

The British mail subsidy was always much less than those offered by other governments.

A new BI service to Madras was vetoed by the Government of India, but overall their existing services were faring adequately. 'I think we are entering on a better period here now for coasting business. The crops in Bengal are excellent and there will be a good demand for grain on the Western coast this year – we have had an uphill fight for several months now.' Mackay's predictions of the turnaround in the company's performance were to come true.

Almost as an afterthought, although it was a matter of great importance to him, he wrote, 'this letter is written at home and my wife is upstairs and has just presented me with a daughter I am told'.

Another insight comes from the reflections of an ex-employee, Shivram Ramchandra. His exaggerated regard for Mackay may have been prompted by a hope for handsome remuneration from the interviewer – Bolitho, writing Lord Inchcape's life in 1936 – but some of his factual reports may be trusted. Mackay lived in a 'chummery' with a fellow merchant, Mr William Bell of Messrs Wm. Bell & Co. and the editor of the *Times of India*, a Mr Curwen. And he still enjoyed a prank:

he rode much on his favourite chestnut horse and occasionally rode up the

stairs into the office to frighten us. After dismounting he would give the
horse a biscuit or so to eat and order it to get down, which it obeyed.

Ramchandra certainly saw Mackay as exceptional among the
Europeans working in Bombay. Most of these would shrink from
dealing directly with Indian merchants and unsavoury, travel-stained
pilgrims, preferring to send trusted Indian assistants. Mackay had no
such scruples, and his grasp of Hindi gave him an advantage over his
colleagues; as far as he was concerned, he was just doing what he
would normally do in London. He went to greater lengths than they
to take every opportunity to expand business, encouraging the
Madras and Southern Mahratta railway authorities to negotiate with
the Portuguese government for the extension of their line to
Marmagod, so he could acquire the agency to supply and transport
the materials required for the construction of the line. His acceptance
of a contract to carry a lucrative consignment of camels despite a
lack of steamers, ferrying them in sailing ships made safer and more
stable with sand ballast, was still discussed with amazement in
Bombay a generation later.

Mackay's fairness to Indian employees, interest in their religious
customs, frequent gifts and small acts of kindness certainly endeared
him to them and helped him succeed in Bombay. Another reason for
his success was his ability to act quickly. He was working at the
Bombay office when the merchant banking firm, Baring Brothers,
suffered a major financial crisis and temporarily closed its doors.
Mackinnon Mackenzie had no money with Baring, but shared an
office in Bombay with Baring's local representatives. On news of the
crash early in the morning, the court registrar promptly sealed the
entire building. The doorman hurried to tell Mackay, who rushed to
his office, broke the seals, and carried the most vital company ledgers
and files back to his own house before anyone in Bombay's business
community knew what was happening.

It was in Bombay that Mackay's usually reliable health first
suffered and, much to the dismay of his seniors in Calcutta, he set off
for home. The normal period of work before the first leave was six
years, and it is possible that if fever had not struck Mackay after his
seven years, he might not have returned home until even later.

Mackay's achievements at Bombay – building up the firm from
indebtedness to an annual remit of over £17,000 in three years – were
rewarded by a coveted partnership in the Calcutta firm. Allowed ten

per cent in the Bombay firm soon after he began to work there, in May 1884 he was awarded five per cent at Calcutta, after William Mackinnon's thirty-eight per cent, Peter Mackinnon's twenty per cent (the Glasgow and London partners retained the lion's share), Duncan Mackinnon's twelve per cent, Alexander's eight per cent, Neil MacMichael's six per cent, though ahead of Russell and Currie's three per cent each. By 1884 his emoluments had increased considerably, being allowed 'Rs 1000 (approximately £90) per month and allowances of Rs 250 for house rent. If needful Mr Mackay also may be called upon to entertain friends at the firm's expense'.

In 1885 Mackay put down £2,000 of his own money in the Bombay firm, but did not immediately take an interest in investing in shares in local businesses and other enterprises. Surprisingly, in view of his later investments and acquisitions on behalf of P&O and the Mackinnon/Inchcape group he was initially reluctant. He had been informed in October 1888 of the availability of a block of Sir William Mackinnon's shares (over £57,000 worth in the Northern Dooars and Upper Assam Tea Companies and in the Rivers Steam Navigation Company). Others had been glad to accept some at a low price, yet 'sometime ago Mackay indicated that he did not care particularly about having a share of these investments, but perhaps he might now wish to have them at the price against each'. Being invited to apply for shares was seen as a privilege extended to valued senior employees, and Mackay changed his mind and quickly instructed that the necessary £3,390 be debited from his account held by the firm in Glasgow which, as was typical of his financial prudence, was also to take care of the resultant dividends. Mackay's share of the partners' £25,000 capital held in Glasgow was only £1,965, and there is no evidence at this stage that this increased. His total credit at Calcutta, Bombay and Karachi in 1886 totalled only Rs 85192 of a total of Rs 3411550 (or approximately £7,500 out of £300,000), at the bottom of the list of partners.

The only other investment of Mackay's noted in the firm's records before 1890 is £20 towards ten Australasian United Steam Navigation Company Limited shares, valued at £480 on the company's flotation in 1887. The AUSN was formed by a merger of two prominent Australian coastal fleets, its capital of £600,000 invested mainly by Mackinnon and his associates, and the shipbuilding firm of Denny. With the Queensland mail contract and the largest fleet on the coast, the AUSN dominated this trade.

Mackay was to increase his holdings and become a director of the AUSN in 1894. His investments remained modest until his return to London, when he was to lead Mackinnon Mackenzie to such prizes as Binny's, discussed in Chapter Four.

Mackay's caution and, to a certain degree, meanness (he prided himself on living frugally and never drawing from his patrimony income at home) did not stem from lack of means. Before he left India, he purchased BI debentures of £900 in 1891 and £600 in 1892, and the marriage settlement he bestowed on his wife, a generous £10,000, was also invested in the shipping line. It was his marriage after he returned to Scotland on leave that fired his ambitions to succeed in his firm and in his money-making plans, so that she (and the several subsequent children) could not only live comfortably, but could enjoy the enhanced social standing that accompanied the position of leading merchant. Climbing to the top of the tree of the firm meant putting his own money into its roots and branches. This Mackay did: nearly half of his total recorded investments were in Mackinnon-related enterprises. They represent a substantial increase in his earnings compared with those on his arrival, reflecting his firm's increased profits.

Mackay became a partner in a range of businesses in India managed by Mackinnon's nephews Duncan Macneill and John Mackinnon, whose managing agency house, Macneill & Co., formed in 1872, handled the affairs of the Northern Dooars and Upper Assam Tea Companies. These had been established after the foundation of the Assam Company in 1839. Macneill also managed the Assam Railways and Trading Co., formed in 1881, and the Rivers Steam Navigation Co., set up in 1865. Mackay also put money into the Bengal Central Railways, and the Oriental Banking Co.

£11,700 was dutifully sent to needy relatives in Scotland and to bail out his bankrupt father-in-law. £4,000 was spent on buying his in-laws' home in Scotland. His only disastrous dabble was in the River Plate Railway Company, the only non-Indian concern in his portfolio, in which he lost £1,050. He always kept several thousands of pounds with Mackinnon & Co. in Glasgow.

Mackay, by the time he left India, earned Rs 2000 (£125) per month emoluments with an additional Rs 600 (£37) for rent and entertaining, substantially more than he might have earned back home. With the income from the investments outlined above, his disposable cash was dependent upon the firm's profits. Tracing the profits of partnership firms is hindered by the lack of a legal necessity to keep accounts, but surviving remittance figures and the pressure from London- and Glasgow-based partners on Mackay to maximise these at all costs, show that nearly all the money earned by the firm went home. In contrast with the postwar period, only a small working capital was kept in India, and Mackay frequently complained that even this was under-employed. A minor speculation he undertook with the firm's 'petty-cash', earning £50 on £5,000 in a month literally by putting the money in the nearest bank, was frowned on by his superiors.

Mackinnon Mackenzie's remittances rose steadily to the equivalent of £32,000 in 1884, £38,000 in 1885, £177,000 in 1888, £580,000 in 1890 and £581,000 in 1891. Although it would appear that these earnings were drained from the subcontinent, this was not really the case at all. The cost of keeping offices and paying clerks, especially in India, was low for a merchant business compared with a manufacturing or processing concern. Mackinnon Mackenzie had no enormous band of shareholders to placate, no artificially high level of dividends to maintain which could prevent expansion of its business. Remittances were largely distributed to the partners, and principally to Sir William Mackinnon before his death on the eve of Mackay's departure from India in 1893. For example, of the £177,000 sent home in 1888, Mackinnon's share equalled a generous £94,525. We can calculate Mackay's share of these remittances reached an overall total of £89,400 (or five per cent of the annual remittance) by the time of his departure, of which nearly half was invested directly in Indian-based businesses. There is also evidence to suggest that other partners were doing likewise: as early as 1884, before the firm's profits really took off, £47,000 was put into Assam tea properties, of which £15,000 was raised by Mackinnon himself. The £50,000 worth of shares which Mackinnon sold to the junior partners in 1888, to which Mackay subscribed £3,390, was only a small part of his overall holdings on behalf of the firm. Besides investments in the BI and various Mackinnon group firms, extensive capital was put into jute mills, coal mines, coffee estates, tea gardens, river steamers, banks and railways.

Munro (1985) has shown that the bulk of the capital in two of the largest and most powerful companies based in India at the end of the nineteenth century – the BI and the Rivers Steam Navigation Co. – was put up by Mackinnon and his contacts. Much of this must have been derived from remittances from his own merchant partnership, Mackinnon Mackenzie. And these were no small sums: the capitalisation of the BI in 1865 was £342,685, of which 17.2 per cent or about £60,000 had been raised by the Mackinnon and Hall families. Mackinnon and his immediate partners also put up 57.4 per cent of the capital of the Rivers SN Co. The rest of the money came from their business associates in Scotland and in London, raised specifically by them.

These direct investments in companies operating in India do not include other ways in which Mackinnon Mackenzie's earnings were spent in the subcontinent. For instance, most of the pay received by European assistants – to say nothing of local staff – was disbursed on day-to-day living expenses. Mackay frequently complained that these were higher than living in Britain, especially in view of high local taxation and the declining value of the rupee.

Thus, it would not be accurate to accuse either individual entrepreneurs like Mackay or Mackinnon or their firm as a whole of showing no interest in the future of the subcontinent and using their earnings solely to feather their nests back in Scotland. Although they did become substantial property owners back home, and put money into non-Indian ventures in East Africa and Australia, their role in capitalising much of the infrastructure and future industries of India should not be underestimated. Of vital subsequent importance to India and the rest of the world was their financial support of Binny's, which was to become a giant among Indian-based textile businesses, to be discussed in Chapter Four. Even so, we do not have complete evidence here that this money was being used in India – if much of it was being put into British-owned Indian-based businesses, was it not still coming back to Britain eventually? And even if Mackinnon Mackenzie were especially interested in investing in India, perhaps they were the exception rather than the rule, and the many other firms in India were draining it of funds. A recent study by James Foreman-Peck (1986), looking at profits from firms and from home charges for the military and administration, has found no evidence of massive capital gains to Britain. Indeed, he argues that 'India seems to have found an extraordinarily cheap source of government and private capital in Britain, judged merely by the rate of return, much lower than Britain actually received from her other overseas investments ... '.

In Mackay's final few years back in Calcutta before his return to England, he was consulted increasingly by the other partners, and began to play a dominant part in all aspects of the firm's affairs.

Less directly concerned with his working life were two particular features of British existence in India also seen in contemporary literature, such as Kipling's: firstly, the popularity of the expatriate community of India as a marriage market for eligible and not-so-eligible young ladies back home, and secondly, the preoccupation of almost everyone living in the subcontinent with the climate. Rather comically and vulgarly known as 'the fishing fleet', shiploads of ambitious young females landed regularly at Indian ports. Many met prospective husbands *en route*. As a result, young men who had summoned their fiancées from home sometimes lost them on the way: four times over in the case of one of Kipling's unfortunate heroes.

Mackay, who had brought out and married his fiancée without mishap, found himself involved in this business when he received a plaintive letter from a distraught young lady who, using her status as niece of the director of one of the railway lines in which Mackay invested, asked for her passage money to be refunded. She could not return to Britain at this point due to what she delicately described as her 'imminent premature confinement' and obviously wanted to cash in her return ticket for ready funds. Finding herself pregnant and left in the lurch by an uncaring rogue back home, she had embarked for India in the first available ship, which happened to be the P&O *Rewa*. With a stronger and more urgent motive than her rivals, she seduced the irresponsible master, Captain Rise. Despite her protestations of the premature nature of the child's birth, Mackay's doctor, sent to verify the truth, affirmed that the pregnancy was full-term. Anxious to avoid scandal, Mackay refunded her money, paid the doctor and gave her a thousand rupees (around £70) out of his own pocket, to help her leave Calcutta as soon as possible. Of the admonished and regretful Captain Rise he wrote: 'I suppose he is not much worse than the majority of sailors except he had the misfortune to be found out'.

Those used to the comparatively equable climate of Britain often underestimated the debilitating effects of the extreme heat of an Indian summer. Mackay's letters are full of references to the weather, not just in relation to his own health and well-being, but to the effect it had on shipping services and on the harvest. Everything hinged on the arrival of the monsoon for the crops: in a typical June he wrote, 'we are still without rains in Calcutta but another week should bring them', but he was still anxiously awaiting rain in mid-July. His wife was unable to stand city heat as summer approached, and Mackay packed her and the children safely off to Simla which, with Darjeeling, was one of the most popular hill-station retreats.

The severity of the climate brought frequent cases of illness and disease. Mackay's wife and children, despite the healthier climate of Simla, frequently fell victim to dysentery and various fevers, and a son named Jamie sadly did not survive to adulthood. Mackay's colleagues and friends similarly suffered. Whilst one partner, Nichol, was sent home with brain fever, Mackay wrote of his friend Rivers Currie, 'I am sorry to hear he is so seedy. It would be a good thing for him I think if he could get employment at home or in the colonies. He will never be fit to work in India'. The word 'seedy' was also used to describe Duncan Macneill, who died soon after his arrival, and William Currie's health was seen as not admitting any longer stay in India. Mackay, on the other hand, enjoyed generally good health himself, and this may be seen as one of the reasons for his love of India and success there. Yet he had his own complaints: 'I am very fit but I am getting horribly fat ... the climate of Bengal seems to have this effect after a certain time of life.'

So when, in May 1893, Sir William Mackinnon's health was failing and he wrote to Mackay requesting his return, the latter decided that, after nearly twenty years, 'there is nothing to keep me in India'. He would not leave, however, until he had negotiated the renewal of the BI's mail subsidy from the Government of India – for the thrice-weekly Bombay to Karachi service – which he won for another ten years. When Mackinnon died later that year, although the chairmanship passed almost dynastically to James Macalister Hall, Mackay's power in the partnership was already firmly established, and his ultimate rise to the leadership of what was to become the Mackinnon/Inchcape group was practically assured.

3

Commercial spokesman and viceregal adviser
Public life in India, 1874–1894

Mackay's first experience in public life shaped his outlook in his future dealings with Government: anger and impatience with bureaucracy, and a strong sense of Britain's responsibility for the economic development of India for its own sake, and not just for the benefit of Britain. In these respects he stood out among his fellow British Indian officials, both in India and at home. This was partly due to his background: he came to public duty without the usual Civil Service training, university education or noble birth. He had no preconceived attitudes towards the role of Government, but saw State affairs with the eyes of a businessman. Mackay's ideals were efficiency, economy and making the most of wealth-generating opportunities: he had little time for moral and diplomatic issues. He was to make many mistakes – through ignorance and over-enthusiasm – but learned a great deal and left India more committed than ever to playing a part in the British administration of the subcontinent.

Mackay's official duties in this period fall into four main areas: his work on the Bombay Chamber of Commerce in 1879–84; his membership and then presidency of the Bengal Chamber of Commerce in the 1890s and work as a commissioner of the Calcutta Port Trust; his election and service on the Viceroy's Legislative Council; and his evidence before the Indian Currency Committee in London in late 1892. How did he gain these positions? What did he achieve? What did he, and the British as a whole in India, fail to achieve?

In Chapter Two, we saw how Mackay's marriage – although few details about it survive – fired his ambition to rise in his firm and to invest in a wide range of businesses in India; it was also the impetus behind his interest in public life. His courtship of Jeannie Shanks on his return to Scotland on leave in 1881 and their marriage in 1883 was to change his life completely and provide him with a new goal: that of heightened social status, a desire for honours and recognition, not for himself but for his wife. Before, as a bachelor, he had been content to mix among expatriate society in the Royal Bombay Yacht Club and Calcutta's Tollygunge Club as a prosperous and up-and coming merchant, enjoying 'chummery' life and was generally unconcerned with social standing.

After his marriage, he wanted to prove himself as an official of the Government of India, convinced that only they, and not the despised commercial class, could receive the prestigious titles and awards, such as the coveted CIE (Commander of the Indian Empire) that conveyed the appropriate social status which he wished to share with his wife. It is not known whether or not she wanted such honours; the significance lies in the fact that he wanted to give them to her. His new ambition was that she should have a worthy place in the rigid social pecking order instituted by the memsahibs of the Raj. He thought she was entitled to this. As their marriage contract recorded, she was 'Jane Paterson Shanks, daughter of James Shanks of Rosely, engineer in Arbroath'; as discussed in Chapter One, Shanks was in fact owner of the town's largest iron foundry. Although Mackay and his wife had been childhood sweethearts, not until he was established could he ask for her hand, and approach Sir William Mackinnon and the other Seniors for permission. Marrying without the firm's permission – or far worse, marrying a native Indian girl – swiftly terminated many promising careers. Employees stayed bachelors until their firms decided that they could afford to maintain a wife in the manner dictated by society in British India. Jeannie's constant and intelligent support was to play a vital part in both his business and public life for the next forty-nine years.

Early useful experience for Mackay's future public service came from his membership of the Bombay Chamber of Commerce committee from 1879 to 1884. The Bombay Chamber was later to proudly boast that 'J.L. Mackay, or Jimmie Mackay as he was then known, afterwards Lord Inchcape, spent the first period of his business career in Bombay and was for a short time a member of the committee'. It was traditional for the most prominent commercial houses to join the Chamber, and as the holder of the BI and

Mackinnon Mackenzie agencies – and many others – Mackay saw this as part of his job.

Issues concerning the Chamber on Mackay's arrival in Bombay were dominated by the income tax question; first levied at three and a half per cent, it was later to rise to over fourteen percent. But Mackay's initial task was to help with a survey of the best use of Indian resources, and the encouragement of Bombay's local exports. He assisted in the promotion of new commodities such as divi-divi (a substance for tanning), india-rubber, China grass, aloe and wild plantain.

Mackay argued that 'nothing should be done to prevent India from finding markets for her manufactures in other countries' but the Chamber would not advocate the abolition of local export duties, on which the port's revenues depended. Mackay then suggested reducing export duties but increasing excise on tobacco, a rapidly expanding and steady trade, which enabled many of these new commodities to develop without restrictions but without Bombay losing revenue. The port was to need all this income and more, as its traffic came to a halt in the cholera epidemic of 1882–3 and much of its grain trade was lost when the local railway rates were increased and grain shipments were redirected to other ports. This trade recovered, and more than half a million tons of grain was being discharged annually at Bombay by 1885.

Mackay then became involved in a debate over the proposed Factory Act. He objected strongly to the definition of children as those aged under thirteen only, argued that at least one hour in twelve should be allowed for the daily meal, and seconded a proposal that factories should close for one day a week. All his recommendations where included when the Act finally received assent in 1881.

In his next task, to introduce a uniform tonnage scale throughout India in cooperation with the Bengal Chamber, Mackay was less successful. Each port dogmatically preferred its own local system. In trying to improve the efficiency of the shipping industry in India, Mackay found himself up against not only Government of India bureaucracy, but strong regional traditions. He complained of the plethora of Indian religious festivals and holidays, which – although he enjoyed being drawn into them, and gained support and affection from Indian merchants and clerks as a result – severely disrupted the trade of the port.

When Mackay and his wife settled back in Calcutta in the mid-

1880s, he was thus already experienced in committee work. With the Bengal Chamber of Commerce, he considered the expansion of Calcutta's trade and a range of local shipping and trading issues, attacked the imposition of Indian income tax, and defended India's opium trade.

Mackay's status with Mackinnon Mackenzie alone ensured his prominence in the Bengal Chamber, even without the reputation for energy and ideas which he had gained in Bombay. At first, he was asked to look at the establishment of telegraph signal stations at strategic points around Calcutta harbour, the appointment of Thomas Cook & Sons as pilgrimage agents for the Government of India, proposals for a uniform system of jute measurement, and the need for extra local railway services for the benefit of shippers using the new Howrah dock. He helped to develop the raw wool trade from Tibet to Bengal, forwarding Tibetan raw wool samples to appropriate mills at Cawnpore and Dharisal, to take advantage of the rise in processed wool prices in international markets. He found the cheapest rates for carrying teak railway sleepers for the new railway for Gwalior State.

In helping develop the range of Indian exports and improving internal distribution networks, Mackay organised a special conference to investigate the building of the Bengal–Nagpore railway. He was told by the railway authorities (it was to be State-developed, as in the case of seventy-five per cent of India's railways) that the country through which it was to pass was uncultivated and undeveloped. Mackay pointed out that in the Central Provinces rice cultivation had doubled since the construction of a local railway and opening up of markets, and argued that the Bengal–Nagpore railway could do the same. As the chief engineer told Mackay, 'if the people found a market, they could produce grain in any quantity'.

The British in India have been criticised for the harm they caused to the Indian textile industry, but Mackay went to great lengths to involve Indian spinners in discussions of the Indian Merchandise Marks Act, designed to regulate the quality of Indian piece goods and yarns for export to France and French colonial markets. Under Mackay's presidency, native Indian merchants joined the committee for the first time. Mackay also insisted that employees of members of the Chamber should be encouraged to sit examinations in native Indian languages, and he made the necessary arrangements with the university authorities.

Of greater importance was the threatened Government of India levy of income tax on shipping and other commercial profits generated in India. Mackay gained the Chamber's support by asking how this would affect partners of India-based firms now resident in Britain who still maintained large investments in India, such as Sir William Mackinnon and others. And what if an employee's salary was paid partly in India and partly elsewhere? The Chamber, led by Mackay, forced the authorities to accept the exemption from this extra income tax of, firstly, investors living in Britain and, secondly, shipping companies, at least those like the BI which were registered in Britain and traded foreign.

The Madras Chamber had been less vociferous in opposing the tax, so the Government of India tried implementing it there first. The tax was supported by the British Government who argued that it was justified by the recent dramatic increase in trade – although Mackay suggested that declining salt tax revenues was a more likely explanation – and the exchange banks were instructed to issue lists of depositors.

Mackay asserted that although such a tax was levied in Britain, the principle had never been officially accepted in India, and he supported the banks' refusal to reveal names. He accused the authorities of trying to renege on their agreement to exempt from tax those deposits where the depositor resided in Britain. With the Bengal Chamber's offered solidarity, the Madras Chamber successfully frustrated attempts to make a test case of a firm capitalised in Birmingham. But in the majority of cases, the authorities ignored the Chambers' combined protestations, and those of other pressure groups such as the European and Anglo-Indian Defence Association, which Mackay had also joined. Some Chamber members – although Mackinnon Mackenzie were fortunately exempted by virtue of their shipping business – experienced greatly increased tax rates. One member's assessment of 1889–90 was more than three times that of 1888–9.

This new tax was in addition to the existing income tax, which was regarded as highly unjust to British expatriates and Indians alike. For example, European employees working in India-based mills found that even the portion of their salaries paid in England were being taxed. Mackay protested strongly that anyone earning under £150 p.a. in Britain was exempt from income tax, but of those paying income tax in India, ninety per cent earned less than Rs 2,000, worth just over £100 with the rupee exchange down to 1s 2d by 1890.

Mackay helped to start an anti-income tax movement to maintain the pressure for reform, organising a special conference at the Chamber in May 1890. He proposed a strategy whereby all commercial establishments would send memorials and telegrams to the Viceroy, and the Chamber would help fight each case in turn. Income tax had been increased in 1885 to defend the North-West Frontier at a critical time, which had now passed. To maintain it, and add a tax on profits at a rate of two and a half per cent, which included all the small markets and bazaars was, he argued, completely unacceptable.

Mackay was more successful in dealing with the opium question of May 1891. Sir Joseph Pease MP, a self-appointed guardian of international moral values, claimed in the House of Commons that the Indian population, to say nothing of consumers in the rest of the world, was suffering mass intoxication and death as a result of the iniquitous opium trade which should be abolished forthwith.

Suitably primed witnesses from various Indian medical and cultural bodies were assembled by Mackay to argue that opium was relatively harmless, and actually beneficial against fever. Moreover, if the Government of India was not reaping the financial rewards of the trade, then the princely states and other countries would, and British India stood to lose six and a half crores of rupees (over £5m) per year.

Raga Doorga Churn Law, representing the British India Association, strongly supported Mackay. He could imagine

nothing so preposterous from a practical point of view as the abolition of the Indian Opium revenue. There could be no doubt that numbers in India, perhaps one-third of the people, used opium in moderation and benefited by it. Opium indeed is better than drinking alcohol ... the people all over India complain of poverty owing to the displacement of manufacturing industries which formerly flourished. If the opium industry is to be stopped in obedience to the outcry in England, hundreds of thousands of ryots [peasant proprietors] will be made to suffer.

No other crop would pay so well as opium. Total revenue had grown from the equivalent of £1.6m in the 1880s to £5m in 1891 alone. On these grounds, as Mackay hoped and expected, the matter was dropped.

Mackay's enthusiasm in contributing to many aspects of public life in

Calcutta, especially those with a bearing on his business interests, also extended to the Calcutta Port Trust, and he became a Port Commissioner in 1885. This was less prestigious and more pedestrian than the Chamber, but equally worthy as a rung on the ladder to becoming an official. It was time-consuming, at least twenty-six long meetings per year, on top of his work at the Chamber which, including subcommittees, involved attendance at least twice a week.

The port certainly had problems and needed efficient management: expenditure on dock works incurred debts of nearly £1m, yet more shipping accommodation was desperately needed to service arrivals of more than a thousand vessels of nearly two million gross tons per year. Shipping calling at Calcutta via the Suez Canal had risen dramatically. In 1870, only fifty-one steamers, of an average of only 1,598 tons entered Calcutta via Suez; by 1883, over 200 steamers of an average of more than 3,000 tons made this journey annually. Calcutta was becoming increasingly dependent on steamer traffic transitting a French-owned waterway completely outside the port's control.

Mackay thus became drawn into a controversy that Britain should have her own canal. Ninety per cent of shipping using the canal was British, but Disraeli held less than half the shares, which had increased in value sixfold since 1870, the Suez Canal Company paying shareholders a dividend of fourteen per cent annually, equivalent to more than £19m. In company with the other port commissioners and most of the shipping interest throughout Britain and India, Mackay believed that shipowners were overcharged, and that these revenues were not helping improve the canal. Delays were increasingly frequent, with transit taking three days and more. It was now too narrow for the increased size and traffic of shipping. Steam barges had to be employed which, according to the shipping press, 'charged usurious rates'. Mackay was also concerned that although he and fellow merchants often endured the imposition of quarantine regulations 'at our Indian ports, where there is not one tithe of the cause for epidemic that there is amongst the crowd of miserable and filthy pilgrims whom the Egyptians allow to huddle together'. The Suez Canal authorities would not risk a decline in revenue from imposing quarantine regulations.

A larger, British canal could avoid delays, ensure a passage of twelve hours, and impose its own rules and standards. The estimated cost was £8m. With 3.7 tons of British shipping passing through the

canal, bringing in nearly £1.6m in dues per year, the proposed canal
could, in theory, pay for itself in five years. It would encourage cheap
wheat exports from India, and help expand other commodities. The
plan was scotched by an overall downturn in freights, and gradually
the British shareholding in the existing canal increased. Mackay
himself was to obtain shares and a seat on the board in the 1920s.

British canal or not, Calcutta's shipping accommodation problems
continued. During Mackay's time as a commissioner, from 1885 to
1984, the running of the port did improve substantially, and local
Indian interests played a larger part. At Mackay's behest, three
Indian merchants joined the Port Trust and, in supervising dock
work costing the equivalent of £4m, he favoured a local concern
despite competing tenders from well-known firms in Britain
including Sir W. Armstrong & Co., the Thames Iron Works Co. and
the West Cumberland Iron & Steel Co.

The new works were funded by the tramway, which brought in the
equivalent of £25,000 p.a., the tea warehouse which earned nearly
£5,000 p.a. and a variety of import and export duties, including those
charged at the petroleum wharf. Calcutta still needed better facilities
for pilgrims: the latrines on the river frontage were completely
inadequate, and the long queues for vaccination disrupted port
traffic. Muslim women, who would not even show their faces in
public, objected to being examined by the medical authorities in
front of everyone else, and had to be provided with a special
building. Similar pressure then came from the Hindu community for
a 'dressing room' for their ladies. More latrines were provided, but,
significantly, ten were built for Europeans, each with four seats,
whilst natives and dock workers made do with four with eight seats.

Mackay was closely involved in all these decisions, and received
hearty thanks for his work: but he was occasionally the butt of
complaints. Mackinnon Mackenzie were accused of bribing assistant
harbour masters to allow their steamers to proceed directly to
Garden Reach – the BI dock – before submitting voyage
documentation, on payment of Rs 16, or just over £1. Mackay
unashamedly replied that the BI thought the extra expense was
worth it, and that the practise should be legalised. It was.

Mackay's talents in public life were recognised at the highest level
officially in late 1890 and early 1891. On 11 February 1891, the
Calcutta daily *Capital* announced:

this morning we welcome to the Viceroy's Legislative Council Mr J.L. Mackay, the resident partner here of the powerful house of Mackinnon Mackenzie & Co. Mr Mackay is a very young man [thirty-nine] for the position he fits so well in Calcutta; he owes that position entirely to himself; for barely a dozen years ago he was an assistant in the building where he now reigns supreme ... his appointment to the Council is an endorsement by the Government of the public approval; it only remains for him to be called to the Shrievalty [he became Sherrif in December 1981] and he will have filled all the offices that merchants here can look to occupy.

Capital was not always to be so generous to Mackay.

How did Mackay win the viceregal attention to such effect? In October 1890, the Director of the Indian Marine wrote to the Viceroy, Lord Lansdowne, that during the recent Burmese expedition, Messrs Swann and Kennedy of the Irrawaddy Flotilla Co., whose vessels had been hired by the Government, 'were given the CIE and Mr J.L. Mackay of the BISN Co. who, in my humble opinion had done more service to the Government in the same expedition, got nothing'. He also mentioned the charter of other BI ships, supervised by Mackay 'who managed a fleet of nearly a hundred steamers' in the expeditions to Egypt and Suakin in 1882 and 1884 respectively, pointing out that 'Mr Mackay's energy and zeal in furthering every wish of the Government was conspicuous, not only in cases where the interests of the company were concerned, but also in those of the Government'. Mackay's CIE was gazetted in the New Year.

Mackay's first direct contact with the viceroy came in response to the latter's request to the Bengal Chamber to produce a uniform weights and measures system between British India and East Africa. Mackay forwarded the suggestions of Sir William Mackinnon, by then back in Britain, for the benefit of his experience with the Imperial British East Africa Company.

Thus Lansdowne was fully aware of Mackay's talents in coming to the help of the Government and the importance of Mackinnon Mackenzie and the BI in the commercial community of Calcutta; but when he required a new mercantile member of the Legislative Council, he did not automatically choose Mackay. Instead, he asked Mackay's colleague Turner, an older and less outgoing character whom Mackay frequently criticised for want of energy and ambition. But Turner did not welcome the extra work and reponsibility. Lansdowne then wrote to Sir A. Scoble QC, a senior Legislative

Council member: 'I am sorry Mr Turner cannot act. We had better ask Mr Mackay. Will you kindly approach him?' This reluctance is slightly at odds with Lansdowne's subsequent note to Mackay that he was 'delighted to learn from Sir A. Scoble that you are able to accept a seat in the Legislative Council. Your presence will be in every way an accession of strength to that body, and I hope you will allow me to add that it is most agreeable to me to have you for a colleague'. If Lansdowne was not at first enthusiastic about Mackay for whatever reason – perhaps he saw him as too pushy and eager for recognition – he was soon to change his mind.

The Council which Mackay joined included representatives of the most powerful authorities in the land: legal, administrative, military and commercial, including four prominent Indians. Mackay was drafted on to subcommittees to discuss bankruptcy proceedings, the Indian Factory Act, Indian merchant shipping and the Merchandise Marks Act, all matters familiar to him.

Mackay's earliest contributions strongly supported local Indian interests. In amending the Indian Merchant Shipping Act of 1880, he insisted on longer contracts for Lascar seamen and free passage for them to return home. In formulating the Registration of Ships Bill, Mackay pointed out that provision should be made for the change of name of merchant ships, in the event of ship sales between Muslims and Hindus, who attached great significance to this matter. On the Factory Act committee to amend the 1881 Act, he made the same points as in the Bombay and Bengal Chamber discussions, arguing for one day off per week and an hour's break for lunch. He objected, however, to women's hours being reduced from a maximum of eleven hours, on the grounds that they should have the chance to earn as much as possible, but agreed that children should be prohibited from working more than seven hours a day.

Mackay also tried to make himself directly useful to the viceroy personally. For instance, when Mackinnon Mackenzie was asked to supply vessels to carry seventy-two Sikh troops and one officer in a private expedition from Goa to Zanzibar, Mackay thought it best to inform Lansdowne, especially when his suspicions were aroused at the Goa agent's refusal to disclose the name of his client. Unfortunately, subsequent correspondence on the matter has not survived.

This and other private acts – including arranging BI passages for viceregal colleagues and friends – brought the two men into closer contact and gave Mackay the confidence to broach more and more important issues with Lansdowne. He took an early opportunity to raise the demoralising effects of the hated income tax, and the unproductive lengths being pursued to avoid payment. In November 1891, Mackay even asked Lansdowne to approve his speech at the important St Andrew's dinner. Lansdowne strongly opposed Mackay's plan to revive the controversial age of consent issue, which aimed to prevent child marriages. Lansdowne told him that this was 'a measure obviously framed in the interests of humanity as apparently simple and innocuous, which had given rise to widespread apprehensions and promised at one moment to occasion a dangerous agitation'.

Mackay quickly regained Lansdowne's confidence with his plan to set up confidential agencies to sell food in famine-stricken Madras. Mackay proposed the despatch of European assistants and supplies from Mackinnon Mackenzie in Calcutta to his agent in Madras. The profits would be strictly controlled just to cover costs, so as not to drive private suppliers out of business, but the Government would make good any net losses incurred. The aim of the agencies, operating entirely on Government account, would be to prevent grain markets being cornered during a famine by profiteering local merchants hoping to raise prices. The plan was never put into force as the Governor of Madras assured Lansdowne that grain was being sold freely, but the viceroy wrote to Mackay that 'I have myself no doubt that the appearance or threatened appearance of your firm upon the scene would lead to the collapse of any attempted corner pushing up grain prices'.

The last two years of Mackay's stay in India were dominated by the Indian currency question. The rate of British investment in the subcontinent had been declining steadily since 1870, earning poor dividends as a result of the lack of protection of Indian industry and of an effective monetary policy. Meanwhile, other nations eager to attract foreign capital, such as Russia, were working towards adopting a full gold standard regulated by a powerful central reserve bank; this was achieved in 1897, and brought in its wake an unprecedented flow of foreign investment.

India had no central reserve bank, and the British Government favoured the maintenance of a silver standard. But the 1880s and 1890s saw the increasing devaluation of the rupee from 1s 9d in 1870

to 1s 2d by 1893, and ultimately a currency panic and the closure of
the Indian silver mints as a crisis measure to force up the exchange
rate. Although a subsequent committee of 1893 recommended a full
gold standard, this never materialised.

Five years later, when Mackay was back in London, it was agreed
to maintain India's silver coinage but to peg it to 'a gold exchange
standard' organised from London. As a means of exchange, the
India Office sold council bills for sterling in London which were met
by rupee payments in India. A measure of stability was achieved and
the value of the rupee fixed at 1s 4d. Britain thus maintained a strong
commitment to supervising India's currency system, which was
arguably generally successful before 1914, at least in avoiding
unnecessary shipments of bullion, but the founding of the Reserve
Bank of India was delayed until 1935. As Keynes wrote in 1913,
although India's gold exchange standard was 'in the forefront of
monetary progress', yet 'in her banking arrangements, in the
management of her note issue, and in the relation of her Government
to the money market, her position is anomalous and she has much to
learn ...'.

What was Mackay's role in the achievement of this limited
solution, and does his work on the currency question help us to
understand why a full gold standard was never adopted in India?
Mackay's election as President of the Indian Currency Commission
followed his presidency of the Bengal Chamber, although he had
little specific experience of currency matters. *Capital* wrote ironically
of how Mackay 'with the courage worthy of a better cause, has
rushed into the presidentship [*sic*] of the Currency Commission, a
place where angels fear to tread'.

Capital had recently reported the collapse of the New Oriental
Bank due to mismanagement and financial profligacy, and was
surprised to hear Mackay claim that this was another victim of the
shrinkage of sterling. The newspaper poured scorn on his suggestion
that adopting gold pieces worth ten rupees each as the basic unit of
currency would solve the problem, and pointed to contradictory
statements Mackay had made in the recent past. In agreement with
Sir David Barbour, the viceroy's financial minister, Mackay had
admitted the difficulties that India would experience in trying to
adopt a gold standard. Yet at the Bengal Chamber, he spoke
confidently of how easy it would be for India to move to gold.
Capital's line throughout the crisis was that gold coinage would

exacerbate the problems. Mackay saw the depreciation of silver against gold as allowing the wealth of the Indian merchants invested in the development of the country to slip through the Government's fingers. Their 30 crores, worth £27m in 1870, was now worth £19m.

Mackay was convinced that his view was more representative of public opinion, and certainly the most desirable solution. As President of the Currency Commission, he was successful in rallying support for his view, especially among the local population, who felt alienated by not being consulted: Lansdowne had decided that only British and European merchants would be able to understand the technicalities. Mackay was inundated with letters of appreciation from Indian merchants, which he assumed to speak for the whole.

This was certainly the message he took with him to England whence he was summoned to appear on Lord Herschell's Committee on Indian Currency. It was a lightening visit by fast mailboat: he left Calcutta in early October 1892 and was back by mid-December. Lansdowne wrote, supportively, that 'you will be able to give the Committee a great deal of information which no-one else could give it, and even if this were not the case, the fact that you will have been consulted cannot fail to reassure the public mind here'.

In London, Mackay found himself among twenty-six witnesses, of whom only one was Indian. Six were fellow merchants, nine were fellow Scots. Eight were full time Government officials, and another eight were directly connected with the banking world. The committee, after interviewing them at length – and Mackay's evidence was longer than most – recommended the closing of the mints against the free coinage of silver, which should be accompanied by a statement that they would be used by the Government for the coinage of rupees in exchange for gold at a fixed rate of 1s 4d. These proposals were introduced in the financial panic of the following year.

Mackay drew attention to the lack of British investment in India, which would only be remedied by the introduction of a gold standard. He produced a sample of the letters he had received from local Indian merchants, pointing out that 'there is a very strong feeling among the native traders in favour of having a common standard with England'. He emphasised the poverty of India as beyond the comprehension of most Europeans: 'I believe that the struggle for existence is greater in India than it was, and I believe a common standard with England would tend to increase the prosperity and wealth of the country'. In the meantime, the rising tax burden to offset the devaluation of the rupee was impoverishing the inhabitants still further.

The doubts which *Capital* raised of his understanding of monetary matters were justified, as Mackay frequently found himself out of his depth. For instance, when asked to consider the price of silver compared with the prices of commodities, Mackay replied, 'I cannot trace the connection between the standard and prices. It is a most difficult thing ... I am unable to do it'. He was not sure how to answer when the committee wondered if one benefit of depreciation might be that Indian textile manufacturers' products would be cheaper abroad, and that their falling price might afford them some protection against the competition from Lancashire.

Mackay was disappointed that his support of the rupee being fixed at 1*s* 6*d* rather than 1*s* 4*d* did not convince the committee, but he accepted that a fixed ratio, even at this lower level, was better than nothing. He admitted that a silver standard would be workable if the United States adopted silver too, but would not be swayed from his belief in the gold standard. He denied that this would cause an international drain of gold to India and a rise in the price of gold, considering that India's requirement would be minimal.

Although the committee took heed of his comments on the sufferings caused by the devaluation of the rupee, Mackay's main arguments were ignored in the final report, and he also failed to convince the members of the Manchester Chamber of Commerce, whom he addressed before his return to India. He spoke at length on how salutary the silver standard had been in India until other countries, such as Germany, went on to gold and the rupee fell by forty per cent. Mackay was seriously worried that it might fall to a mere 10*d* from a high of nearly 2*s* in the 1870s.

He argued that India needed a gold standard because of its close trade links with gold standard countries such as Britain. Indian export prices were rendered lower, but she was now having to pay out more for imports. This, Mackay suggested, was leading to a deeper and deeper trade recession. And whilst India was desperately trying to raise revenue for economic development, the falling value of the rupee meant that she was paying out the equivalent of £16m a year in gold to Britain to cover the costs of defence and administration.

Mackay accepted that the British system of allowing the free circulation of gold with a limited issue of silver in small denominations would not work in India, as she could not afford enough gold, but there were far more very small transactions in India than in Britain, and an extensive gold coinage would not be necessary. After all, Mackay pointed out, France had had a gold standard since 1873 but still maintained the unlimited circulation of silver five - franc pieces. The Manchester Chamber members bombarded Mackay with questions which he could not adequately answer, especially in their assertion that if gold were introduced into India, it would be hoarded just as silver had been.

His address was reported in India by *Capital*, who considered that 'Mr Mackay's speech was smart, but very shallow' as 'Mr Mackay treats the trade of India with the gold-using countries as of overwhelming importance, whereas that trade is a trifle compared with the home trade with the silver-using countries'. Trade with Britain, Germany, France and other gold standard countries was indeed only one-twelfth that of India's trade with silver-using countries of the Indian Ocean and the Middle and Far East. Although the Indian rupee had indeed depreciated by forty per cent against gold, commodity prices had fallen by only about five per cent.

Mackay was vindicated to a certain extent by the escalating devaluation crisis which came to a head in the late summer of 1893. Between January and July, eleven crores – nearly £7m – was coined in India, more than in the whole of the previous year. The level of taxation rose accordingly, and Mackay warned the Legislative Council that:

It seems to me that, if we decide to continue on a silver basis, and England decides to retain us as a dependency, before many years are over half of our population will be engaged in the occupation of collecting taxes for the State, while the time and intelligence of the other half will be devoted to devising means to avoid the payment.

Mackay's representations certainly brought attention to the need for financial stability in India, but he went too far in asserting that India should have a full gold standard. She was not yet poised, as was Japan – and, to a certain extent, Russia – for economic take-off, and needed much more than the foreign-capital attracting powers of a gold standard for economic development on modern, western lines. India's financial infrastructure and level of technical education was almost nonexistent. But most of all, a gold standard would have

given India far too much fiscal independence for Britain's
interpretation of their colonial relationship. Mackay saw India for
herself: after his return to London for good in 1894, he saw the
subcontinent in a different light.

A final achievement of Mackay's before he left India was the
establishment of the Calcutta Royal Exchange under the auspices of
the Bengal Chamber, as a market for shippers and traders on the
lines of the Baltic Exchange in London. One hundred and ninety
members immediately enrolled: the organisation had been long
awaited. Tribute was paid to this, and to all Mackay's achievements,
in a plethora of farewell addresses on his departure.

The Bengal Chamber had already acknowledged its appreciation
of Mackay's leadership by re-electing him an unprecedented three
times, and drew members' attention to their president's work on the
Indian Factory Act and with the opium revenue. A request that he sit
for his portrait was signed by every member, British, European,
American and Indian alike. In his reply, Mackay expressed gratitude
that the merchants, planters, miners, manufacturers and shipowners
of India were finally being taken seriously by the Government,
thanks particularly to Lansdowne's sympathetic administration; on
his arrival, they had been largely shunned.

Mackay's work on the Port Commission for nine years and as 'the
head of every important social movement of recent years, and the
supporter of many charities' was acknowledged by the Dalhousie
Institute. They saw the passing of an Act supporting the idea of a
gold standard, which was to lead to the 'gold exchange standard' of
1898 as very much Mackay's work, through injecting new life into the
Currency Commission which had lain dormant for eight years. They
also attested to Mackay's support of the sporting activities of the
British community in India, such as pig-sticking at Ahmedabad,
duck shooting in Chullumbheel, camping in Sikkim, following the
hounds in Bombay, pheasant shooting among the Simla hills, snipe
shooting throughout Bengal, and yachting on the western coast.

Mackay was also officially thanked by the Calcutta Trades
Association, the BI Club, the Port Commissioners and over a
hundred members of the Indian mercantile community. The
Committee of the Chamber concluded that 'it was rare indeed for a
merchant to leave India with so many expressions of goodwill, and
such lengthy acknowledgements of the services he has rendered to the

community as Mr Mackay'.

Mackay's business career in India was outstanding in any case, but no other merchant played such an important part in public affairs: Sir William Mackinnon and his nephews confined themselves entirely to commercial matters. In contrast, Mackay devoted almost unlimited time and patience to his public tasks, supported by a trustworthy team at Mackinnon Mackenzie whom he could leave to carry on with the job in his absence. Work generally was in any event speeded up by two developments which revolutionised daily working routine in the offices of Calcutta, the typewriter and the telephone, both supported enthusiastically by Mackay. The former has greatly facilitated interpreting the documentation of Mackay's life: the latter has, of course, made the task more difficult.

In developing new trades, supporting merchant shipping needs, advocating factory reform, assisting in the adoption of uniform systems of measurement, arguing the case for the opium revenue, and improving facilities at the ports of Bombay and Calcutta, he made a lasting impact. That he was less successful in reducing income tax, or in the adoption of a gold standard for India, is not surprising: these matters were far out of his hands. Even had Mackay become viceroy, and Chapter Five explains how near he came to the ultimate seat of power in India, he could not have pushed through such changes single-handed, and in opposition to the British Government.

Yet his experience of public life in India were not necessarily the best preparation for public life in Britain. His feeling of pride in his achievements on leaving Calcutta was to a certain extent exaggerated by the relatively small size of the expatriate community. Here, it was easy to feel like an important political figure, and Indian social and economic reforms were so far behind Britain that it was similarly easy to feel progressive and enlightened.

And Mackay was only too aware of the failures of the British in India, especially in terms of inadequate investment in the subcontinent. As seen in Chapter Two, Mackay personally invested the bulk of his disposable income in India, but unfortunately others did not share his enthusiasm. Argentinian railway stocks and Russian government bonds were much more attractive, paying higher short-term dividends. Mackay was ultimately to reap handsome rewards from his Indian investments, but apart from those in Mackinnon Mackenzie itself, these were not forthcoming until the First World War and in generations to come.

Funds for developing India's economic infrastructure were woefully inadequate. For example, port improvements and extensions were financed by local earnings only. The railway network was a mere 17,000 miles long in 1889, and could not pretend to unify the country and assuage the effects of famine. State famine relief barely paid lip service to the country's needs: less than 60,000 persons were in receipt of state benefits throughout the 1880s and 1890s, when more than that number were starving in Ganjam district alone in the 1889 famine.

The total British investment in India stood at £160m in 1870 and rose to £380m by 1914, but this was not enough to lift India from poverty, and was already declining in terms of its proportion of the total of Britain's capital invested overseas. The heavy tax burden prevented the development of a strong internal market which could have stimulated local manufacture. Mackay was aware of a certain 'drain' – although he would not have called it that – in servicing India's public debt and paying for the administration of India from Calcutta and London. He had often criticised the huge expenditure on defence, which has been estimated to have taken up thirty per cent of Indian Government revenues annually in the 1870s.

Mackay frequently advocated an increased development of Indian coal mines and textile mills: he invested in both, and was impressed with their quality and the scope for large-scale production. But this would not have suited the interests of the British Government at home, who saw India above all as a market for British products, at a time when Britain's staple exports were cotton piece goods and textiles from Lancashire, and coal from the north-east coast and South Wales.

Mackay pointed to the invisible earnings from shipping which could be increased, and suggested that the size of the Indian Ocean market was such that more goods could be absorbed without Britain's trade suffering. The frustration of many of his plans, hopes an ideals was expressed in a rather plaintive statement he made to the Herschell Committee: 'I believe that there is a very strong feeling that the country is getting into a state of great poverty ... it has not developed in anything like the way it ought to have done with the opening of the Suez Canal. An enormous extent of country with great capabilities wants developments'. With his return to London, he did not forget these sympathies; he was more determined than ever to increase his influence in British Indian politics.

4

Shipowner and empire builder
Business life, 1894–1914

The affairs of Mackinnon Mackenzie in India were still vastly important to Mackay back at home, but now these duties were augmented by new responsibilities in Australia, and work with Gray Dawes in London. In 1894 Mackay was very much the expatriate finding his feet, experiencing executive power at head office for the first time. His new duties included negotiating with Scottish shipbuilders, London bankers, British Government officials: all strangers to him after nearly twenty years away and only short periods of leave in England. By 1914, however, he had become the greatest shipowner in the land, respected for his leadership of the BI and his shrewd merger of the BI with the mighty P&O on such favourable terms. He became well known as a skilled and trusted commercial plenipotentiary for the Government, as we shall see in Chapter Six. Simultaneously, he had become financially and managerially involved in several prominent companies, far extending the shareholdings and partnerships he had held whilst in India, which built on the old Mackinnon group that he had inherited, and anticipated the future Inchcape group.

Just before he left India, Mackay had negotiated the renewal of the thrice-weekly Bombay to Karachi mail contract. In the mid-1890s the BI, managed by a network of satellite agents orbiting round Mackinnon Mackenzie, sailed weekly between Calcutta and Chittagong, Akyab, Rangoon and Moulmein; monthly to Singapore, twice weekly to Bombay, fortnightly to Madras, and monthly to Rangoon. Bushire, Bandar Abbas, Jeddah, Aden, Port Said, Algiers and London could be reached by a monthly connecting service, and a similar line was provided via Zanzibar and Mombasa. One in five steamers calling at Indian ports at this time bore the familiar BI funnel rings, and more than two-thirds of the rest were owned by British concerns. Only a handful of vessels called from Germany, France, Norway and Italy, and there were practically no large, locally-owned steamers until after the First World War.

If Mackay was lucky in his timing on his arrival in Calcutta in 1874, and in Bombay in 1878, he was especially fortunate in returning to London in the winter of 1893–4. The old generation of the Mackinnon group was dying out and making way for the young. Sir William's death was closely followed by that of A.M. Monteath, one of Mackay's old senior partners in Calcutta, and J.M. Hall retired soon after he had taken over the chairmanship. Duncan Mackinnon, Sir William's nephew, in replacing Hall and succeeding his Uncle, was past his prime and no longer very effective. *Fairplay's* report of the 1894 AGM reminded them that Sir William (who 'has helped forward in the world more natives than would man all the BI steamers') had left no direct heirs, at a time when the BI and Mackinnon Mackenzie desperately needed new blood.

The BI was in trouble in 1893, facing depressed trade and poor exchange rates, and had to transfer £50,000 from the insurance fund to pay a ten per cent dividend on the paid-up capital of £694,800. The net earnings of the steamers had been only £54,387, and it was essential to leave a balance for next year. Although the subsidy from the Government of India was assured for another ten years, the BI was expected to provide more, and faster steamers, for no extra reward.

Business began to pick up when trade on the Indian coast increased in the mid-1890s. Mackay's suggestion of building four new steamers of over 5,000 gross tons each, while prices were low, was accepted. He then successfully advocated introducing a new service to Colombo and Mauritius from Calcutta, helped negotiate a new contract to Australia, and argued that the weekly Rangoon and Moulmein service should be increased to three times weekly. He also suggested that the monthly service to Zanzibar, Mozambique and Delagoa Bay should be resumed and a new fornightly service to the Straits begun. Mackay was also instrumental in developing a BI service carrying Indian workers from the Coromandel coast to Burma, Malaya, East Africa and Mauritius; and by the new century, his proposed new lines to South Africa, the Seychelles, Java, Siam, China and Japan had been established.

A contemporary notebook, an *aide-mémoire* of practice and

procedure, has survived describing the workings of these services. Mackinnon Mackenzie had their hands full advertising sailings for passengers and shippers, organising ballast, insurance, coaling, through freights, repairs at their own Mazagon and Howrah Docks, port charges, pilotage, lighterage, warehousing and onward shipments by rail. They also acted as agents in Bombay and Calcutta for the McIver Line, the City Line, the Anchor Line, P&O, Shepherd Shuster and the Asiatic Company, and would ship goods on behalf of fellow merchants such as Parry & Co. in Madras.

Space was being booked on the BI service to Karachi and onwards to London six months ahead of departure, merchants putting down £1 per ton. Mackay told his old colleagues, 'you are in a splendid position'. Subsidies payable to the BI each year totalled nearly Rs 300,000 – about £18,000 – and Mackinnon Mackenzie received generous commissions. The BI paid them four per cent on freight and passenger bookings, with an extra two and a half per cent when payable at the destination and four per cent on transhipment cargo. Thomas Cook & Son allowed commission of Mackinnon Mackenzie's work in handling their passages from Australia and India. The P&O agreed a ten per cent reciprocal rebate with the BI on through bookings on each others' lines. The few surviving details of Mackinnon Mackenzie's profits of the later 1890s suggest they approached £750,000 annually.

Between 1893 and 1899, the annual net earnings of BI steamers rose from just over £50,000 to nearly £123,000. This appears less dramatic compared with their agent's earnings, but the BI had a fleet worth £1,855,514 to maintain, compared with the minimal capital costs and running expenses of Mackinnon Mackenzie. Twenty-eight new ships, most of them over 5,000 gross tons, were purchased in this period, principally at Mackay's suggestion. The BI was lucky: a threatened collapse of trade with an outbreak of plague in Bombay in 1898 and cholera all over southern India was offset by the hiring of ten BI steamers by the Government of India for troop movements and for famine relief, and these high earnings continued.

The BI's financial success in the late 1890s was achieved despite a strike of many of its officers in February 1898. This was fully documented at the time in a 143-page printed report, 'for the information of the Directors'. That the entire episode – a strike at Rangoon of all BI officers and the formation in sympathy of 'Officers' Guilds' in Calcutta and Bombay – was handled without disrupting services or leading to bad feeling, was almost completed due to Mackay's intervention. The strike then became a showpiece of his management skill and energy, and enabled him to prove to any doubtful members of the BI Board in London and the agencies all over India, that he was more than capable of running the whole shipping line.

How did he do it? He went straight to Calcutta to talk to old Mackinnon Mackenzie colleagues and meet the officers who were threatening strike action and had refused to take command on Rs 200 a month, about £16. They would allow only their Guild secretary to negotiate with Mackay on their behalf: Mackay completely refused to recognise the status of this individual. He argued that the BI would not discuss the issue with a body known to be so openly antagonistic towards the company, without talking to the officers involved, and they agreed to disband the Guild. The Calcutta officers then suffered coercion from their more militant fellows at Rangoon and Bombay, and a partial strike went ahead as planned, from 7–15 February, with ships being run by chief officers. Mackay would not talk to anyone except the officers involved on an individual basis, and demands for half pay whilst unemployed were refused. Instead, he widely advertised a 'forgive and forget' attitude to those officers who wished to be re-employed on the old terms. At Calcutta, nearly all drifted back, mindful of the future income they might have been forsaking.

Yet none felt that their action had been in vain, as Mackay toured Calcutta and published his impressions of their hardships, meeting enough grievances by improving local conditions and placating local animosities to prevent further actions, but not agreeing to an increase in pay. Mackay somehow convinced them that the BI could not afford pay rises, quite an achievement in view of the BI's record earnings. It is understandable that the profits generated by Mackinnon Mackenzie as a private partnership were unknown to BI officers, but they could easily have discovered the BI's results, published throughout the shipping and financial press.

Placating the Bombay and Rangoon strikers, who completely refused to work, was more difficult, as they were more determined and better organised, and no one could be found to go to sea for only Rs 200 a month. By standing out against the strikers in mid-February, and refusing point-blank to accept their demands, at a loss of Rs 50,000 (around £4,000) in delayed steamers, in Mackay's words 'we had right on our side, and the only course open to us was to fight it out till we conquered' and this loss was 'well worth our while to sacrifice in the circumstances'. As he summed up to the directors at home:

The Company has vindicated the position it took upon my assuming charge in Calcutta on 31st January, [of refusing to give way to the strikers], the officers have had a severe lesson, the impossible Guild has been dissolved, the officers have undertaken not to form another, and we on the other hand have had an experience from which we should not fail to profit in the future.

Soon afterwards, Mackay's second ranking in the Mackinnon Mackenzie organization, behind Duncan Mackinnon, was officially recognised in a deed of co-partnery. This document describes the dynastic structure of the organisation Sir William had left behind, which Mackay effectively inherited. It enabled Mackay, once established, to consolidate his authority. Only Duncan Mackinnon and Mackay were designated as 'Seniors' and only they could nominate new junior partners and determine the firm's business at all ports for a period of fifteen years from 1905. Profits were to be distributed on the basis of the capital invested, of which the latter totalled Rs 5,000,000, about £400,000, of which Mackinnon held thirty and Mackay twenty-five per cent. The Seniors were not obliged to live in India, and this concession was also allowed for their sons who may become partners, who could inherit their shares. Mackay's son Kenneth, and his grandson – also Kenneth – were to take advantage of this in due course.

Mackinnon Mackenzie maintained their status as the most prominent British shipping agency house in the years leading up to the First World War. Besides purely commercial activities, they were called upon by the Foreign Department of the Government of India to help investigate German activity in the Gulf pearl industry. In return, they would receive every support in extending their business. The tonnage of BI steamers calling at Gulf ports had quadrupled in the penultimate decade of the nineteenth century, and by the early 1900s, entrances by BI ships at Bushire, Bahrain, Bandar Abbas, Lingah and Basra reached over 200,000 tons annually, and dominated the traffic by between seventy and ninety per cent. The Foreign Department concluded that the German firm of Wonkhaus were not a permanent threat to Gray, Paul & Co, the BI agents, who were closely linked to Mackinnon Mackenzie and Gray Dawes. The term 'flagships of imperialism' has been used in reference to the P&O; it was also certainly true of the BI.

Although profits were still buoyant for the BI in these immediate prewar years, Mackay with Mackinnon's support argued that they should issue £1m in four and a half per cent debenture stock in September 1912, to raise funds for future growth. The BI's existing capital was £1,657,200 of which £957,200 was fully paid up, and its ships – 108 steamers of 458,722 tons – were, with other assets, worth £4 ½m.

This issue was designed partly to pay for a new acquisition which Inchcape – as he had become in 1911 – found particularly appropriate for the BI. The Apcar Line had been owned and run by two Armenian merchants based in Calcutta, and since 1901 they had enjoyed a cargo pooling agreement with the BI. Apcar's assets were worth Rs 1,500,000 (around £120,000) and Inchcape paid only Rs 800,000, or £64,000, as the two merchants were keen to sell up and leave what they regarded as an unreliable trade. This was followed by the purchase in 1912 of Archibald Currie's five large steamers in the India/Australian trade.

Inchcape's weekly letters to the Mackinnon Mackenzie junior partners in Calcutta also looked at more day-to-day issues. As a result of the previous strike, he agreed to pay officers their full salary whilst in hospital, to try to make the BI service as attractive as possible. He agreed to a joint coaling arrangement with the Asiatic Company. He tried to offset competition with the Mogul line in the pilgrim trade by negotiating with their agents, Turner Morrison. An attempt to purchase the Eastern Shipping Company, worth £78,000 and for which he offered £50,000, came to nothing.

The Gulf trade continued to flourish, making approximately £100,000 in the first half of 1912, and £141,000 in the second half, but the ships on this line needed at least three-quarters of a million pounds spent on new tonnage. Meanwhile, Inchcape was negotiating with the Turkish Government to gain monopoly trading advantages in Mesopotamia, free of official tax. New ships would be needed for this too.

The greatest threat, Inchcape realised, now came from the Japanese. He sent his son Kenneth, already installed and working with Mackinnon Mackenzie in Calcutta, to Japan on an extended tour to analyse the country's maritime potential, and the young man kept an illuminating and fascinating diary. As Inchcape pointed out to Sir Edward Grey and other Foreign Office officials at home: 'I don't know what the upshot of this Japanese attack on our coasting trade will be. We are precluded from entering the coasting trade of Japan while the Japs are free to come into the coasting trade of India'. Kenneth informed his father that a new Japanese company, connected with the Nippon Yusen Kaisha, was planning to offer an Indian coastal service, apparently subsidised by the Japanese government. Meanwhile Inchcape instructed Turner, who managed BI affairs in Liverpool, to help obtain tonnage to build up the fleet of the Bombay & Persia Steam Navigation Company, with which the BI enjoyed cooperation, to offer a cheaper service and undercut the Japanese.

The BI was facing competition on all fronts, as well as problems in India itself. The strike which he had handled so effectively was a taste of things to come. Inchcape's solution to local unrest was a mixture of paternalism and understanding which worked very well among those with whom he did business, but inevitably was not the panacea for large organised movements. Certainly he could always get the best from his Indian staff and individual Indian merchants and entrepreneurs.

His son Kenneth described how he was working at Mackinnon Mackenzie just before the outbreak of war when his father came out on one of his periodical visits. One morning Kenneth looked up from his desk to see waiting before him, 'a pitch black Indian man, with cast marks over his shaven head and torso, wearing only a loin cloth and a piece of white linen negligently draped over his shoulders'.

Kenneth had no idea what to do when the apparition asked for an advance of a lakh of rupees, about £8,000,

as the sum was absolutely unheard of wealth to me and considering he had no signs of affluence, the costume he was standing in could hardly have cost more than 1/6, I realised this was a situation I was unable to cope with, so I took his card to my father's room. He knew him perfectly well, spoke to him in fluent Hindustani, and when he was finally ushered in and repeated his request my father tore a slip off a pad and wrote him out a 'chit' for a lakh of rupees which he told him to take to the cashier. I was absolutely astounded but my father told me he was a perfectly respectable man and wanted some money to finance a rice shipment to Madras, the freight of which would go to the BI.

Unknown to Kenneth, his visitor was 'Chitty', from one of the most powerful merchant and banker families of Bengal.

The years between his return from India and the First World War saw the expansion of Mackay's geographical and entrepreneurial horizons. As he had shown in his sudden trip to Calcutta to try and forestall the BI officers' strike, he could be very effective as a troubleshooter. In the same role he visited Australia for the first six months of 1900.

Mackay was interested in the Australasian United Steam Navigation Company (AUSN) for professional and personal reasons: it was managed by the British India and Queensland Agency (BI&QA), so it was within the Mackinnon orbit; and he was a director and substantial shareholder, having gradually increased his investment in the company since it was floated in 1887. The problems of Australian coastal shipping, and especially the AUSN, have been more than thoroughly documented elsewhere, yet Mackay's contribution in completely turning round the fortunes of this company has never been examined in detail before.

Mackay's part in the AUSN recovery has a modern ring to it. Indeed, many of its problems were timeless. Reasonable profits were achieved in the first few years after the AUSN's existence in the late 1880s, thanks to the Queensland Government mail contract and its dominant position among Australian coastal firms, in which its forty-six steamers of over 31,000 gross tons represented twenty-seven per cent of the ships and twenty-three per cent of the tonnage. The net earnings of the AUSN steamers then declined drastically, with the company making a net loss in 1893–5 and 1897. The spheres of influence which the AUSN had established with the other companies had broken down, with others pre-empting AUSN bids for lucrative flour and sugar contracts. The Melbourne to Sydney passenger service had become so competitive that fares no longer covered costs, and the coal trade had become a cut-throat free-for-all. Meanwhile, everyone was trying to cash in on the gold rush at Coolgardie and Kalgoorlie. The AUSN, with its eight luxury passenger services, the ships with electric lighting and all mod cons, was especially hard hit. There had been a massive wave of strikes in the early 1890s among crews and sheepshearers, causing disruption throughout the whole economy, especially when English holders of fixed deposits in Australian banks lost confidence and did not renew them provoking a severe financial crisis.

The AUSN fleet, lacking funds for renewal, was declining in efficiency and advancing in age. From 1887 to 1898, twenty-four vessels had left the fleet but only nine had been added, mostly comparatively small vessels of 3,000 tons. Mackay sold off the outdated tonnage, and invested £600,000 in large, modern liners, totally reorganising the focus of the AUSN's business away from passengers to cargo. The AUSN's profitability was restored, rising from £24,000 soon after Mackay's departure to a peak of £54,000 during the First World War.

Mackay achieved this turnaround by, first of all, selecting the best man for the job of taking over the AUSN management. B.W. Macdonald was an old India hand who, like many others, was unable to cope with the climate, and had been sent to Australia. With another able junior, David Hamilton, he had not been promoted due to a lack of mobility among the top managers, many of whom were not to survive Mackay's visit. One was Bland, the Australia head office manager – who apparently lived up to his name – who met Mackay on his arrival at Albany and took him to Perth and Fremantle.

Mackay was coolly objective in his dealings in Australia; he did not care for the place as he cared for India, and the subsequent labour troubles which were to blight all his businesses there did not make him change his mind. As he wrote to Duncan Mackinnon, 'The climate here is delightful. The harbour is very fine, the whole place is pretty – if it was only peopled by the natives of India the place would be a paradise, but the people here are ... by no means attractive ... '.

He left no stone unturned in his searches on ships, in warehouses and harbour facilities or – particularly – in offices. Hamilton represented the AUSN at Perth, immediately winning Mackay's approval. Bland – one of the most senior managers – angered Mackay by writing to the representatives of the BI&QA at all the ports telling them they must accept a twenty-five per cent cut in salary. Mackay was annoyed that Bland was overriding his authority, and that he had only this very unimaginative solution to saving money. Macdonald, based at Cooktown, was among the first to object. Bland had already taken one stupid decision whilst Mackay was there. He had sold one of the surplus steamers to the secretary of the Burketown meatworks, on the understanding that she would not be sailed against the AUSN; but he forgot to add the proviso that she should not be sold to an AUSN competitor, which is what happened almost immediately.

All the time he was with Mackay, Bland was determinedly going behind his director's back, and trying vaguely to improve some of the most glaring of the company's problems before the hawk-eyed Mackay spotted them. He tried to sell off the worst of the old storage hulks, and to land new contracts. After a week, Mackay was convinced that 'he is not equal to his position'. Bland meanwhile blamed the directors for issuing orders at odds with the situation, and claimed that he was often instructed to pursue policies which he knew would be disastrous. But, as Mackay wrote to Mackinnon, Bland had never voiced any fears of the outcome of his decisions. His days with the AUSN soon came to an abrupt end.

Mackay was glad to then move to 'the Eastern colonies which are more civilised and less cut off'. There he met the rival companies, the Adelaide Co., Burns Philip, McIllwraith McEacharn, Howard Smiths and Huddart Parker with the aim – to be successfully realised – of making pooling agreements. Northcote, the AUSN's Melbourne manager, was also destined for the axe. Not only had he not tried to reach agreements with his competitors, he was *persona non grata* with most of them because of his high-handed attitude. Mackay also attended the Shipowners' Federation meeting, which Northcote had avoided. It turned out to be a useful instrument in deciding strategy to deal with labour unrest and many common problems.

One of Mackay's first moves in each AUSN office he visited was to bring in a professional auditor, whose findings were:

somewhat startling. He says that the accounts have been grossly neglected for the last five or six years and that items amounting to £10,000 which have been eliminated as debits against the steamers and passed to the debit of the Agents, and which as a consequence are now shown as assets belonging to the AUSN which will have to be written off.

Unlike many fellow-directors, Mackay had developed a shrewd eye for dubious accounting practices. Managers who assumed that such a lofty personage from the London head office could be blinded by science, by having the ledgers thrust upon him without explanation, were making a mistake when they tried this ploy on Mackay.

Mackay thus pinpointed the problem as a breakdown in office management, which was 'disgraceful in the extreme. Nobody appears to have any control of the business'. Newsham, in the accounts department, was 'altogether useless and incompetent'. Barnes, at the head office in Brisbane, was 'unfit to be left in charge'. Leresche, at Sydney, was 'quite unequal to the appointment'. Mackay decided to appoint Macdonald to run the whole business from Brisbane, close down the Sydney office and sack Bland, saving £3,500 a year from his salary alone. Hamilton would run the important Adelaide office, and the others would be demoted to posts more suited to their capacities. Among the lower echelons, Mackay fired several office clerks whose sole job had been to make unnecessary copies of all correspondence. He went through all the manifests to make sure the cargoes shipped actually tallied with those on the income ledger: an alarming number did not.

Every lunch and dinner was spent entertaining competitors and Government officials, with Lady Mackay pulling her weight in supporting the AUSN's and the BI's interests. Her role is never entirely clear because she and her husband destroyed their own voluminous personal correspondence. But she was with him at all times on this trip, as on every subsequent assignment, and his diary suggests that each morning they discussed the objects of the day's visits, and went through the latest correspondence together.

By the end of his tour, Mackay had organised local shipowners to make a joint working agreement within the Queensland trade. He examined every important coastal contract and helped Macdonald plan a strategy to obtain them for the AUSN. The auditor was to carry out a quarterly inspection of all the books. Each office was markedly slimmer, in numbers and in salaries. Macdonald took over the running of the whole business, and was willing to accept only £800 a year. Mackay was not sorry to then sail from Sydney, and no doubt Bland and Northcote were glad to see him go. The AUSN was transformed.

Six days out, Mackay was already thinking of other things. Off Melbourne, he invited a series of prominent Australasian businessmen to dine with him in his cabin aboard the P&O *Britannia*. Among them was Sir James Mills, the Chairman of the Union Company of New Zealand. This meeting was to lead to one of the most crucial business deals of Mackay's whole career.

Back in London, Mackay wrote weekly to Macdonald. He involved the AUSN in every new BI venture. One in particular was his acquisition for the BI of the Currie Line from Captain Archibald Currie, whose ships were brought into the BI's India to Australia service, and Macdonald's advice was sought on how they could best be employed. Mackay stayed in close correspondence with many of the rival companies' chairmen, especially James Burns of Burns

Philp, and thereby gave Macdonald the authority to stand up to them. With the outbreak of war, Mackay – then Inchcape – paid Macdonald and Hamilton the supreme compliment of closing down the BI&QA and making the AUSN agency over to them, calling it Macdonald Hamilton & Co. Not only did this give them added influence in the management of the shipping line; it also gave them the income. Inchcape knew more than most that it was the agencies which made the profits, not the liners.

By the 1890s, the business of the BI's London manager, Gray Dawes, was expanding beyond its original shipping and merchanting functions. It had offered banking facilities for several years, in the same way as the Scottish arm of the Mackinnon group, Wm Mackinnon & Co. of Glasgow, who handled Mackay's finances when he was in India. It also handled the shares not only of its directors but also of several small investors from outer London and the Home Counties. Edwin Sandys Dawes and Archibald Gray had successfully developed the business from when Sir William had created the niche in the 1860s.

Mackay was less closely concerned with the running of Gray Dawes than he was with Mackinnon MacKenzie and the AUSN, but he took a great interest in its financial business and stock dealings, especially with firms in India. There was good reason for this. In 1906 he was the impetus behind a major investment on behalf of Mackinnon Mackenzie which was to become one of their most successful acquisitions, far into the future. Binny & Co., founded in the closing years of the eighteenth century was, by the outbreak of the war, the largest merchant firm in Madras (see Jones, 1986, for a detailed discussion of its origins).

In 1906 Binny's was in a very weak state. Arbuthnot & Co., a prominent bank with extensive business in the Madras presidency, was forced to suspend payment in that year, causing mass panic in the local banking community, including Binny's, who suddenly faced an unprecedented run on their banking department. Although the assets of the firm were more than adequate to meet their liabilities, they were not sufficiently liquid and Binny's too suspended. The partners had already come into contact with Mackay through their shipping business with the BI, and they called on him for help. Mackay realised that here was a valuable firm available at a bargain price. Its office premises, godowns (warehouses), three textile mills, oil mills and coffee-curing works, nine wholly-owned coffee estates with eight partly-owned, to say nothing of the goodwill of more than a century, were well worth the equivalent of £50,000 that was being asked for it. He persuaded Duncan Mackinnon and George Mackenzie to join him in supporting the venture, and organising the firm into a limited company.

A description of Binny's in a guide of 1914 shows that Mackay's initiative of 1906 benefited both rescued and rescuer. By 1910, with Mackay's help, they gained the BI agency at Madras: earning four per cent freight and passage money and four per cent on transhipment freight, the same arrangement enjoyed by Mackinnon Mackenzie in Calcutta. Binny's then acquired steam and petrol launches, thirty-five barges and thirty lighters, and handled 'a very considerable proportion' of Madras's imports. They were agents for the Madras Port Trust, transhipping immigrants from the Straits and Rangoon. The cotton and woollen mills quickly recovered from the firm's near collapse, and the coffee estates boomed, with 3,500 acres producing up to 700 tons of coffee in a good season. Binny's meanwhile represented four important banks in Madras, including Baring Brothers of London, and fourteen insurance companies. The first half-yearly dividend of ten per cent was paid at the end of 1906.

Mackay also increased his investments in the Rivers Steam Navigation Company, which had pooled its fleet in 1889 with a rival line, the India General, operating then as the Joint Steamer Companies. Except for a cyclone in 1909 which destroyed much of their property, the firms enjoyed good business carrying tea, jute sacks and coal, paying handsome dividends in the final years before the war, despite heavy competition from the State-subsidised railways. Mackay had helped the Joint Steamer Companies negotiate with Lord George Hamilton, Secretary of State for India in the late 1890s, to come to a working arrangement with the railways, so that goods could be booked through to travel on both rail and river steamer services. In one six-month period, the half-year ended December 1899, regarded as a relatively bad time, the India General alone made a net profit of over £31,000.

The Joint Steamer Companies were managed by Macneill & Co. who also controlled several tea estates in which Mackay had an interest. The Macneills were related to the Mackinnon family as cousins. During the 1890s, they handled the affairs of twelve tea companies with estates in Assam and Cachar, including the largest and oldest, the Upper Assam Tea Company, in which Mackay had

invested before he left India. Macneill's business flourished despite
the death of Duncan Macneill in 1892, especially helped by a great
rush for land in all the tea districts throughout the 1890s, with a rise
in the demand for Indian teas and their continuing popularity against
China teas. John Mackinnon, a cousin of the founder, wrote that
'next to Darjeeling in point of excellence for tea planting comes
Upper Assam, and we should not lose an opportunity of picking up
any blocks of land available'. Macneill's tea estates were consolidated
and expanded, spurred on by intense competition from Sir John
Muir of Finlay, Muir & Co. who tried to create a monopoly of
Indian tea estate ownership and tea production. Mackay followed
these developments closely. The tea companies – and river steamers –
represented an important long-term investment for the Mackinnon/Inch-
cape group which he now led with Duncan Mackinnon. The
Macneill interest came to this group in 1915 after the death of the
Mackinnon heirs, from the Government of India, who insisted that
this business could not be left to minors, and asked Inchcape to take
it over. To take the single year of 1910, the Upper Assam Tea
Company produced 55,000 maunds of tea which sold at £8.80 each
on the London market, bringing in gross proceeds of nearly half a
million pounds – a valuable business indeed.

With the death of Duncan Mackinnon, Mackay – then Inchcape –
rose to the head of the existing Mackinnon empire. The twenty years
between his return to London and the outbreak of war saw a second
apprenticeship as a top-ranking shipowner. His contribution to the
management of the BI and the AUSN, as we have seen, was
remarkable in increasing their profitability and developing new
trades and opportunities. This improved performance was dependent
on a supply of the latest and most efficient tonnage. Mackay's
growing banking interests, through his directorship of the National
Provincial Bank of England, and the Royal Bank of Scotland,
helped obtain cheap finance to maintain the strength of the fleets, but
he also had to make the best possible deals with the shipbuilders.

Working at the BI's head office in London, Mackay first dealt
directly with shipbuilders, and for the first time was in a position to
contract personally for new tonnage, for both the AUSN and the BI.
At first, he was unsure exactly how to handle these businessmen who
were as powerful as himself but, capitalising on the fact that times
when shipbuilders were begging for orders were more common than
times when shipowners were begging for yardspace, he made sure

that shipbuilders with whom he dealt obeyed the dictum, 'the customer is always right'. In terms of the specification, overall design and price of vessels he purchased, Mackay was usually able to call the tune, especially after a few years' experience. He developed very close relationships with a number of shipbuilders, and this manner of buying ships was to become characteristic of the British shipbuilding industry from this period and even arguably to the present day. Such builder– client patronage has been blamed for the industry's lack of responsiveness to market changes and ultimate decline in the latter half of the twentieth century, but that is another story.

Before the First World War, Mackay (as a representative of the BI and AUSN) dealt in particular with four Clyde shipbuilders: Denny, Russell/Lithgow, Barclay Curle and Stephen, especially Denny at first. Denny's – an old-established unlimited company with close links to the Mackinnon group through investments as well as shipbuilding – built twenty-four steamers, three AUSN ships, seventy-seven paddle steamers and motor launches for the Indian river steamer companies, thirty-seven barges and one tug for the BI&QA before 1914. Although Duncan Mackinnon was still nominally in charge of the BI, Mackay played a vital part in its ship-building programme, and quickly developed a good working relationship with Denny. Mackay's orders between 1895 and 1914 accounted for a major proportion of Denny's business: of the 487 yard numbers issued, 142 or twenty-nine per cent were BI and related orders.

Mackay did not feel tied to Denny's, especially when he became convinced that their prices were too high. Russell/Lithgow built two AUSN steamers, and Barclay Currie built nineteen new BI ships in the pre-1914 shipping boom, including the *Neuralia* and *Nevasa* of over 9,000 tons, the largest of the BI's prewar vessels and highly popular with passengers. Between 1905 and 1914, the BI's orders claimed over a third of Barclay Curle's output. Detailed insight into Mackay's dealings with one shipbuilder in particular is provided by his correspondence with Frederic John Stephen of the firm of Alexander Stephen & Sons Ltd. This shipbuilder–customer relationship between the two men, who both died in 1932, lasted for over thirty years.

Before the outbreak of hostilities, fourteen BI and AUSN ships were launched from Stephen's Linthouse yard. F.J. Stephen was the fifth of seven generations of Stephens, one of the oldest Scottish shipbuilding families, a private partnership for over 150 years.

Stephen had a solid training in naval architecture, joining the firm's shipbuilding department in 1887 and acting as salesman in negotiating orders for his company with shipowners such as Mackay.

In the early stages of their relationship, Mackay was influenced by Stephen's opinions, as in the case of the building of the 4,058 ton AUSN *Wyandra*, launched in 1902. Mackay made the initial enquiry, expressing an interest in a 2,300-ton general cargo steamer with sophisticated and expensive hydraulic cargo gear and refrigerating machinery. Stephen pointed out that Mackay's specifications would make the vessel exorbitantly expensive: Mackay, to whom costing was always crucial, backed down.

Stephen had these convictions because in 1900 the firm had decided to opt out of general cargo building and concentrate on larger, higher-class cargo liners and passenger vessels. The coincided with their adoption of limited liability status, with a capital of £350,000, the brothers keeping firm control of the voting stock and ordinary shares. Thus Stephen was disappointed at Mackay's order for a small general cargo steamer, and urged him to consider a 4,000-ton vessel, almost twice the size originally envisaged. Mackay then considered a midway compromise, but the *Wyandra* was built as Stephen had planned. The price of £49,750 was fair, but Mackay was to have reservations in dealing with Stephen in the future, and it was 1908 before they built another ship for him.

In the six years between 1902 and 1908, Mackay and Stephen negotiated, abortively, for six separate contracts, requiring long-winded, time-consuming work for the shipbuilders in compiling estimates. Mackay could not accept that costs had risen so sharply. To facilitate payment, even at the risk of a less profitable deal for themselves, Stephen suggested building the proposed vessel on a 'commission principle': instead of naming their price at the time of completion of the contracts, the shipbuilders were prepared to pass over to their customer the exact costs of building the vessel, with a modest five per cent profit on the final sum. This principle differed from that adopted by Mackay in his dealings with Gray's of Hartlepool whereby an agreed sum was paid, half on delivery and half during the course of building in the form of discountable bills.

Stephen pointed out that 'on this principle you would get the benefit of any fall in costs there might be during the building of the boat', referring to the fact that he had already purchased enough steel for the entire job, at a price considerably lower than that prevailing.

Three of their current orders, he continued, were being executed in this fashion to the advantage and satisfaction of the owners. In Mackay's case, Stephen was also prepared to offer a fixed maximum price, at the danger of reducing his own profits almost to nothing. When Mackay abandoned the deal, Stephen's patience was obviously stretched to its limits, for he announced that it would be some time – if ever – that prices would come down to a level which Mackay would deem acceptable, and that there was no point in going any further with the matter.

Stephen doggedly pursued every chance of another BI or AUSN contract. That so much effort was spent cultivating his custom is a reflection of Mackay's growing prominence as a shipowner. In 1903, Mackay approached Stephen again, for a copy of the *Wyandra*, but ten feet longer. Stephen's estimated price of £104,500 was more than twice what the *Wyandra* had cost, but reflected the overall rise in costs, particularly of steel. Then Mackay changed his mind again. By 1905, despite their intention to specialise in larger, quality vessels, Stephen considered Mackay's proposal for a 270-foot steamer for £49,500. This quickly fell through; yet another possibility in June 1907 was more protracted, but also ultimately unsuccessful. The long-awaited contract for the 6,338-ton AUSN *Wyreema* was finally agreed at the end of 1908, five years after the first discussions.

These negotiations are revealing of the problems a shipbuilder faced in dealing with a very important – although not necessarily knowledgeable – customer. The small steamer that Mackay wanted turned out to be almost impossible to build – the hull and engine specifications were mutually contradictory. They would require such an immense beam in proportion to length as to render the vessel possibly unseaworthy. The seriousness of Mackay's enquiry is questionable: certainly he did not hesitate to take up Stephen's time with the most far-fetched proposals.

Another case was the building of the BI *Levuka*. Mackay wanted a 350-foot vessel with his own design of ballast tanks and bunker arrangement, until Stephen pointed out that with the ballast tanks full and 100 tons of coal in the bunkers, the ship's propeller would not be adequately immersed unless all the machinery was moved aft and the vessel was trimmed to aft. Eventually, more workable specifications were agreed, and the 6,129-ton vessel, with full refrigeration machinery and quadruple expansion engines, was completed for £133,500.

How much profit was Stephen making out of the BI and AUSN? The period before 1914, although one of difficulty in obtaining orders and raw materials was, despite Stephen's protests to Mackay, one of great success for these shipbuilders. In the fourteen years before war broke out, their dividend payments totalled £225,453 on an issued capital of £261,000. The return on the ordinary shares, principally held by the Stephen family, frequently reached twenty per cent and was to be even greater during the war. So Stephen could afford to be indulgent to Mackay's whims and fancies, especially when his customer took a stake in the equity in 1917.

Before this, Mackay and Stephen had already entered into a joint venture with the American and European Shipping Co. who operated steamers on Lake Erie. Stephen had undertaken to build their vessels and had accepted shares in lieu of payment; Mackay had lent them money. In July 1909 they went bankrupt, and subsequent rescue attempts were at Mackay's behest by McKenzie, president of the Canadian Northern Railway, but there is no evidence that either party received compensation.

Mackay's extensive business responsibilities never prevented him from closely supervising every aspect of Stephen's work for him, which comprised nine more vessels before war broke out. This was principally in the interests of saving money. For example, in the case of the 4,066-ton *Abhona*, Mackay saved £340 out of the total of £75,000 by using pitch pine instead of teak for the living accommodation.

Mackay was not always strictly fair with Stephen. Although the contract price for the building of the 5,196-ton *Ellenga* and her sister ship the *Ellora* was agreed in advance, Mackay insisted on the installation of expensive additions – including specialist sidelights – for no additional cost. Stephen was the first to be informed of any complaints arising from his work. When Mackay drew his attention to the rapid deterioration of the woodwork of the *Levuka*, Stephen almost pathetically replied, 'We really did all we could to ensure success, and certainly would not have grudged to spend another fifty pound note above even what we did spend, to try and make her perfect'.

Demand for tonnage for the shipping empire controlled by Mackay reached a peak in the immediate prewar years, stimulated by the increase in traffic on the Persia service, the Mesopotamian concessions and the growth of the frozen meat trade from Australia.

By the outbreak of the First World War, the BI comprised 120 steamers of 708,678 tons, with a book value of £4.3m; the AUSN was at an all-time peak of twenty-four vessels of 63,953 tons. When the P&O/BI desperately needed new tonnage in the face of wartime casualties and increased demand for carrying space, the long-standing relationship between shipowner and shipbuilder was certainly advantageous, and mainly to the shipping line.

The merger between the BI and the P&O was one of the most shrewd deals of Inchcape's life. It is a remarkable case of a company apparently selling itself out to a more powerful rival, whilst in reality gaining control of that rival. Why did Sir Thomas Sutherland, regarded as one of the most powerful shipping leaders, allow this to happen?

Sutherland had joined the P&O within fifteen years of its first contract in 1852, when he was only eighteen. Two years later, he had been sent to Bombay, but it was in Hong Kong that he really made his mark. By the time he was twenty-six, he had been appointed superintendent of P&O's Japan and China agencies and a member of Hong Kong's Legislative Assembly; Inchcape was thirty-eight before he had achieved comparable prominence.

As Inchcape was to benefit from the vacuum of power at Mackinnon Mackenzie and the BI with the increasing age and timely death of Sir William Mackinnon in 1893, so Sutherland rose to power whilst the P&O founder, Arthur Anderson, was reaching the end of his life. Appointed managing director in 1872 after four years as assistant manager and after an extensive tour of all P&O's operations worldwide, he revolutionised the whole organisation. Facing severe difficulties with the opening of the Suez Canal in 1869, Sutherland implemented drastic economy measures within a company whose finances had been cushioned by generous subsidies.

Successfully predicting the principal trends in the ocean carrying trade, Sutherland built up the P&O, moving its base from Southampton to London, and contracting for a series of new, efficient vessels. Under his able leadership, the P&O rose to great power and influence, establishing unique national prestige. Like Inchcape, he played a significant role in public life, being elected Liberal MP for Greenock in 1884 and achieving his knighthood in 1891.

By 1913, the P&O had a secure financial base and extensive network of routes, such that it felt strong enough to negotiate a merger with a similarly powerful shipping company without compromising its position. It had a paid-up capital of five and a half million pounds, sixty ships of over half a million tons and a dominant position on the prime mail routes through Suez to Bombay, Yokohama and Sydney. Meanwhile, the P&O 'Branch Line' to Australia via the Cape ran a monthly service for emigrants with the *Salsette*, and the company maintained over 200 overseas agencies.

A second factor in persuading Sutherland to look sympathetically upon a merger with the BI was the increasing trend in the early twentieth century for shipping combines to grow in size and swallow up others. For example, P&O had already taken over the Blue Anchor Line in 1910, and the AUSN had been created through the ASN and QSS merger. The BI had acquired Apcar and Currie.

Thirdly, Sutherland himself, eighteen years older than Inchcape, was nearly eighty in 1913 and seeking retirement. Although other members of his Board, such as Sir Walter Lawrence, certainly saw themselves as possible candidates for the chairmanship, it was not until Inchcape had established a prominent position in the BI that Sutherland felt confident he had identified a worthy successor. All along, to Sutherland at least, the possibility of a merger with the BI was tied up with Inchcape's ultimate leadership of the combine.

The surviving documentation within the P&O archives charts Sutherland's interest in the BI. The BI was closely comparable in size and complementary to the P&O, rather than competitive, in its operations. The BI had 120 steamers of over 700,000 tons; although the P&O had only half the number of ships, it could muster a similar aggregate tonnage. The BI dominated the Indian Ocean trades, the P&O the long haul routes and home lines.

The BI certainly appeared financially sound: it could afford to distribute £130,720 in dividends (five per cent on the preference stock and ten per cent on the ordinary shares) with £15,666 to carry over for 1914. It was expanding its fleet, with four new vessels delivered since the end of 1913, four more nearing completion and two cargo steamers on long-term contract had been purchased outright. Six old steamers had been disposed of in early 1913. Meanwhile, debentures totalling £211,860 had just been paid off. The book value of the BI fleet was placed at £4.3m, with further capital and reserves worth £6m.

Duncan Mackinnon, who had officially acknowledged Inchcape's pre-eminence in the BI for at least the previous three years, retired owing to failing health in 1913, and with the death of the Duke of Argyll – a valued and prestigious outside director – in the same year, the old guard was fading away, and with them the opposition to a merger with the P&O.

On 19 May 1914, the P&O Board passed a resolution to make an offer to the BI to buy its ordinary and preferred stock. The two boards were to be 'fused', still working separately but under a single controlling body, 'in which the Directors of the P&O will possess a preponderating voice'. Despite the P&O board's insistence on this clause from the outset, it was subsequently completely ignored. Sutherland was not worried, despite private letters from colleagues voicing disquiet that this future board might not adequately protect the interests of its P&O element.

Freshfields, the P&O solicitor, on investigating the advisability of this decision, revealed a fourth reason why Sutherland welcomed the BI merger. Apparently, the capital powers of the P&O were almost completely exhausted. An increase in its capitalisation was necessary before any further expansion could be envisaged. An extraordinary general meeting to authorise the raising of extra capital was to be held, irrespective of any merger plans.

At this meeting shareholders first heard how the P&O board proposed to come to an agreement with the BI whereby BI shares would be exchanged for P&O stock. Each BI ordinary share (nominally £50) was to be paid for in P&O deferred stock, valuing each at £33 6s 8d, and each £1 BI five per cent preferred stock acquired by £1 fully-paid P&O five per cent preferred stock. The increase in capital which this represented was £700,000 for the preferred stock and £638,133 for the deferred stock, totalling £1.3m, making the P&O's total capital £4.8m.

Sutherland, in presenting the case for the merger, insisted on referring to it not only as a good deal financially, but essentially as 'a combination', and that the aim was 'to strengthen the position of both companies, to promote economy, eliminate possible rivalry and generally to increase the efficiency of their joint work'. He emphasised that the conditions agreed were the 'only possible terms on which this operation could have been carried out'. He tried to placate the anxieties of P&O stockholders and directors alike by reiterating the resolution that the P&O would maintain 'a preponderating voice' and that P&O business would continue under the same management and agencies. But his audience were suspicious of Inchcape's motives, and the policies he might adopt when he succeeded to the chairmanship.

That the prospect of Inchcape as their chairman was not altogether welcomed by P&O stockholders is plain. Sutherland maintained that the P&O was fortunate to acquire Lord Inchcape's services – there was no need to dwell on his reputation, this was well known to the whole shipping world. One of the two dissentients (such interventions were comparatively rare at P&O AGMs, such was the respect in which Sutherland was held) thought that Lord Inchcape's remuneration should be decided at a public meeting. Sutherland considered that this was but a small matter, and that it was ungentlemanly to raise it.

On 22 May 1914, Sutherland despatched a telegram to his fellow P&O directors:

Inchcape and I decided this morning in view of rumours in the Press about impending events that it would be desirable to announce our intentions to prevent unwise speculation and also to facilitate the business of the BI meeting on Tuesday where questions would certainly be asked. The notice which will appear puts an end to the secrecy which has been so well kept.

The final agreement came five days later on 27 May 1914, whereby the BI duly transferred all its issued stock to the P&O. All twelve P&O directors were now also directors of the BI, and all eight BI directors were to have a seat on the P&O board. At this stage, Inchcape was to continue as chairman of the BI for a term of ten years only, and there was nothing to say he would be the next P&O chairman. The BI closed its books on 30 September 1914, and officially ceased to exist. But, in reality, it was stronger than ever.

If the P&O really wanted to cut out rivalry with the BI in an age of fierce competition, and at the same time take over its property and goodwill, why was the BI not liquidated? Sutherland argued to P&O stockholders that BI shareholders wanted to retain an interest in their own company through the P&O, 'and we will have a controlling power in both concerns'. The BI, he said, was as large as P&O, too big to be immediately taken over, and it needed to be managed separately. Mackinnon Mackenzie would remain managers for at least the next ten years, and its commission business with the BI – although very extensive and remunerative – was necessary for the BI's effective running. The two companies operating side by side would have a wider base of security for future profits.

Yet this was not the full story. The directors' minutes record that when Sutherland opened negotiations with Inchcape in March 1914, he had advocated the liquidation of the BI, but objections were anticipated from the Board of Trade in view of the monopoly this would create. Also, the P&O could hardly have managed the heavy outlay of capital that would have been necessary to pay off the BI's debenture issue, which amounted to £1.6m. So, in a nutshell, the P&O's shortage of funds meant that the future independence and power of the BI, especially combined with the influence of its powerful leader, was assured.

By June 10, Waltons, the BI solicitors, informed Freshfields, representing the P&O, that the P&O offer to BI shareholders had been accepted by the requisite majority, and the acceptance documents were duly issued. Significantly, in the final proof of the notification to the press, all references to the P&O having 'a preponderating voice' had been eliminated.

The last meeting of the old P&O board was held on 22 July. Any hopes of a last-ditch attempt to assert the power of the P&O in the new arrangement were lost at Sutherland's insistence that all the actions of the previous few months should be taken as confirmed so that no minutes would need to be read at the first meeting of the new board in October. At the new board meeting, all seemed to proceed as planned. There was no immediate cause for alarm. It seemed just a formality when Sutherland successfully proposed that Inchcape's salary as a managing director of the P&O should be the same as that which he received from the BI as chairman – £5,000.

However, this meeting marked a turning point in P&O history more far-reaching than was realised at the time, except by Inchcape himself and possibly by Sutherland. Inchcape had written to his friend Lord Kilbracken, 'I have after much labour fixed it up with P&O. I think the settlement is an uncommonly good one and perfectly fair to both companies'. Sutherland agreed with this, or at least attempted to persuade himself, his fellow directors, and the P&O stockholders that he did. He would have been less happy to read another private letter of Inchcape's, boasting that he now had nearly 2m tons of shipping under his control, governing a 'single traffic system' which touched 'every conceivable port of the British Empire'.

That Sutherland's powers of persuasion were not altogether successful was shown in the reaction of a stockholder at the

Extraordinary Meeting of the P&O on 24 June. Drawing attention
of the high price finally paid for BI shares (£96, when the market rate
was £83, and the original agreement was £33), he complained that,
'the British India Company had made a very good bargain indeed.
Whether the P&O had done the same was open to doubt'. We have
no evidence of insider trading, but were rumours of merger alone
enough to push up the BI share price by nearly 300 per cent?

The steady accumulation of power by Inchcape, his assumption of
the chairmanship and two and a half per cent of the net profits, and
the new prominence of the BI and Mackinnon Mackenzie men and
interests *vis-à-vis* the P&O, saw the realisation of many P&O fears
over the next few years. Contemporary oral evidence, such as that
attested by Wilfrid Mizen, who joined the P&O in 1913 and rose to
the position of general manager before his retirement, confirms a
general feeling of usurpation of the P&O by the BI. But none
necessarily anticipated that this regime would continue for nearly a
quarter of a century, and that in the hard times that were to come the
BI and the Mackinnon/Inchcape group would play a vital part in the
shipping line's survival.

5

Plenipotentiary and government watchdog
Public life 1894–1914

Back in England, Mackay was now Sir James Mackay, his work for Indian currency reform bringing him a much coveted KCIE. He plunged eagerly into the affairs of the Council of India, cultivating secretaries of state Hamilton and Morley as he had done Viceroys Dufferin and Lansdowne, and became increasingly involved in British home affairs. This period saw a huge number of Government select committees examining almost every imaginable aspect of British commerce at home and overseas. As Mackay built up a reputation for his willingness to take part and for providing a sound businessman's approach, he was drawn in more and more. His service on seventeen committees in this period was remarkable in terms of his energy and patience alone. But did he make a real, unique contribution or did he just make up the numbers and lend weight? How were his efforts judged by the politicians of the day? Does his committee work show a widening range of knowledge and experience, or was he looking at the same question again and again in a different context?

One of Mackay's first public duties was his service on a Board of Trade Committee of 1898 considering 'the dissemination of commercial information', with the intention of expanding British trade overseas, at a time of mounting concern over Anglo-German commercial rivalry and the fear that British trade was losing out to foreign competition. The committee agreed that such information should be more systematically collected and distributed, and that consuls could play a valuable role. Mackay objected, insisting that a special note should be appended to the report:

Hitherto the discovery and exploitation of new markets have been the outcome of individual effort, unaided by the State, and there is no reason to suppose that there is any abatement in the energy of the British Nation.

This was typical of his attitude: he had a tendency to see everything from his point of view, assuming similar experiences of others, despite hours of evidence from a plethora of witnesses on this and other committees. In this particular case, extensive work on consular correspondence of this period has shown that British and foreign merchants relied heavily on help from their diplomatic represent- atives in finding new markets and sources of supply. But Mackay was especially outspoken against consuls supplying British traders with information on the solvency or otherwise of businesses in their areas, helping recover debts or advertising British goods.

Yet there was some value in wider publication of commercial information generally. Mackay agreed that

if the working classes were acquainted with foreign trade competition and the cost of raw materials and production, then such information might tend to prevent disputes and stoppages of work, which generally result in the success of competing countries.

But, overall, Mackay argued that spreading information would help less enterprising businessmen: they should not be placed on the same level as those first in the field, who should be allowed to keep this advantage. The report's conclusion to promote commercial knowledge would, Mackay argued,

retard rather than further the development of British trade, because men are induced to embark in commerce not with the object of increasing the volume of the country's trade, but in the hope of obtaining some substantial advantage for themselves. Lessen the prospects of obtaining that advantage and the volume of the country's trade will decrease.

Mackay worried that Britain's competitors might make more use of the information than Britain's entrepreneurs.

Mackay's own conclusions inevitably determined the line of questioning he adopted, which aimed to prove that most of Britain's overseas trade was built up by individual effort, not by Government aid. The merchants and traders called as witnesses naturally confirmed this view. No one pointed out that Mackay's own com- mercial success was heavily influenced by Mackinnon Mackenzie's work as agents for the BI, who received substantial Government subsidies, in mail contracts and in transport work. Mackay's contribution to this committee shows a somewhat blinkered and unreasonable attitude to those less commercially successful than himself, and he offered no constructive suggestions to aid British commerce against German competition. He was more interested in the role of the individual businessman than the wider context of national well-being and used this committee as a platform for his views, when it was really more narrowly concerned with improving the commercial infrastructure. Did Mackay maintain this attitude in later committees?

Closely related in purpose to the Commercial Information Committee was that of four years later, which enquired into the constitution of the Consular Service. This was the first of Mackay's contacts with Bonar Law, the future Prime Minister. They worked together on the age structure, entrance requirements, salaries and grades of consular officials, and possible methods of improving consular knowledge of commercial matters. It seems surprising that Mackay was brought in at this point after his outspoken attack against the use of consuls in commercial expansion in 1898. His complaints that many consuls lacked competence was borne out by one of the principle findings of the committee, that 'the Consular Service as it exists at present offers no attraction to capable young men', when they were badly needed to support British trade.

In any case, many consuls found themselves inundated with such duties as the engagement and discharge of British seamen and the administration of the Merchant Shipping Act, to the extent that they were unable to attend to British subjects who needed their help, commercial or otherwise. Mackay's questions revealed that 'the most successful traders have no desire to invoke the assistance of our Consuls, and that they consider themselves able to obtain more useful information for their business than the best Consuls can supply', confirming his conclusions of 1898.

Yet the Consular Service was not helped by the fact that for too long it had attracted the less able Civil Service recruits, especially for the less attractive and more remote postings. Bonar Law, despite Mackay's scorn, still maintained that their role was valuable, and therefore argued that recruits should have languages, numeracy, and training in commercial geography, the elements of political economy, British mercantile law and shipping practice, with time at the commercial branch of the Board of Trade.

But the salaries offered were derisory. Mackay was reluctant to increase government spending on Civil Service salaries, but, he pointed out, how could one hope to attract able young men from leading commercial houses if the maximum reward for a Consul-General was only £1,200 and junior vice-consuls received as little as £300? Mackay himself, probably the sort of recruit they were after, would have had little incentive to enter the Consular Service except patriotism. If he had joined at the age of thirty-two, with ten years' experience at Mackinnon Mackenzie, he would have received £500 p.a.; this bore little comparison with his salary by 1884 of £924, with £215 house rent and extra for entertaining, not to mention the opportunities for investment at preferential rates. When Mackay left India, aged forty-two, he received £1,680 in salary and £480 in rent allowance, and his share of the profits as partner totalled nearly £90,000 during his stay. If he had then joined the Consular Service, he could not have hoped for as much as £1,000 a year.

On the other hand, Bonar Law and his Government colleagues saw public service as an honourable duty, attracting gentlemen of private means who were not influenced by salary scales. Mackay was not confident of the prospects for the report's recommendations. He felt frustrated dealing with the niceties of the Civil Service. His next assignment was much more to his liking.

Mackay's first major task on behalf of the Council of India began when he was called upon to represent the India Office in a matter which was very close to his business interests: a proposed mail service to East Africa under the British flag. The whole matter had wide imperial implications. Lord Salisbury at the Foreign Office was most concerned at 'the danger to which British commercial interests are exposed by the competition of heavily-subsidised lines under foreign flags'. This interdepartmental committee, meeting in 1898, considered the adequacy of the existing steamer service, the political and economic grounds for extending it, the possibility of doing it other than by direct subsidy, such as the carriage of Uganda railway material, and the feasibility of inviting tenders from the major companies.

Despite Mackay's protestations of the crucial importance of this line, which had been served by the BI since 1894 without subsidy in a constant struggle against the French and the Germans, the question was constantly postponed due to Salisbury's reluctance to provide Government support.

To advance his case, Mackay described a simple experiment he had conducted whereby Mackinnon Mackenzie had sent specie, valued at Rs 550,000 (about $258,000 or approximately £35,000), from Calcutta via Bombay to Zanzibar by three different lines: the BI, the French Messageries Maritimes and the German national line. The BI was by far the most expensive: Rs 639 compared with Rs 601 charged by the French and only Rs 503 by the Germans. The reason was the advanced age and small size of the BI's vessels on this route, which was not profitable enough to allow them to be replaced. The BI made some money on the coasting trades of East Africa, but their efforts to maximise business opportunities were not always successful: for example, Hindu passengers, who objected on religious grounds to travelling in close proximity to cattle on the BI ships, were lost to rival lines.

On the previous two committees, Mackay had spoken at length against State 'interference', and in support of completely free enterprise: but here he lobbied strongly for Government of India funding for the BI's shipping services. To no avail though. It was not necessarily the case that Mackay's persuasive powers let him down: the Government of India faced more important problems – heavy expenditure in India itself on irrigation projects, famine relief and railway construction – than to care about British political and economic representation in East Africa. The BI had to abandon this service in 1908, much to Mackay's chagrin.

His motives were much less selfish in his next major undertaking. Honest and sincere patriotism – combined with a sufficient business income to work for little or no remuneration – led him to agree to take charge of the negotiation of a new commercial treaty with China in late 1901, following the suppression of the Boxer Rebellion. The India Office sought Mackay because of his experience in dealing with 'natives', compiling detailed commercial reports and, perhaps most significantly, his willingness to undertake what was expected to be a long and frustrating task. So it proved, and Mackay was to spend nearly a year between Shanghai and the other commercial outposts, kept mostly in inactivity by the shrewd leader of the Chinese delegation, Sheng-Ta-jen, who kept pretending to be indisposed and thereby continually missing and cancelling meetings. At home, the controversial new treaty faced a mixture of opposition and support. In finally achieving a partial abolition of *likin*, and helping to regularise and encourage British trade with China and offset Russian, German and French competition, Mackay's GCMG was well earned. Although the total abolition of *likin* did not take place until 1931, Mackay did call a stop to the destructive internal customs duties on goods imported into China from Britain. British exports did still pay imperial maritime customs dues on entry, however. Hamilton at the India Office paid enthusiastic tribute to 'the first treaty of its kind which has not been negotiated with shotted guns behind the British negotiations'.

The China treaty, according to a diary Mackay kept during his travels, was the most trying task of his entire career. The diary described not only the complex, time-consuming and exasperating nature of the negotiations, but provides an insight into the contribution of Lady Mackay at every stage of the proceedings.

Mackay began the diary in early June 1902. His interviews with Sheng to abolish the *likin* duties were then at a critical point. A delaying tactic which the wily Chinaman employed was to question each individual commodity affected by the *likin* abolition proposals. The salt and opium *likin* barriers would have to remain, he said, unless he could get each individual ruler of the regions of China – known as viceroys – to agree. This was a major blow to Mackay. One of the main reasons for eradicating *likin* was to facilitate the movement of such valuable trade goods as salt and opium throughout China, to the benefit of British commerce. Mackay sought and received wider powers of authority to negotiate with the viceroys to win their individual agreement to ending both *likin* and salt barriers, and began a tour of regional centres of China, accompanied by his wife and eldest daughter, Margaret.

The viceroys were initially completely unhelpful. For example, at Hankow, viceroy Chang Chi-tung was reluctant to come to an agreement with Mackay without Sheng, who was suffering another bout of 'illness'. When Sheng finally appeared, talks began. The meetings at Hankow were lengthy and tiring in the extreme, lasting up to ten hours each day. They reached a climax two weeks later at a session at the British Consulate stretching from 9.30 a.m. till 7 p.m. in which Mackay felt he had nearly tied up *likin* and salt tax abolition, at least as far as it related to Hankow. Lady Mackay helped in drawing up the details of the treaty as it then stood. The Mackays then wanted to leave as soon as possible, especially as one of the diplomatic staff attached to their party had gone down with dysentery and needed urgent medical attention.

Yet the very next day, Chang disputed another fundamental clause, and Mackay described the 'very hard work to get the thing through – great fight over the opening of the treaty ports'. A day later, a letter from Sheng's sickbed agreed with Chang against Mackay. After another ten hours of negotiations with Chang, all articles had finally been agreed in such a way to please all the Chinese leaders, and Mackay sent yet another wire to the Foreign Office with the news.

Mackay returned from this meeting in triumph to his family, but to his horror found his daughter at death's door with typhoid. Despite this, he and his wife spent three hours ciphering the telegrams to the Foreign Office – all official and most commercial wires were coded at this time – including a particularly urgent one to Lansdowne at the India Office asking that they might come home as soon as possible. The next day they waited for replies. It was 'very muggy and steaming, awfully dull day, with nothing to do and waiting on in anxiety'. His worries about his family's health were compounded by the news that the gatekeeper, whose post was just outside their bedroom window, had just died of cholera.

Leaving Hankow after hearing from the Foreign Office, the party proceeded to Xamen, where another viceroy was persuaded to agree to Mackay's proposals. Then the Mackays went on to Nanking, Margaret having to be carried on board their steamer. Several more viceroys had to be visited, Mackay complaining all the while that he never wanted to see the Yangtze valley again. At Chungkiang he obtained newspapers, and read of Lansdowne's encouraging statements in the House of Lords. At Woosung he took three weeks to come to an agreement with the old viceroy Chingstee Toung, staying in the royal palace all the while, living solely off pigeon's eggs, with the temperature never falling below 100 degrees in the shade. But now he had a new worry: his wife too had developed typhoid. As the treaty went to the printers, all but Mackay were ill with diarrhoea or worse, and he now pushed Sheng hard to come to a final agreement, arguing that if he objected to anything more at this stage, Mackay would complain to the Foreign Office that he had 'been subjected to a gross breach of faith'.

At the beginning of August, the treaty, and the lives of his wife and daughter, hung in the balance. Sheng would give nothing away, despite the agreements that Mackay had won from the viceroys. In desperation, Mackay contacted the ambassador, Ernest Satow, as Sheng was claiming a lack of authority to settle the outstanding clauses concerning the opening of more treaty ports in China. Mackay tried another way of forcing Sheng to finalise the treaty: starting the process of translating it into Chinese. Fortunately Lady Mackay had recovered enough to supervise the translators and cipher all the queries to the Foreign Office. For most of August, Mackay spent between five and ten hours with Sheng each day, and by the beginning of September he had obtained Sheng's signature and received Lansdowne's formal congratulations. He then returned home, making short commercial tours of Japan and the Pacific ports of the United States on the way.

Mackay's patience and negotiating skills had been stretched to their utmost. Had it been worth it? The proceedings, which fill two 300-page volumes, represent an exhaustive examination of British commerce with China. With the abolition of *likin*, British trade, particularly in goods from India, resumed its importance in this vast and largely undeveloped region, on the scale it had done before *likin* had been reintroduced. Mackay's work also had the wider significance of helping to offset Russian competition, which had always remained free of duties and had been making great headway.

As in the case of the mail contract to East Africa, the need to abolish *likin* in China reflected a mixture of political and economic aims, stimulated by a form of passive imperialism. Britain did not necessarily want the expense of establishing British colonial rule in East Africa or China, but she wanted to ensure that no one else did. Mackay was thus flying the flag by, firstly, persuading China to agree to abolish *likin* duties throughout the Empire in return for an increase in duties paid by the British on imports of Indian goods and exports of local Chinese goods and, secondly, by extracting an agreement from the Chinese authorities that 'British Indian subjects and goods are to be treated on an equality with Russian subjects and goods'.

Mackay's committee work back at home after his return from China ranged from a Secretary of State for India's Committee to enquire into the expediency or otherwise of retaining Cooper's Hill College, a seminary originally instituted by the East India Company for the training of its recruits for India; a Board of Trade and Local Government Board Committee of 1903; a conference of representatives from Britain, the USA and Mexico concerning the introduction of the gold standard into China and Mexico; an enquiry into the organisation of the department of the Controller of the Navy; and a Royal Commission on the natural resources and trade of the British Empire of 1911.

Worth considering in more detail were a committee of the Board of Agriculture of 1904 to enquire whether preference was given by English railways to produce from abroad being conveyed over English lines; a Treasury Committee investigating Government workshops in 1906; and an enquiry into Indian railway finance and administration of 1907–8. Mackay also concluded negotiations concerning British trade on the Tigris and Euphrates rivers and the Baghdad railway concession of 1913; and finally, on the eve of war, a subcommittee of the Committee on Imperial Defence looking into the question of the insurance of British shipping in time of war. Such a wide range of enquiries highlights Mackay's great energy and enthusiasm for government work in this period.

Early in 1904, Mackay was asked to join a committee to investigate differing railway rates, appointed by the Board of Agriculture and Fisheries. Seen as contributing an external business perspective among the Board of Trade officials and economists who dominated the committee, Mackay reviewed the rates charged by rival companies and reported on whether or not preferential treatment was given by them to foreign and colonial goods – mainly garden, farm and dairy produce – compared with rates for home-produced items.

As a large-scale, important trader himself, Mackay supported preferential rates for produce in bulk which travelled regularly and was of a uniform shape. These rates, he argue, were available to both home and foreign producers. Overall, he was in favour of maintaining the status quo –'the local trader cannot expect for small, irregular, and often ill-packed consignments, the same rates and facilities as are given to the large, regular and well-packed consignments'. Foreign produce was given preference, but only because it came in whole trainloads from the ports, and home produce came piecemeal in wagonloads. In many respects, foreign produce had the advantage. For example, frozen meat could be packed more tightly than fresh. Traders who felt disadvantaged by 'the great companies' were allowed to demand equal rates and the Board of Agriculture and Fisheries would act on behalf of a trader in offering conciliation.

The committee sat for seventeen days stretched over a year from June 1904, of which Mackay was present for nine. His questions were practical and searching. He asked a representative of the Board of Agriculture how a farmer would go about sending a consignment of goods by rail for the first time, and heard a suprising admission of ignorance, and then the worrying remark that a rate quoted by a clerk would not necessarily be the same as that charged in the end. He thus revealed the breakdown in communications between the board, the railway companies and the public.

Mackay constantly supported the coasting trade as an economical alternative to rail in order to lower costs. He argued that some ports, such as Goole, would be better off without a railway altogether. Witnesses representing the Great Northern Railway, who objected to the idea of railways being confined to places without water transport, were shocked.

Above all, Mackay saw the whole issue as a practical business matter. He thought it reasonable that the railway companies arranged their rates to get the best return. But he did call attention to the unjustified power of the middlemen acting between farmers and railway companies in keeping rates high and preventing the sort of cooperation between farmers that could help them in bargaining. He made a substantial contribution to the discussions, always asking for points of clarification, exact quantities, prices and timings.

Almost as soon as the Railway Rates Committee completed its work, Mackay was asked by the Treasury to join the Government Factories and Workshops Committee, to enquire whether or not Government production could be advantageously replaced by private enterprise. Before the changes wrought by the First World War which increased Government influence in everyday life and business, private enterprise had been encouraged in an atmosphere of *laissez-faire* which reached a peak in the first decade of the new century.

The committee looked first at the Enfield small arms factory, suffering a falling off of demand for its output after the Boer War. The other Government small arms factory at Sparkbrook in Birmingham had already been sold to private interests. This had been welcomed because it added to the resources of the private sector upon which the Government could call in wartime and maintained a reserve of productive power for national emergencies. Mackay agreed that the Government arsenal 'must be adequately equipped for tiding over the first few months of a critical period', but after that, 'private enterprise may be trusted to meet national requirements to a certain extent'.

Mackay and his colleagues had no conception at this time of the enormity of the need for armaments in wartime. Lloyd George's Ministry of Munitions would have been inconceivable in 1906, when future hostilities were envisaged on a scale similar to that of the Boer War. So Mackay pushed strongly for leaving resources to private enterprises, especially as 'trade was certainly in a better position than the arsenal to face the inconvenience of a fluctuating demand', because trade was not tied to one customer nor to specified products. Unit production costs at the reduced arsenal would unfortunately rise but this would be offset by the advantages of a greater power of expansion. Woolwich Arsenal was retained in preference to others as 'rapid expansion is most easily effected when manufacture is carried on in close proximity to a large centre of population where other industries (besides the manufacture of munitions of war) are conducted'.

Mackay and the Treasury officials with whom he sat felt content in 1906 that the country was well prepared for war. They cannot be criticised for taking such a view at that time, and Mackay was merely acting as their ally in helping reduce State costs and encouraging private enterprise.

The first committee of which Mackay acted as chairman followed in 1907–8 and reported on the Indian railway finance and administration, especially the alleged inadequacy of the existing arrangements for railway traffic in India.

Although there had been an increase in funding allocated to the railways of over £4m (from £5.3m in 1900–1901 to £9.7m in 1906–1907), there were many complaints of inadequate rolling stock and a severe shortage of crossing stations and sidings. Mackay recommended providing 13,000 more wagons, and went on to consider how much money could properly and advantageously be raised for more equipment. The committee looked forward to the time when the existing 30,000 miles of railway could be increased to 100,000: 'we believe that even this estimate of mileage is short of that which will ultimately be found to be necessary'. The problem hinged on the amount of capital that could be raised by the Government in Westminster each year, and how much could realistically be borrowed. Mackay, with financiers Lord Rothschild and Lord

Swayttling, decided to allocate £7.5m from India's budget for railway costs, with another £5m expected to come from railway revenue.

Mackay recommended direct Government borrowing by the issue of India stock, together with an issue by the railway companies in India of guaranteed share capital offering dividends which would share in surplus profits. Fears of high interest rates and heavier expenditure than expected kept the committee's recommendations cautious.

In raising more money for India's railways, the committee upheld the principle that providing equipment and improving existing lines should take precedence over the construction of new lines. Thus they concentrated on making the communications of British India more efficient, rather than extending them to open up more areas within the subcontinent. This was subsequently to be one of the greatest areas of contention among historians when considering the impact of the British on India – that railway networks were geared exclusively for strategic movements of troops and for the import/export trade via the ports of British India, with no concern for allaying the effects of regional famine and raising the standard of living over the maximum area. Mackay's attitude to these inequalities was reflected almost universally in Government and British commercial circles.

Overall, Mackay's efforts to improve Indian railways were rendered only partially successful by administrative confusion and fears of heavy debts. The service offered was woefully inadequate, and railway mileage compared with land space and population was still amongst the worst in the world. Yet his efforts went some way to relieving its problems, and were rewarded with the Order of the Star of India, his second knighthood, in January 1910.

On the eve of war, after his peerage conferred in 1911, Inchcape became involved in another foreign and colonial matter in which, even more than in the East Africa mail contract discussions, his public and business interests were inextricably intertwined. This was an Anglo-Turkish joint venture on the Euphrates and Tigris rivers in Mesopotamia. Through the Ottoman Company, Britain aimed to contain and control German competition in the area. H.F.B. Lynch, whose company had managed a British steamship service on the rivers since the 1840s, proposed to manage jointly the new steamers with Inchcape, who had been brought in as a representative of the Foreign Office. Inchcape took a firm stand from the outset: he was to have the upper hand, and the Foreign Office agreed that the BI would continue carrying mails from India on this route.

A concession was provisionally agreed in September 1913 that the new company, in which British, German and Turkish interests were to be represented, was to enjoy monopoly rights on the rivers for sixty years. But neither Inchcape nor the Foreign Office, in the person of Sir Edward Grey, felt they could trust the Turkish authorities, led by Hakki Pasha. For instance, the Imperial Ottoman Government had begun various new irrigation schemes in Southern Mesopotamia, employing a British firm to carry out the necessary preliminary surveys. But the Ottoman Government had not awarded the subsequent contract to this firm. Grey was concerned that British businesses were working on false pretences, and that the Ottoman Government might offer the job to a foreign firm, undercutting the British bids and availing themselves of work already completed in the meantime. Hakki Pasha would not give a satisfactory answer to Foreign Office enquiries.

Inchcape and Lynch were to hold a forty per cent interest in the construction of rail terminal facilities at Basra and Baghdad, the railway materials for which were to be carried by the steamers. Inchcape's insistence that the Baghdad–Kuwait stretch of the railway should be kept under British control led to the establishment of an informal protectorate over Kuwait in 1914. Meanwhile, the negotiations with Hakki Pasha came to nothing. The outbreak of war interrupted Inchcape's ambitions in international commercial diplomacy, but they were soon to be resumed.

With the possibility of war becoming more and more apparent, Inchcape was asked to investigate the implications of insuring British shipping in time of war. With representatives from the Liverpool Steamship Owners' Association and Lloyd's, the committee tried to ensure that overseas trade would not be interrupted because British shipowners could not afford war-risk insurance.

Inchcape was adamant that, much as he supported Government protection of merchant ships in wartime, this should not be seen as a gift. Thus he recommended that, in the case of hull insurance, the Government should share the costs with the existing mutual clubs, reinsuring their policies. The Government should charge a flat fee for cargo insurance, irrespective of the voyage or character of the cargo. With the uncertainties of war, Inchcape emphasised the importance of all premiums and claims being paid in cash – the latter on the spot.

The meetings were held in conditions of great secrecy, to prevent any of the British Government's wartime arrangements being leaked to the enemy. Inchcape estimated that probably ten per cent of British ships would be at sea in enemy waters when war broke out, and would be liable to immediate capture. He considered that another ten per cent might be lost in the following six months. The Board of Trade argued that freights would rise dramatically to compensate for ship losses. But Inchcape pointed out that many companies traded under long-term arrangements to stabilise freights, and these needed six months' notice to amend. Shipowners would not send their vessels to sea unless they could be assured of a degree of Government cover. No one had any idea of the scale of the conflict to come, of the nature of dislocation it would bring, or how long it would last. Inchcape's attitude could still be light-hearted. At the proposal to set up Government bureaux to handle insurance claims, he remarked 'I wonder what office hours they would keep'.

Looking at this record of public service as a whole, to what extent does Mackay's peerage of 1911 as Baron Inchcape of Strathnaver reflect the quality and importance of his contribution? It could be argued that fifteen years on the Council of India and service on so many committees were in themselves worthy of such recognition, but Inchcape did not enjoy sufficient regard from the Prime Minister to explain the honour bestowed. Asquith apparently did not think highly of him. In writing to Venetia Stanley in 1915, he described a dinner party where 'I found a most boring company, Lord and Lady Inchcape, Lord Justice Banks, Sir Guy and Lady Granet, and one or two other dim people'.

Instead, Inchcape's peerage was the result of an offer by Morley, at the India Office, of the viceroyalty of India in succession to Minto, in 1909. Yet Morley did not consult the Cabinet. Mackay's wildest dreams were coming true until shattered by Asquith's decision that it would be a mistake to appoint a man with so many commercial interests in the sub-continent to such a powerful position. In this light, his peerage may be interpreted as something of a consolation prize, and it does reflect Asquith's apparent desire to retain his services for the future. The new Lord Inchcape wrote to his friend Godley, the Under-Secretary at the India Office,

Of course I am very pleased to get it, more for the sake of my wife and family than myself. I must candidly admit I think it is a reward much more than I deserve ... but I shall always have the satisfaction of feeling that I never asked for it and that I did not pay for it.

Yet a peerage was a poor substitute for the viceroyalty. If it had gone through as Morley had planned, Mackay's whole life would have been changed. It would have been a complete turning point. Aged fifty-seven then, he would have remained in politics after his return from the Indian Railways Committee and his term as viceroy, and could well have been a member of the War Cabinet in 1914–18. His business career would then have taken second place, and it is unlikely that he would have succeeded to the leadership of the BI and then the P&O.

Despite his disappointment at not gaining the viceroyalty, Inchcape was himself convinced of the value of his contribution to Government work before the war and, like many of his contemporaries, faced the outbreak of hostilities with more optimism than pessimism. By 1918, his outlook had changed completely, and his attitude to his public duties was radically altered. It was not that he then wished to avoid such work – quite the contrary, he far surpassed his already prodigious record in public service – but his outlook was different.

His concerns before the war were chiefly with consolidating the role of the British Empire in the world from a position of strength, not weakness. He could afford to pour scorn on the efforts of consular officials to further British trade, he could accept the Government decision not to subsidise the BI's Bombay–Zanzibar service, and he could force through the abolition of *likin* in China. He could oppose Government interference in the matter of preferential railway rates in Britain, and any further spending on Government workshops. He could allocate large Government sums for the reorganisation of India's railways. He upheld Britain's interests over Germany in Mesopotamia, and was brought in as the spokesman of the British shipping interest to comment on the state provision of maritime insurance.

Inchcape was confident of his authority, and the authority of the British Empire. None of these concerns appeared to be matters of life and death at the time. It was important that the flag should continue to be flown throughout the world, and the Empire did not feel immediately threatened. Government intervention in business and in public welfare was still limited, and an overall attitude of *laissez-faire* prevailed: it appeared to Inchcape and many others that most people did not want, or need, Government help. Inchcape's contribution was to bolster these feelings, and he showed a remarkably consistent and predictable attitude to the problems he was asked to consider. But these views were no longer necessarily appropriate during the war or, more important, in its aftermath.

6

'Let us get on with the war'
Business and public life, 1914–1918

As the head of the world's greatest shipping combine at the outbreak of the world's greatest military and economic conflagration, Inchcape's political and business influence reached its highest point. His experience and track record of service on Government Committees, combined with his position of ascendancy in the shipping world, at a time of such national and international crisis, accelerated an already rapid process of public recognition of his work.

The four years of war witnessed the peak of Inchcape's achievements: despite enormous casualties, the P&O and the BI, together with the enterprises within the Mackinnon/Inchcape group, emerged stonger than ever. Meanwhile Inchcape's public services on behalf of the Government became almost indispensable. How did he steer the P&O, the BI and all his concerns so effectively through the war? What was his role in the national war effort?

The survival and flourishing of Inchcape's business interests during the First World War may be understood only through a year by year analysis of problems faced and solved. Under Inchcape's guidance, disruption of trade, losses of ships and men, Government acquisitioning and tonnage shortages were overcome. How was this achieved?

The first result of the outbreak of hostilities was a rise in general labour costs: general staff who had joined the armed services as volunteers were still paid. Inchcape decided that they should not suffer a reduction in earnings, so meagre army and naval pay was topped up, and meanwhile the lack of their services was felt. The P&O in particular not only lost men, but younger directors, such as Kenneth, Inchcape's son, and William Mackinnon, a descendant of

his namesake who had served on the BI Board and then joined P&O.
Another immediate and unforeseen difficulty concerned settling
debts outstanding to Germans. Accounts due to German firms were
being held up in various P&O, BI and Mackinnon Mackenzie
departments after Britain's declaration of war against Germany in
August 1914, which included a clause that no payments whatever
were to be made to the enemy. Companies incorporated in Germany
were classified as enemies, and the Government suggested that
payments should be made only to German or Austrian firms with
businesses confined to Britain. Despite public anti-German
demonstrations, Inchcape decided that he would meet payments to
firms that were still allowed to trade.

The impact of war on the fleet was also immediate, with the loss of
the *Chilkana*, a brand new 5,000-ton BI cargo ship, in mid-October
1914, sunk by the German cruiser *Enden*. Then the *Rohilla* was lost
off Whitby, followed by the small *Harlington*, and the *Lorara* was
hired by the Government in India in November 1914.

Yet by the end of 1914, the P&O had recovered from the cashflow
problems it suffered at the time of the merger with the BI. Helped by
income from Government hiring and the rise in freights, receipts rose
to over £200,000 per month, which managed to keep pace with
running costs and enabled the P&O and BI to complete all
outstanding payments on new ships. At his last AGM before
Inchcape took the helm, Sutherland described 1914 as one of the
Company's most successful years. Gross revenue reached £4.8m,
allowing a cash profit of £750,000, £500,000 for depreciation, a
£70,000 balance for 1915 – much larger than usual – and a generous
topping up of the reserve fund, which stood at £2m. This success, he
argued, justified continuing to pay a dividend in wartime.

The expansion of business generally in 1914 led Inchcape to search
for enlarged premises for the P&O and the London headquarters of
his overseas firms, and he successfully negotiated the purchase of
119–120 Leadenhall Street for £25,000, a good investment and a
large, well placed office. To acknowledge the particularly heavy
administrative work caused by the war, in cargo, passengers and
special works, Inchcape granted £5,000 for distribution among the
London staff.

Despite the reluctance of many P&O shareholders to accept
Sutherland's resignation and, more to the point, Inchcape's
succession to the chairmanship, there was no apparent opposition at

board level. It was accepted that the outbreak of war was no time for disputes of leadership. An early sign of Inchcape having already gained a powerful position was the fact that he signed the minutes of the December 1914 board meeting, before Sutherland had actually resigned and whilst Sir William Adamson was nominally in the chair. Sutherland was voted £40,000 and an extra £15,000 to compensate for his immediate loss of earnings, indicative of the value of two and a half per cent of the net profits of the P&O, on which his earnings had been based since a vote of thanks from his board in the 1880s. At this point Inchcape officially received £50,000 as managing director, but he was to claim Sutherland's entitlement in due course.

1915, Inchcape's first full year of P&O chairmanship, saw the war gather momentum, with escalating ship losses. Two 8,000-ton P&O mail steamers, the *India* and the *Persia*, were torpedoed, and the BI *Umeta*, requisitioned by the Government, was sunk by a submarine, an early warning of the menace which would wreak havoc amongst British shipping. British commerce-raiding against the Germans, and the slow stranglehold they exerted on German trade routes, were ultimately effective, but not before the U-boat had done its damage.

The commandeering of P&O and BI ships by the Government rose from twenty steamers of 167,676 tons in February 1915 to thirty of 242,741 tons by November the same year, and persuading the Government to accept war-risk insurance became one of Inchcape's first objectives. This he achieved by mid-1915. No record survives of the development of P&O and BI vessels during 1915: not surprisingly, printed proceedings of AGMs drew the attention of the censor, but the internal board meeting records are also strangely silent.

Thus little is known of the management of the fleet overall, except snippets of detail: Inchcape took immediate advantage of the rise in shipbuilding prices by selling six old and unwanted ships at a large profit. But he could not replace them and, with soaring coal prices, it became more and more difficult to carry on the mail service. Not only did he have fewer ships at his disposal, but crews were increasingly hard to find, not just due to those joining the services. For instance, on several BI steamers, frightened Lascars fled home, leaving the passengers to work the ships.

The paralysis of trade since August 1914 continued. Sutherland, still advising the P&O board, likened the situation to the slump which followed the opening of the Suez Canal. P&O usually carried at least 200,000 tons of cargo from the Continent per year: this was hopeless now. There was still a large demand for tonnage to the USA, Argentina and the Mediterranean but, apart from the export trade to Australia, the situation favoured the tramp rather than the liner. However, Inchcape was to find during the course of 1915, the huge Government demand for shipping as transports and the rates they paid more than adequately offset this early disadvantage.

Inchcape's chairmanship, from the outset, was marked by the assertion of his ultimate loyalty to the BI and the Mackinnon/Inchcape group. Naïve P&O directors and shareholders, who still believed Sutherland's pre-merger promise that P&O interests would predominate, were soon disillusioned. For example, in March 1915 Inchcape insisted that the P&O *Mata Hari* be transferred to the BI on the grounds of preventing competition on the Penang to Singapore route, and that the P&O agent at Singapore should be under the control of Mackinnon Mackenzie in Calcutta. The BI's Mazagon Dock in Bombay was enlarged and reorganised to take over the property, stores, barges and moveable plant of the P&O as well as the BI. P&O and BI banking arrangements at Port Said were amalgamated under the auspices of the BI, saving £30,000 p.a. Despite criticism at the time, these moves helped streamline the P&O's operations and considerably increased its prestige and resources overseas. This integration went to the extreme of the hanging of portraits of past BI chairmen – Sir William Mackinnon and James Hall – on the P&O boardroom walls. These were signs of more to come.

The war's impact on the shipping industry tended towards a pooling of resources rather than an intensification of competition, indicating an overall problem of maintaining services. In August, Inchcape successfully proposed an arrangement between the BI, the French Messageries Maritimes and British Union Castle to accept each other's tickets held by passengers to make the best of the irregular services between Europe and East Africa. Similarly, when he found the BI short of tonnage in the Far East, Inchcape was able to charter vessels from the Indo-China Steam Navigation Company, thanks to his contacts with Jardine Matheson in Hong Kong.

He kept the P&O and BI war effort to a maximum by helping sustain patriotism and a strong sense of purpose. Thus he effusively congratulated captains who survived attacks, such as the commander of the *Karoa*, shelled at Sulva Bay, who manoeuvred his ship so successfully that only one in thirty projectiles hit their target. He frequently forwarded to the press letters from his officers describing their ordeals, especially highlighting the bravery of the lower ranks, such as Lascars and firemen. To a country starved of news, when military movements and the many disasters were kept secret for months, if not years, and when terrifying rumours of German barbarism abounded, Inchcape's stories of BI and P&O heroes did much to maintain morale.

Inchcape brought attention to another aspect of the P&O and BI war effort: the channelling of P&O and BI capital into war bonds and other Government investments. In March he bought £40,000 exchequer bonds, £20,000 French treasury bills, and put £50,000 on fixed deposit with the National Bank of India; his £44,000 investment in Argentine Government treasury bills was less directly patriotic and more profit orientated.

In June, the P&O put a further £100,000 into British treasury bills and £60,000 in East Indian Railways, followed later that month with £180,000 in British treasury bonds. The Board then approved an investment of £650,000 in new war loans, which was topped up to reach £1m by July. As 1915 progressed, Inchcape systematically divested foreign investments from the P&O portfolio, usually at a profit but not always: he lost £3,600 on £10,000 three per cent German bonds. These investments on behalf of the P&O and the BI were not just a patriotic gesture: all earned over 3.5 per cent, some nearly five per cent.

New tonnage to replace vessels sunk, and to cope with the increased level of business, now became one of Inchcape's greatest problems. He exploited his powerful position with shipbuilders to the full: in November 1915 he persuaded Stephen's to reserve the next two yard numbers for him for P&O, BI or AUSN ships. Supplies from British yards were never adequate throughout the war. Inchcape was already on the lookout for whole fleets to acquire.

Reviewing 1915 at his first AGM, Inchcape highlighted difficulties such as maintaining services and coping with coal prices of three times their prewar level. Conscious of containing the wave of patriotism leading men everywhere to rush to join the ranks – over 500,000 joined in the first month of Kitchener's appeals, and more than three million voluntarily accepted the King's shilling during the course of the war – Inchcape emphasised that officers and men staying with the P&O were providing an equally valuable service to their country. It already had a splendid record. Four hundred and eighty employees had joined up, of whom twenty-seven had been killed and sixteen wounded, with a boy of eighteen winning a VC: but maintaining P&O services was paramount.

Then Inchcape had to justify why, at a time of increased profits – nearly £300,000 on a gross revenue of £5.1m, more than double that of ten years before – the dividend on preferred stock was not more than five per cent and fifteen per cent on deferred stock, and why nearly £80,000 was held in reserve for next year. He pointed to the special levy on profits implemented by the Government which had to be provided for; he maintained that neutrals were doing much better than combatants, and many British firms were selling out, which the P&O, with its mail contract commitments, could not do; and insisted that the rates paid for commandeered vessels were low compared with those on the open market. In this patriotic duty, P&O had carried two and a half million officers and men, 320,000 sick and wounded, nearly a million horses and two and a half million tons of stores, with only 0.1 per cent loss of life. No one knew how long the war would last, and what might happen.

Privately, Inchcape was more confident. To Mackinnon Mackenzie colleagues in Calcutta, he acknowledged, 'As you are aware, our earnings during the last year have been abnormally large ... we have made enormously large profits'. The BI had remitted home more than £1.4m from Calcutta for 1914. The total for the first six months of 1915 has not been discovered, but over £400,000 was remitted during the second half year. As Inchcape wrote to his old India Office friend Lord Kilbracken, who had since become a BI director, this was enough to pay for all the P&O's and the BI's new ships.

Inchcape took the opportunity of the apparent success of his first year in office to forward a resolution that he be paid a comparatively modest £2,000 for the year ending September 1915 or – significantly – a percentage of the P&O's net earnings at the same rate paid to Sir Thomas Sutherland, whichever was the higher. Together with a recommendation that directors be paid their emoluments free of income tax, this was not opposed, and Inchcape's personal wealth, already substantial, was assured.

By the end of 1915, despite worrying signs of heavy casualties, beginnings of U-boat attacks and the sinking of the *Lusitania*, the spirit of jingoism in Britain had been sapped but not entirely eroded. Inchcape, like many of his contemporaries including Churchill, tried to retain an air that to a certain extent it was still 'business as usual'. Government control of shipping at this stage was minimal. For instance, the P&O handbook of October 1915 was very much the same as always, except for a sticker printed in red on the cover advising that calls and sailings from Tangier and Brindisi were temporarily suspended and that the boat train from Liverpool Street had been retimed.

Inchcape showed considerable enterprise in maintaining as many services as possible, by effecting the resumption, at considerable cost, of the P&O special sleeping-car train from London to Marseilles, which had been suspended a year before. He offered a special £90 tour for the many who always wanted to winter outside Britain, but who now found that Continental resorts were unattractive and dangerous. This tour was scheduled to take three months, including first class accommodation from Marseilles to Bombay by mail steamer, with a first-class excursion rail service across India, and the option of touring Egypt. The war was not to be allowed to impinge on the P&O's lucrative first-class passenger trade, and all new-found opportunities for profit were to be maximised.

Inchcape was able to maintain public confidence in the P&O when the prices of other shipping lines' shares were falling. By the end of 1915, P&O £100 deferred stock had reached £295, much higher than that of the Royal Mail Group, for example, whose results had been disappointing. P&O directors were beginning to see the advantages of the merger with the BI, and of Inchcape's chairmanship.

1916 was dominated by Inchcape's acquisition of the New Zealand Shipping Company Limited for the P&O. The significance of this decision for the war years and later is such that the background merits examination in some detail.

The New Zealand Shipping Company was founded with the aim of improving shipping services for passengers and emigrants on the long haul to and from England. Formed in 1873, with a nominal capital of £250,000, it operated seventeen sailing ships by 1877. Excited by the prospects of the frozen meat trade, the company increased its capital to £1m, built five new steamers and experimented with seaborne refrigerating equipment. After proving the commercial viability of this trade the company received, in 1884, a £30,000 annual subsidy

from the colonial Government for five years. Financial support then
was offered by Edwyn Sandys Dawes of Gray Dawes, a prominent
partner in many old Mackinnon groups businesses, including the
AUSN.

In 1889 New Zealand Shipping acquired the bankrupt Canadian–
Australian Royal Mail Line for only £142,183, and offered a joint
service on this route with the Union Company from 1901. From the
1880s until its accounts were consolidated with the P&O Group in
1916, the New Zealand Shipping Company achieved a healthy
annual profit of between £25,000 and £45,000. By the turn of the
century, the fleet was transformed from its initial 13,253 aggregate
sailing ship tonnage to steamers of 87,117 tons. The growth of the
refrigerated meat trade across the Pacific to London rose rapidly
from the year 1886, when 20,000 tons of New Zealand mutton of a
total of 30,000 tons was landed at British ports. New Zealand
Shipping's steamship tonnage exceeded that of its sailing fleet from
1885 onwards. In this year the company had received a new mail
contract from the New Zealand Government to provide a monthly
service alternating between San Francisco and London.

A glimpse of the company's workings is given in a surviving
individual voyage profit listing for 1896–7. An especially successful
voyage, that of the brand new 6,688-ton *Mataura*, earned £33,775.
She carried 90,000 carcasses of mutton from New Zealand via
Montevideo, Rio and Tenerife to London, earning over £11,000, and
brought cargoes worth another £22,000 back from London via the
Cape. Earnings of individual ships averaged around £20,000 each per
year, supporting a steady building programme.

In 1910, New Zealand Shipping won a Canadian government
contract – taking advantage of the lack of substantial competition
from North American lines – to link eastern Canadian ports with
Australia and New Zealand. A further entry into the Australian trade
came with the acquisition in 1912 of the Federal Line, which
increased total tonnage to 144,357. The Federal Line had been
founded twenty years before, itself having acquired Money Wigram,
prominent in the Australian trade since 1837 when they were one of
the first shipowners to transfer from the Indian trade when the East
India Company lost its monopoly. Detailed records of the cargoes
carried by New Zealand Shipping in the First World War – before
they first used the Panama Canal in 1916–17 show the prominence of
the company in the trade not only to the UK but to America, Canada

and the continent of Europe. In 1914–15, for example, New Zealand Shipping and the Federal Line carried more than half of total sheep carcasses.

These two lines retained their dominance in the trade between Britain and New Zealand, carrying more than three-quarters of total sheep carcasses arriving from New Zealand in the UK in 1914–15, and more than half of the 1915–16 total, in competition with Shaw, Savill & Albion, the Clan Line and the Commonwealth and Dominion Lines. Jointly with the first-named firm, New Zealand Shipping established a tight control over the market's supply side, establishing backward linkages with local meat and wool companies. Their high earnings (over £1.4m in 1916, with management costs of only 2.03 per cent and a clear profit of £106,551) together with a large modern fleet, made the acquisition of New Zealand Shipping one of Inchcape's best deals.

The severe shortage of tonnage, and lengthening delays at every shipyard in Britain, with an increasing rate of Government requisitioning and wartime losses, had made the purchase of additional tonnage from any source Inchcape's first imperative as early as mid-1915. As he pointed out in his speech to shareholders at the December 1916 AGM, because of a lack of ships, the P&O were benefiting less than other companies from the steady rise in freights. Almost half the ships were now in Government hands, earning less than prewar rates, and having to carry mails, which incurred greater costs and left less room for passengers. In 1916, four P&O and four BI ships were lost to the fleet. The company did not suffer monetarily as a result, but sorely felt the loss of their services. New vessels cost almost twice prewar rates if they could be bought at all.

The P&O had acquired ships before by absorbing other companies: the Blue Anchor Line in 1910 and the BI and AUSN in 1914. Through Blue Anchor, the P&O gained its first foothold in Australia and New Zealand, and meanwhile the BI had provided a service between Britain and Queensland under contract with the Queensland Government, jointly operating with the Federal Line and occasionally with New Zealand Shipping, who were also linked to the BI through Gray Dawes.

Thus Inchcape's proposal to fuse the interests of the BI, New Zealand Shipping and the Federal Line appeared logical to all parties, and agreement was quickly reached. According to Inchcape, the assets of New Zealand Shipping and the Federal Line, taking into account depreciation at five per cent amounted to £3.184m, when the ships, taken at 1916 values, were easily worth over £5m.

Inchcape suggested that New Zealand shareholders should be offered P&O deferred stock to the value of £906,720. The New Zealand share would be held in trust by BI directors, who would pay to the P&O their approximate market value, judged as £300 per £100 nominal, or a total of £2.72m. This arrangement may be interpreted as a means of diverting BI cash to the P&O, and as New Zealand Shipping also had investment assets totalling £2m, the BI was depleted by only £700,000, and the P&O had a much-needed new fleet.

New Zealand Shipping was undoubtedly a bargain: thirty-one steamers of 240,000 tons, with an average age of just seven and a half years, two of which had only recently been launched, with two more about to come off the stocks. Inchcape was accurate in describing the ships as 'of a fine money-making type, with large refrigerated capacity'. He anticipated further growth in this trade after the war, and pointed out that the P&O was thus buying itself into a trade now which it might otherwise have to fight for later. The P&O fleet at the time comprised 236 steamers and fifty-seven tugs – over 1.5m tons – with a capital of £7.5m. Inchcape received the congratulations of fellow shipowner Sir John Ellerman on an outstanding deal.

Inchcape naturally also saw this acquisition within the context of the Mackinnon/Inchcape group. He argued, on the grounds that he had his hands full with running the P&O and the BI, that Mackinnon Mackenzie should run New Zealand Shipping and Federal, and receive the same commission for this as they already enjoyed from their BI agencies. BI directors already received half per cent of the gross earnings of BI ships, and Inchcape suggested that this should include the newly acquired fleets. BI directors (including himself) would naturally forsake this if the companies fell on hard times, 'looking to the fact that we have all benefited very materially by the very exceptional prosperity which shipping has enjoyed during the last ten years'.

The New Zealand Shipping fleet, and the Union Company, acquired in 1917, turned out to be exceptionally profitable investments. According to an independent investigation into P&O profits during Inchcape's chairmanship – discussed in Chapter Seven – the former's contributions to P&O earnings grew from £36,232 in 1916 to over £100,000 by the mid-1920s, when the Group was in great need.

1916, like 1915, saw Inchcape showing further support of the Government through the purchase of Government securities on behalf of the P&O, but for the first time he openly criticised Government policies and attitudes. Whilst £1m of P&O funds were invested in five per cent British Treasury Bills in January and February 1916, followed by another £1,148,000 by the end of the year, at the P&O AGM in December 1916, Inchcape launched into a bitter attack on the Government and voiced deep-rooted fears for the British shipping industry in the future.

British shipping, Inchcape argued, owed nothing to the Government which, instead of protecting its interests, subjected it to heavy tax – twenty five per cent of net earnings in income tax, and sixty per cent on any profits in excess of those made on the average of the two prewar years. In October, Inchcape deposited with the Inland Revenue nearly £400,000 to pay excess profits duty for 1914–15, and a further £4,000 towards 1915–16. Meanwhile, the current agitation for the nationalisation of shipping, apparently condoned by the Government was, according to Inchcape, potentially disastrous.

If the British Government was unhelpful, said Inchcape, then various international shipping authorities were no better. For instance, the International Bulkhead Committee laid down rules intended to help ships to stay afloat when damaged. According to the captain of the P&O *Mantola*, his ship, badly shelled, would certainly have sunk if he had implemented the new rules. In describing this story to shareholders, Inchcape added dryly, 'We are learning a lot from this War'.

Inchcape continued to integrate BI and Mackinnon/Inchcape group interests with the P&O, pointing to the success of the Mazagon Docks. When, in April, the London to Calcutta service was temporarily suspended and there was no work for the P&O Calcutta agent, Inchcape took the opportunity to transfer the agency to Mackinnon Mackenzie. The P&O Bombay agency was also taken over by Mackinnon Mackenzie, in September, at the suggestion of the P&O agent himself, because of the added prestige and business this would, and did, bring.

Inchcape's dealings with BI agents and captains in 1916 gave him more reason to criticise the Government. In May, he was informed that rates of hire paid by the Government of India for merchant ships were too high, and should be reduced to Rs 15 per ton, about £1.50. This was when the BI themselves would pay Rs 30 per ton to charter much-needed tonnage. Ships were in such short supply that in February the BI had had to turn down a potentially lucrative offer from the Anglo-Persian Oil Company to carry their general cargo and passengers from Indian ports to the Persian Gulf.

Inchcape hated being at the mercy of Government officials in determining rates of hire, and it stuck in his throat to have to offer a £3 discount to the Government of India in carrying horses from Australia at the already low rate of £20. Despite this, he could still be courteous and obliging to Government advisers and others close to power, and shrewdly offered P&O and BI passages to them, such as in the case of Lord Cunliffe's journey to Bombay in February 1916. This was important in maintaining the image of the P&O as the nation's premier shipping line in the eyes of the Government and the public.

Lobbying the India Office, worrying about where extra shipping was to come from – although this was to some extent allayed by the New Zealand Shipping purchase, finally signed in September – fearing more shipping casualties almost daily, and increasingly cynical about the future, Inchcape's normally robust health showed signs, at sixty-two, of letting him down.

Returning from a few weeks' holiday to more clashes with the Government, he found that it had now commandeered two BI vessels being built by Barclay Curle, turning them into oil tankers. The shipbuilders immediately laid down two more, but they would cost at least double, and meanwhile the BI lost two year's worth of earnings from them. Investment in war bonds with the money they would have spent brought them five per cent, far less than they could have earned with the ships.

Turning to Gray's of Hartlepool as another source of supply of new tonnage, Inchcape found prices even higher. Calling in the Board of Trade to arbitrate was little help: they supported the builders. Stephen was finally allowed by the Government to go ahead with building the *Vasna*, but the P&O and the BI were still badly in need of ships. Thus Inchcape began considering investing in shipbuilding, and in June 1916 applied for 30,000 £1 shares in the Standard Shipbuilding & Engineering Co. Ltd. In October he reached a new agreement with Harland & Wolff for new steamers, and in December with Cammell Laird.

Yet for all his complaints, at the 1916 AGM Inchcape was satisfied with the P&O results. The declared profit after depreciation and insurance of £654,000 was nearly double that of 1914, and that was after putting aside over £85,000 for the next year. But, with uncertainties ahead, he felt justified in reducing the dividend on the preferred stock to two and a half per cent, and on the deferred stock to twelve per cent.

In order to set aside wartime earnings for future use without shareholder pressure to raise the dividend, Inchcape suppressed detailed information within the Report & Accounts on the grounds that it was not desirable that this should be available to P&O's competitors overseas. Keeping the published accounts to a minimum became, after the war, a convenient device whereby Inchcape concealed the true picture of the financial state of the P&O and the role of the BI and Mackinnon/Inchcape group firms in its survival during the 1920s and early 1930s. This was revealed only on his death and under Alexander Shaw's chairmanship.

The financial press described the P&O's new Report & Accounts as 'a very meagre document as compared with the old statements sent in under the Sutherland regime. There are no details whatever of operating charges'. There was speculation of an inadequate allocation for depreciation, when previously this had been allowed for on a liberal scale. Yet this was, in the main, overshadowed by praise for the P&O and the BI, in coping with the submarine menace and trying to maintain services with thirty five of their ships hired to the Government: they could proudly boast that not a single mail departure had been abandoned since the outbreak of hostilities. Public confidence was maintained at an even higher level than before, with deferred stock closing the year at £351. It then dropped to £307 on rumours of total Government control of British shipping, as unpopular with Inchcape as it was with shareholders.

Inchcape was able to offset 1917's mounting ship losses through continuing his acquisitions drive, adding 113 vessels to the P&O/BI fleet. The P&O lost nine ships in 1917 and the BI lost eight, so Inchcape's policy was warmly greeted by directors and shareholders alike. In May he announced the progress of negotiations with the Union Steamship Company of New Zealand; in October the offer for the Hain Steamship Company, in November the purchase of the Nourse Line and in December the acquisition of the Mercantile Steamship Company.

The Union Steamship Company of New Zealand had been

founded in 1875 through an amalgamation of several coasting lines,
and initially confined itself to providing local Australian coastal and
Antipodean and Pacific Island services. It was substantially financed
by the shipbuilder Peter Denny, also an investor in the AUSN and
associate of Mackinnon's. From only five sailing vessels of 2,126
aggregate tons in 1875, the Union company expanded into the trans
Tasman trade and summer cruising and, doubling its capital to half a
million pounds in 1879, began to look even further afield. A stronger
stake in the Fiji and Pacific Islands trade was acquired in 1881. In
1885, it won the joint New Zealand and New South Wales
Government Contract – limited to three years only – to provide a
monthly mail service between Sydney, Auckland, Samoa, Honolulu
and San Francisco. To supply extra vessels and provide a more
extensive service, they brought in the American Oceanic Steamship
Company.

Further acquisitions followed. The Tasmanian Steamship Company brought eight small steamers of 9,892 aggregate tons for only
£185,000 in 1891, making a total of fifty-three vessels of 57,737 tons.
In 1900 the San Francisco service came to and an abrupt end with
the annexation of Hawaii by the USA, debarring foreign vessels from
plying between American ports. Union then turned to the Canadian–
Australian Line, founded by James Huddart in 1873, and took over
its Sydney–Vancouver mail service. Jointly with New Zealand
Shipping, Union operated what became known as the 'All Red
Route', between Sydney, Brisbane, Honolulu and Vancouver, later
including Fiji.

In 1911 the New Zealand Government awarded the Union
Company a small subsidy to include Auckland, and the monthly
mail service to the UK was resumed in this year. The call at San
Francisco was reinstated in 1909 as part of a monthly service via
Wellington and Tahiti, alternating with the Vancouver Line.

When Union was bought by Lord Inchcape in 1917, it had
declared a net profit of £155,973, on operating thirty-two passenger
ships of 131,759 gross tons, and seventy-three cargo ships of 227,188
gross tons, in several coastal and intercolonial trades and its two
Pacific mail services. It did not compete with New Zealand Shipping
in the same ports, but Union also relied heavily on the frozen meat
trade, and benefited from its rise in freight – from 4d to 5d per pound
– in the early years of the war.

Inchcape's announcement of the proposed acquisition described how the company had worked jointly with the BI for a lengthy period, that Mackinnon Mackenzie were their agents in Calcutta, and that, with the AUSN, they had operated a service in the Australia-Fiji trade. Inchcape offered Union shareholders 10*s*' worth of P&O deferred stock and 30*s* in cash for each £1 ordinary share. With £500,000 of P&O stock valued at £1.5m and with the same amount in cash, Union would receive £3m.

Inchcape pointed out to the P&O board that the average profits of the Union Company for the previous eleven years, after depreciation, had been £236,000, and he calculated that the net earnings of Union steamers would need to be only £75,000 per year to cover P&O expenses. With the opening of the Panama Canal, Inchcape's new fleets were poised to capitalise on the expansion of the Pacific trade.

Mills, the Union chairman, and his shareholders overcame their initial reluctance when they realised that they would receive the equivalent of £3 for each £1 share, then valued at 46*s*, and that operating under the P&O umbrella would conceal their earnings. Inchcape noted that at the back of Mills' mind was the desire 'to hide away the profits which have been and are being made by the Union Company of New Zealand from the public in New Zealand', to prevent the loss of the mail contracts.

The Union Company in the future was to make an even greater contribution to the P&O group earnings than New Zealand Shipping. Payments exceeded £100,000 by 1918, and in 1928, its regular annual 'special bonuses' reached over £1m.

The press saw the offer as very satisfactory to both the P&O and to the Union shareholders; *Fairplay* considered that Inchcape had got a fantastic bargain. But the episode stirred up a controversy of a different sort: much Fleet Street ink was spilt on the danger of monopolistic practices as a result of such a fusion.

There were particularly strong objections in the Australian newspapers, who speculated on the reasons for the speed of the negotiations in selling off what they saw as Australia's 'most national concern': a shipping line ranked seventh in the carrying trade of the British Empire. 'Is it expected that New Zealand will lightly stand aside and see this great concern wrested from our hands and pass into the control of a company which employes lascars, coolies and Chinese in manning its ships?' The antagonism of Australian shipping interest increased in the years to come.

The acquisition of the Hain Steamship Company followed in

October 1917. Originating as a small sailing fleet in the 1830s, the business had been taken over by Sir Edward Hain in 1878 who then operated steamships on the single-ship company principle, with full limited liability after 1901. By 1917, as Inchcape reported to his board, Hain comprised twenty-three high quality cargo steamers of 164,366 aggregate deadweight, averaging only eight years old. Valued at only £12 per ton, totalling £1.9m with cash assets of £2.4m, and only £400,000 outstanding on delivery of four new vessels of 31,680 tons, the Hain fleet was another excellent deal at £4.4m.

All the Hain ships had been requisitioned, and even at the relatively low Blue Book standard rates imposed, had made over £200,000 net profit in the previous year. The fleet would continue to be run by the existing owners for the time being, but with Gray Dawes in overall control, for which they contributed £100,000 of the purchase price. Gray Dawes' role was explained in terms that it was important to keep the Hain fleet a separate entity, as its steamers were worked on more economical lines that those of the P&O, although the groups' fleets were coaled together.

The acquisition arose from the recent death of Sir Edward Hain, the founder and principal owner. At the close of the deal in December, after acceptance from eighty-four per cent of the shareholders, Inchcape calculated that the P&O had already made £406,024 profit.

The Hain Line marked a new development in Inchcape's acquisition policy: its fleet, unlike the P&O/BI, carried cargoes only and worked as tramps, not liners, and was not specifically connected with the East. The method of purchase, by cash rather than by paper, was another departure from the norm. In a wartime situation, beggars could not be choosers, but the fleet was purchased not merely because of a desperate need for tonnage, but as part of a strategic plan for the future of the P&O to diversify its interests.

The acquisition of the Nourse Line's six steamers of 23,496 tons followed in November 1917. It was passed without the agreement of the P&O board, Inchcape seeing no need at all to justify its purchase. The Nourse Line had established connections with the East, and fitted in well with existing BI services. In another cash deal, of £42 for each of the 16,000 £10 Nourse shares, the P&O bought six badly needed new vessels for less than their actual cost.

The Nourse Line dated back to 1861, carrying contract labour – coolies – between India and British Guiana, the West Indies, Natal and Fiji. By the end of the century the fleet had expanded to over twenty sailing ships of nearly 2,000 tons, and had branched into the Atlantic and Indian Ocean cargo trades, employing sailing ships when others had long since gone over to steam. These were sold on the death of the founder, Captain James Nourse, in 1897, and limited liability status had been adopted in 1903.

Inchcape's final acquisition of 1917, that of the Mercantile Steamship Company, reveals his determination and patience as a negotiator. Mercantile operated tramps, initially to trade between UK ports, its original capital of £300,000 having been raised by five shipowners in London, Hull and Liverpool in the 1860s. The fleet had suffered particularly heavy losses in the war, its 1914 fleet of fourteen ships reduced to only six by the end of 1917. These were between 4,600 and 8,100 tons, half new and half old.

Mercantile's loading brokers and managers, Glover Bros, were loathe to lose their business of two and a half per cent commission on the net profits of voyages. They considered that Mercantile's capital of £328,000, fixed assets of £1.7m and cash assets of over £850,000 were worth at least £664,000 (minus cash assets), valuing the fleet at £15 12s per ton. This was much more than Inchcape had paid *pro rata* for the Hain ships, despite the fact that the Mercantile fleet earned much less, with 1917 net profits of a modest £20,000.

But Glover Bros knew that by the end of 1917 anyone with ships to sell could name his own price. Acting through Hain rather than the P&O, not wanting to connect the prestigious national liner service with a small tramp outfit, Inchcape offered £1.46m, which included a pay-off to Glover Bros. But they would not accept a lump sum purchase, especially as they valued the ships at only £14 10s per ton, 'a great deal less than we can sell them at individually'.

Inchcape, much to the consternation of F.C. Allen of the P&O who assisted in the negotiations, refused to offer Mercantile more, and in fact offered them less. They wanted £624,000, he offered £575,000. When they turned it down, Allen suggested £593,000, Inchcape offered a final £563,000. Finally, after pretending to drop out of the deal completely, Inchcape was offered the ships for £604,000, with the whole business for £1.5m, when Mercantile had originally refused to contemplate a lump sum sale at all. It was more than Inchcape wanted to pay, but substantially less than Mercantile hoped to get. The P&O still made a profit of £150,000. Mercantile was another good buy, its profits rising to over £80,000 in 1918.

Inchcape's work as P&O chairman throughout 1917 continued the pattern set in 1915 and 1916. He bought more Government stocks on its behalf: Bonar Law was well satisfied with P&O's application for £7½m of the new war loan. By December 1917, Inchcape had purchased another £4m worth 'from my various interests, steamers, trusts, firms and private resources'. He continued the process of integrating P&O agencies with Mackinnon Mackenzie, readily approved by the board for all the Australian and Far Eastern ports as an effective economy measure.

As business continued to expand, Inchcape arranged the purchase of further office space, next door in 117–18 Leadenhall Street, for £31,800. He then acquired the lease on 114–16 Cockspur Street for only £60,000. Both were seen as excellent investments.

Profits continued to rise, exceeding £762,000 for the year ending September 1917, with dividends maintained at the cautious level of two and a half per cent on the preferred stock and twelve per cent on the deferred stock, carrying over nearly £100,000 to the next year. One of Inchcape's greatest problems now was minimising excess profit duty: he effectively hid directors's remuneration under the general category of working expenses.

Inchcape's correspondence on BI matters with Mackinnon Mackenzie in Calcutta reveals continued annoyance and impatience with Government interference. He could cope with losing ships and the disruption of trade, but he hated having his hands tied. He complained to MP A.H. Steel-Maitland about the prohibition of coal cargoes to India and the problems of P&O and BI steamers in coaling of Bombay. Inchcape then faced the Ministry of Shipping's investigations into the earnings of British vessels in the Australian trade, which he described as 'inaugurating still another department for checking shipowners' accounts'.

Inchcape strongly opposed total Government requisitioning of ships. As he wrote to the BI agent in Liverpool, 'I am afraid they [the Government] are to requisition the whole of our steamers on the coast [of India] and make us run them on Government account. It will be a horrid nuisance but we can't help it. Lloyd George sold us to the Labour Party for his premiership.' The latter remark appears to refer to Labour's nationalisation policies, which appalled Inchcape.

The BI's high rate of profitability continued, but because of taxation had to be closely guarded from the authorities. Mackinnon Mackenzie's commission, which appeared in the accounts in

London, was instead debited as it was incurred from voyage accounts. 'The amount was so large last year and the year before that the income tax people questioned it, and they threatened to levy excess profits duty on the amount, but found they were wrong and had to abandon the idea', Inchcape described with relief. Mackinnon Mackenzie's extra commission from the BI, on the basis of 5s 10d per annum per ton on a total fleet tonnage of 617,747 tons, for the year ending September 1917, was £180,000. This was approximately a quarter of the total charge to voyage accounts, which also included £325,630 for repairs and dockings, largely to the benefit of the company's own docks and yards. So Inchcape was able to absorb into fleet running costs several items which would incur excess profit duty and thereby conserved funds which were to help the P&O and BI in the future.

Throughout 1917, Inchcape continued to strongly support the P&O and BI war efforts and spoke positively about the future, but privately he felt increasingly pessimistic:

the loss of life and the destruction of property, the impoverishment of the Country, the burden of taxation which is in store for us all for at least a generation are terrible and it is not pleasant to contemplate the likelihood of a complete upheaval of the whole of our social structure, after the war. If we manage to tide over without a revolution and something akin to anarchy we shall be fortunate. The whole social life of the country is completely altered and the existing conditions are by no means agreeable. But I am afraid they will be worse before they are better.

But it was not all gloom and despondency. The P&O's role in the war had its elements of great heroism and even irony, seen in a typical story by F.A. Hook, later Inchcape's personal secretary. A P&O captain, commanding a fast, armed merchant cruiser, was sent to watch a certain undisclosed port on the coast of mainland Europe to prevent the landing of a rare mineral believed to be finding its way into Germany. The P&O captain spotted the vessel, but could not avoid being noticed by the local inhabitants, many of whom had entertained British seamen at the local brothel; this time, the captain put it firmly out of bounds, as he rightly feared a ruse to divert the British ship from its prey. When the suspected cargo was about to be landed, the P&O captain discovered he had run out of supplies. In order to make the four-day run for replenishments without losing his chance to stop the enemy, the P&O captain engineered a strike of local stevedores to prevent anything being unloaded there. When he finally approached the vessel, which contained 300 tons of contraband valued at £300 per ton, it was scuttled by the Germans at the last minute.

The P&O group continued to help in diverse aspects of the war effort, including providing ambulances and scout aeroplanes.

Inchcape was also concerned with keeping up the spirits of P&O and BI officers in POW camps, sending food and clothing parcels. Nine officers from the BI in 1917 alone were being held captive in enemy territory.

Despite the acquisitions of 1917, Inchcape still needed tonnage, and was especially interested in oil-burning ships, by which he could benefit from his agreement with the Anglo-Persian Oil Company; but these were particularly hard to come by. He was able, on the other hand, thanks to his contacts, to acquire surplus Ministry of Shipping vessels, those released from war work and not then required by their previous owners. In October 1917, he concluded an agreement with Harland & Wolff of Belfast on behalf of the P&O to reserve five ships for his exclusive use for the next ten years. He was to pay five per cent over and above raw materials and labour, on six months' drafts, enviously seen by other shipowners as a good deal at a time of high shipbuilding costs.

The 1917 AGM noted a personal loss. Young William Mackinnon, the son of Duncan Mackinnon, the chairman, was killed in France. Thus the last Mackinnon heir died and the Mackinnon Mackenzie companies fell into Inchcape's hands. Ship losses had been great in 1917, the high water mark of the submarine menace but, as Inchcape pointed out, of a total of 625 voyages to and from the East and Australia, only 1.12 per cent had ended in disaster, reflecting great credit on the protection afforded by the Royal Navy. Vital and valuable cargoes of bullion between India and Australia had been delivered successfully.

Profits were maintained, with a 'net result' of £762,400 and twelve per cent dividend on the deferred stock, despite the Government's forcible commandeering of new BI ships straight from the shipyards, and the failure of Inchcape's attempts to retrieve the difference in building costs and loss of revenue in the meantime. Inchcape's views on this were enthusiastically supported by shareholders:

I don't know what our socialistic friends would say if a Government official walked into their houses or on to their small holdings and cleared out their belongings on the same conditions. It is the sort of thing we might possibly have to endure if the Germans got over here but scarcely what we would expect from a British Government.

The shareholders, now becoming used to the severely truncated reports and accounts, were informed that the cash resources of the P&O, normally put into new ships which could no longer be had, were being lent to the Government to finance the war effort, and they were called upon to do the same, by spending their dividends on war bonds. These Government issues did not reduce trading in P&O stock, the share price reaching £343 in 1917. Despite all his reservations concerning Government policy, his mounting pessimism and his increasing conservatism after the Bolshevik Revolution, Inchcape realised that the war must be won before anything else, and this was the spirit with which he faced 1918.

1918 was marked by more ship losses: five P&O and seven BI, with New Zealand Shipping, the Federal Line, and the Union Company losing thirteen vessels between them. The war thus constantly starved the P&O group of its fleet resources, despite Inchcape's constant attempts at resupply from a variety of sources, but it is possible to argue that some ship losses were a blessing in disguise, clearing out obsolete, ancient and undersized craft.

Inchcape certainly made the best of the situation. He used his leverage at the Ministry for Shipping to extract the maximum compensation from the authorities. By the end of 1918, the combined P&O fleets had lost sixty-six ships, of over 440,000 gross tons. They had originally cost nearly £8.3m, their depreciated value by their date of loss was only £.7m, and they had been written down in the P&O books to only £1.8m. Yet Inchcape, through determined bargaining in every case, won over £12m in compensation. The BI did particularly well: Twenty-three ships originally costing £2.2m, written down to just over £½m, earned nearly £4m in compensation.

Inchcape minimised the book value of his ships for the purposes of calculating the 'net result' and for tax purposes, but maximised them for Government pay-outs. Some particularly old and almost redundant vessels nevertheless brought large sums to the P&O coffers. The BI *Golconda* and *Mombasa* for example, both relatively small vessels of under 5,000 tons, torpedoed in 1916 when they were over twenty-seven years old, were compensated for to the tune of over £100,000, though for many years they had been regarded as worth nothing on the books.

The New Zealand ships were especially well compensated, Inchcape receiving almost double their original building costs, and the seven Hain ships lost, valued at nil in the accounts, raised nearly £1m although they had cost less then £300,000.

Inchcape's best deal was undoubedly the *Ballarat*. Lost in 1917, this 11,120 ton liner had cost £176,000 new five years previously, and was written down to only £15,000. On approaching Sir Joseph Maclay, head of the Ministry of Shipping, and two of his officials, Inchcape was told that the maximum compensation was £395,000. He argued with them for more than an hour, saying he would accept £420,000 but no less. He then announced 'I will retire into the next room and smoke a cigarette and leave you to talk the matter over amongst yourselves'. Within ten minutes they called him back and humbly declared, 'Lord Inchcape, you have been extremely useful and helpful to this Ministry all through the War. No words of mine can express the gratitude we feel. I am convinced you would not ask more for your ship than you consider you are entitled to get and we have decided to pay you £420,000'. In describing this incident to his friend Lord Kilbracken, Inchcape commented, 'I think I did a fairly good hour's work for the P&O in getting this extra £25,000, and I drove back to the City feeling rather pleased with myself'.

Yet Inchcape could easily counter accusations of profiteering by pointing to the P&O's enormous investment in war bonds, which reached over £16m by the end of 1918, not counting a further £19m subscribed by the National Provincial Bank, of which he was a director.

Moreover, it was all very well to receive such compensation, but as Inchcape would have been the first to point out, it was almost impossible to obtain new vessels, and prices had rocketed. In February 1918, after much negotiation, he was finally authorised to sign agreements with the Egis shipyard on the Clyde to build seven new vessels of standard design, to be engined by William Gray of Hartlepool, priced at twenty per cent over net cost.

Inchcape made further investments in ship and repair yards, acquiring a majority interest in R.H. Green and Silley Weir, who undertook eighty per cent of all steamship repair work on the Thames, including all P&O and BI jobs and much Government work. Their turnover in 1916–17 had been £1.6m and their profits, even after excess profits duty, were £90,000 on a capital of only £200,000, a return of twenty-four per cent. With the prospect of much repair and reconditioning work after the war, especially in readapting hospital ships and armed merchant cruisers, Inchcape easily convinced the board of the advisability of this latest acquisition. To minimise liability for excess profits duty, at Inchcape's suggestion large batches of shares were held by the New Zealand and Federal companies, and individual P&O/BI group directors took a personal interest; Inchcape himself purchased three and a half per cent of the equity, and thus Weir joined the P&O fold as an associated rather than a subsidiary company.

Inchcape's shipbuilding investments continued in 1918 with discussions with the Admiralty concerning the purchase of the Chepstow Shipbuilding Company and another 102,000 shares in Alexander Stephens. But most of all he wanted ships already built and trading.

At the end of 1918, after protracted negotiations, the board approved Inchcape's announcement of the purchase of fifty-one per cent of the £5 deferred shares of the Orient Steamship Company, for a cash payment by the P&O of £2.2m. This meant paying £125 each for these shares, but Orient had six ships of 72,295 tons, less than ten years old, which had originally cost £2.2m, now worth £1.5m after four per cent depreciation, and Orient also had liquid assets of nearly £2m. Furthermore, the company had made annual average net profits before the War of nearly £370,000.

This acquisition was a natural follow-on from the New Zealand and Federal lines, as Orient, which had traded from London to the West Indies and Australia since the early nineteenth century, worked with the latter on the Australia to Pacific America run. Established as a limited company in 1878, its mail and passenger service to Australia was especially attractive to the P&O. In their turn, Orient welcomed the chance to rebuild their fleet and its business under the P&O umbrella, whilst their brokers, Anderson & Green, held forty-nine per cent of the equity. Orient was to play an important part in expanding the P&O's Pacific trade after the opening of the Panama Canal and, like the other subsidiaries, made substantial contributions to the P&O coffers, rising from £13,291 in 1919 to over £70,000 a year during the 1920s.

The management of the Orient Line, as in the case of many other acquisitions, was undertaken by Gray Dawes. The latter's profits, mainly from commission earnings, rose to over £200,000 per year, an impressive sum for a shipping agency business with only £50,000 in fixed capital and a modest staff of cleerks each paid 45s per week. It was liable for excess profits duty at eighty per cent but even so, Inchcape, who held thirty per cent of the shares in this private partnership, received £13,476 in 1918.

With the end of the war, the Shipping Interest presented a united front in opposition to continued Government control, and in this process Inchcape, with his powerful influence in Government circles, emerged as leader. This is apparent from his announcement of 21 December 1918: 'I'm glad to say that at a meeting of a War Cabinet Committee presided over by Sir Eric Geddes yesterday afternoon at which I was present representing the Chancellor of the Exchequer, it was decided to free the shipbuilding trade of the country from all restrictions'.

Inchcape himself was among the first to capitalise on this. Earlier that same month, he had concluded an agreement with Barclay Curle to keep two of their berths at the BI's disposal for ten years, with a supplementary arrangement that they would also supply propelling-machinery for the entire P&O group. Inchcape's terms of twenty-two and a half per cent on top of the cost of materials – to cover labour, establishment charges and profits, with payments on three and six months accounts pending the final settlement, were certainly to his advantage, and reflect his leverage within the industry.

A sense of relief, but exhaustion, is evident from the December 1918 AGM. The 'net result' of £782,400 after insurance and depreciation reflected continued high earnings, but Inchcape still ensured that a substantial sum – nearly £100,000 – was carried over to next year, with an unchanged dividend. The price of P&O deferred stock rose to £470 in the autumn of 1918, the highest figure ever recorded.

But, with no detailed balance sheet, how did shareholders or anyone else know if this was the true picture? They were forced to rely on Inchcape's assurances. Firstly, he painted a bleak picture: how the war had brought such a total change to P&O's business that there had been only one ship running to India over the last few months, and meanwhile the sea-lanes were dominated by cruisers, despatch vessels, hospital ships, transports, or vessels carrying

Government cargoes only. Passenger traffic was down due to convoy restrictions on the carriage of mails.

Then he announced his plans: the P&O and the BI would resume their ascendancy in the Indian Ocean and Far Eastern trades, and the recently enlarged P&O group would flex its newly-found muscles in Australia. Inchcape saw these plans within the context of the Mackinnon/Inchcape group as a whole, which could continue to bring new business opportunities and provide financial support. Oral evidence, from Wilfrid Mizen (referred to at the end of Chapter Four) suggests that Mackinnon Mackenzie's profits exceeded £500,000 per year, of which commission earnings from the P&O and BI made a substantial contribution. By subsequently offering rebates, Inchcape was able to repay these funds back to the P&O when in need.

Mackinnon Mackenzie was not only the nerve centre of the P&O's and the BI's operations overseas but also the dominant agency within this shipping network. As the centre of the Mackinnon/Inchcape group, it also managed a wide range of largely Indian industrial and commercial concerns, some initially created by Mackinnon and many subsequently developed by Inchcape. These included the Macneill & Barry tea estate, jute mill and coalmine ownership and management business, of which Inchcape had acquired outright control in 1915, and Binny's textile mills, bought by Mackinnon Mackenzie in 1906 at Inchcape's behest. Both had achieved considerable growth and paid large dividends during the war; Binny's, by 1917, was supplying over a million yards of khaki per year to the Ordnance Department, and paid dividends of twenty per cent. Another significant member of the Mackinnon/Inchcape group, the Joint Steamer Companies, enjoyed increased business with the need for transport on the rivers of India and Mesopotamia.

These firms supported the war effort just as the P&O did: the jute mills and river steamers within the Mackinnon/Inchcape group contributed over £1m to the Government of India's five-year treasury bills. The P&O and BI had already gained advantages from their links with these firms, and were to benefit enormously later from having this commercial and industrial empire behind them in India at a time when trade was difficult and cargoes were being fought for tooth and nail. The Clan Line – which originated from the BI and subsequently became a strong competitor – had the same mutually advantageous arrangement with another commercial house, James Finlay. Membership of this group was crucial to the P&O's survival,

and Inchcape planned its future accordingly. This perspective was by
no means apparent to shareholders at the time.

Instead, Inchcape warned against expectations of high profits by
arguing that despite the fact that the proposed nationalisation of
shipping had been abandoned by the end of 1918, there was still
strong Government attachment to DORA – the Defence of the Realm
Act – under which Government power could be exerted almost
arbitrarily. Furthermore, excess profit duty was still being levied.

The shipping industry was by no means free of restrictions, and
suffered as a result of the standard ships policy, whereby yards were
taken over to produce vessels of standardised design and tonnage in
the interests of speed and minimising costs. Inchcape criticised this: it
was not a long-term solution to the problem of the shortage of good
quality tonnage which could be adapted to postwar needs.
Introduced in 1917, when more than three million tons of British
shipping had been sunk by enemy submarines – 500,000 in April
1917 alone – this development may be seen as the pinnacle of
Government control. Inchcape, typically, led a petition to the
Ministry of Shipping against the policy, having rallied to the cause
the most prominent of his fellow shipowners: Alfred Booth of
Cunard, Sir John Ellerman, Richard Holt of Ocean and China
Mutual, Owen Philipps of the Royal Mail Group, Harold Sanderson
of White Star and Shaw Savill and Martland Kersey of Canadian
Pacific. They argued, correctly as it turned out, that specialised fast
liners could be more profitable than the slow standard ships, despite
the savings gained from interchangeable parts which could be
quickly produced in bulk in the shipyards.

At the close of this 1918 AGM, a shareholder rose to pay tribute to
Inchcape's leadership of the P&O during a time of prolonged crisis,
exclaiming that despite many anxious moments, the chairman never
showed any emotion. This was a more profound comment than he
probably realised. Although Inchcape indeed felt deeply and
emotionally about the tragic losses of the War, they hardened him
and removed his general air of optimism. Oral evidence from a
contemporary confirms this. Wilfrid Mizen occasionally had to take
over the duties of the resident clerk during weekends and holidays. It
fell to him to telephone his chairman three times daily, a harrowing
task when ships were being torpedoed and crews drowned, which
was exacerbated by Inchcape's slight deafness and compounded by
bad telephone lines. Despite brave words at AGMs, Inchcape was

already depressed at the prospects for British shipping in general and the P&O in particular. The P&O had indeed emerged more powerful than before, thanks to his shrewd acquisitions policy, large compensation pay-outs, and close supervision of all aspects of the business: but it had to face still worse crises to come.

Inchcape had much on his hands with the problems of managing the country's largest shipping line in wartime, and these years also saw an expansion of his banking interests, with his merging of the Union Bank with the National Provincial. Yet these concerns did not preclude his enthusiasm for public work. One of the most important committees on which he served in this period was that concerned with the home production of food in England and Wales which met first in mid-1915. He was apparently persuaded to join the investigation at the behest of Sir Eric Geddes, who afterwards maintained that Inchcape, like Kitchener, was one of the first to appreciate the possible duration of the war, and one of the first to urge that the amount of shipping exposed to submarine risks could be reduced by curtailing the demand for food in Britain.

Appointed by the Board of Agriculture and Fisheries, the committee's brief was ' to consider and report what steps should be taken, by legislation or otherwise, for the sole purpose of maintaining and, if possible, increasing the present production of food in England and Wales, on the assumption that the War may be prolonged beyond the harvest of 1916. Chaired by Viscount Milner, the committee of nine examined seventeen witnesses in sixteen meetings – members of the Board of Agriculture and Fisheries, the Agricultural Labourers' and Rural Workers' Union and the Farmers' Club. Inchcape, with Sir Harry Verney MP, strongly disagreed with the other members of the committee, to the extent of refusing to sign the final report.

Key points raised in the discussions included the necessity to restore poorer grassland areas, which had been unchanged since the 1870s, to arable cultivation, especially of wheat. Somehow an incentive must be provided for farmers to increase their wheat production at the expense of sacrificing the comparative certainty of present profits. The committee considered that farmers would have to 'change some of their methods, alter their rotations, and increase their area of arable cultivation in the face of a shortage of labour. In addition, they will have to run the risk, not only of uncertain seasons, but also of a fall in the price of wheat at the Conclusion of the War'. In view of having to make this sacrifice and to hasten momentum, the committee proposed that the Government should 'guarantee a minimum price for home-grown wheat for a period of several years'. Despite the insistence by all the witnesses that such a guarantee was crucial, the committee members hesitated, but finally agreed to 45s per quarter for a period of four years.

Communication and organisation of the policy had to be discussed in detail. Every county council must survey the amount of land under the plough, and acreages under wheat, oats, potatoes and other crops. District committees with 'target contributions' were to be set up, and a central authority would closely monitor progress. By the time that the final report was issued in October 1915, the Government had rejected the recommendation that a minimum price for wheat should be guaranteed by the State for four years. They were partly influenced by the partial cessation of the worst extremes of the submarine menace – as far as the Government was concerned, one of the main reasons for appointing the committee in the first place was now less apparent. Certainly, the threat of enemy submarines cutting off imported food supplies was a strong factor in the committee's interim recommendations.

The main bone of contention then became the question of increasing output generally by stimulating more intensive cultivation. Was the 'permanent interest of the nation' at stake here, or just the need for short-term wartime measures? Those who signed the final report felt, showing considerable foresight, that 'the intensification of our agriculture will be even more necessary after the War than now, for then the nation's indebtedness will have reduced its purchasing power abroad'.

Inchcape objected particularly strongly to a footnote signed by the other members advocating the production 'within the country [of] a very large proportion of the foodstuffs and other agricultural products natural to its soil, but now purchased abroad at a cost of nearly £300m p.a. two-thirds of which are derived from countries outside the British Empire'. The importance of bulk agricultural cargoes to fill the holds of merchant ships, especially as return freights for exports and re-exports from Britain, was understandably more of a priority to Inchcape than to his non-maritime fellow members.

Inchcape's and Verney's separate minority report questioned the whole issue of the long-term benefit to the country of the majority's proposals.

We expressly abstain from adhering to the opinion that the nation's purchasing power will hereafter be reduced, or that it is necessary and possible to raise in this country a very large proportion of nearly £300m worth of food now purchased abroad. We are not prepared to say that, even if possible, there would be an economic gain in doing this.

Inchcape agreed in principle with the 45s guarantee on wheat suggested in the interim report, but took the Government's side in arguing that 'the submarine menace [was] well in hand' and there was no need for 'extraordinary measures to ensure a home-grown supply'.

The concluding paragraph of the minority report distanced its authors still further from their colleagues.

The question as to whether it would be an ultimate advantage to this country after the War to give a bonus to agriculture at the expense of other great industries, or at the expense of the general taxpayer, is a very large one. It is not, in our opinion, within the terms of our reference, it has not come within the scope of our enquiry, and upon it we consider we are not called on to offer an opinion.

Inchcape emphasised the practical impossibility of favouring with subsidies one branch of the British economy over another. He was especially against subsidies for an industry concerned with home production for home consumption only which was not contributing to increasing seaborne commerce. He was confirming his reputation for caution, non-intervention and protecting the taxpayer's purse. His attitude was in every way consistent with that expressed before the war. He does not appear to have fully appreciated here the seriousness of the food crisis.

Inchcape's reputation for advocating opposition to State interference was such that in August 1918 his writings on the subject were being reprinted in bulk – 10,000 copies – by an association in London formed expressly to rally supporters of this popular cause. He wrote voluminously on this and many other topics, his article on the 'present and prospective financial condition of the country' receiving high praise from Bonar Law and from Sir John Bradbury at the Treasury.

Another literary effort attempted to stir up opposition to the war among German merchant shipping magnates, such as Ballin, the creator of the Hamburg Amerika Line. Ballin had abandoned his previous stance of support for the Kaiser once the United States entered the war and he found much of his business destroyed. The Norddeutscher Lloyd and the Hansa Company were also hard hit. Inchcape composed an eight-page appeal to German shipowners and entrepreneurs – including Henniken, the Chairman of Norddeutscher Lloyd and a colleague of Inchcape's on the board of the Suez Canal Company and Gwinner, the governor of Deutsche Bank – in September 1918, but there is no record of any results.

Of his other Government committee duties during the war, the most crucial to his own interests was that concerned with the hire of merchant shipping in wartime. Vessels were requisitioned – thirty-seven per cent of British tonnage by 1916 – to carry essential commodities, such as wheat, meat and sugar, with all refrigerated space and later all grain space taken up by the Government. Such vessels, including a large number of P&O ships, earned freights at predetermined, fixed 'Blue Book' rates. The whole system worked unsatisfactorily, as far as Inchcape was concerned, when free market rates outstripped Blue Book rates by up to 200 per cent. Nevertheless, he was not able to change this system.

On the Port and Transit committee, appointed in November 1915, Inchcape achieved more positive results. Turnaround efficiency was much improved across the board. In 1918, Britain imported 31m tons of cargo with only 6.25m tons of shipping; in 1913, 13m tons of shipping had landed only 35m tons. Another success was his help in organising a general convoy strategy in the summer of 1917, whereby ninety per cent of overseas voyages were protected, drastically reducing losses. Inchcape was constantly on call at the Ministry of Shipping; for example, he was asked to use his influence with the Suez Canal Company to release tugs which had been taken over by the naval authorities in Egypt.

Inchcape's multifarious public activities in the war years included his membership of a Board of Trade committee on uniforms for the merchant marine, chairmanship of the London General Shipowners' Society, vice-presidency of the Royal Society of Arts, and treasurership of the Royal Merchant Seamen's Orphanage. He was a member of the executive committee of the National Committee on Sea Training, the Cobden Club, the Anglo-Belgian Union, the City of London Volunteer Regiment (Scottish Section), the Council of King

George's Fund for Sailors and, at the behest of Winston Churchill, the board of the Great Western Railway.

Inchcape's public work in this crucial period reached such a magnitude to receive an accolade in *The Times* that 'probably no civilian outside the Cabinet discharged during the war a greater range of administrative activities'. His work was regarded as so important that he was one of the few private individuals awarded a petrol allowance for his motor car. In May 1918 he was informed by Lloyd George that he had been awarded the honour of Knight Grand Cross of the Order of the British Empire for his war efforts. A scribbled note in pencil at the top of this letter instructed his secretary to ask that his name should not be put forward, and the accompanying form requesting details of his particulars was never completed and returned. Inchcape, who had striven so hard for recognition as an official in India, already had enough honours. This was no longer the main motivating force behind his public duties; instead, his goal was the preservation of the freedom of capital in Britain.

Looking at Inchcape's management of the P&O and the BI in a wider context, it is clear that he helped Britain's shipping industry play a decisive role in the Allied victory over Germany. The P&O made a major contribution to the Admiralty's achievement of providing 23.7m safe individual passages; it has been estimated that this was equivalent to roughly twenty-four times the average annual immigration into the USA in the ten years before the war.

Furthermore, 50m tons of military stores (excluding food and materials for munitions) were carried by Government requisitioned ships to the theatres of war, equal to the total imports into the whole of Britain in an average year. Many common wartime destinations were covered by P&O services. Requisitioning was most widespread in the Indian trade (over fifty per cent) in which the BI was dominant; in Australian waters (seventy-five per cent) where the AUSN, the New Zealand, Federal and Union Companies were powerful; and in the Far East, where nearly every ship was called up for service, including many P&O ships which frequented such ports as Hong Kong, Singapore, Batavia and Yokohama.

For these services, the British shipping industry made large profits – as in the case of the P&O – but paid a heavy cost. It has been conservatively calculated that the liner companies as a whole

increased their reserves by nearly £24m between 1914 and 1918. High
wartime freights encouraged speculation: in one year alone, 1915, as
many as ninety-four new shipping companies were formed in Britain,
spurred on by the record earnings of £262m by British shipping in the
first two years of the war.

On behalf of the P&O, Inchcape was able to capitalise on wartime
opportunities to the utmost by maintaining public confidence in the
P&O as one of the nation's premier shipping lines, keeping the share
price, and corporate morale, at a high level; by adding tonnage to the
fleets from every conceivable source, making several brilliant
acquisitions; fighting tooth and nail with the Government for every
penny of compensation for ship losses; channelling the combined
management and financial resources of the entire Mackinnon/Inch-
cape group behind the fleets; and constantly supporting the bravery
of officers and crews at sea and of port staff all over the world. These
efforts were considerably aided by Inchcape's power and prestige in
Government circles: he saw his public duties not only as a crusade for
the defence of private business, but also as a way of storing up
goodwill upon which he could draw later.

But, at the end of the day, 7½m tons of shipping (thirty-eight per
cent of 1914 tonnage) was lost, from which, arguably, British
shipping never recovered, especially as it was hit harder than that of
any other combatant. The role of British shipping in world trade was
never the same again, losing not only tonnage, but also markets and
the privileges which came with its traditional prominence. How did
Inchcape come to terms with this?

7

'Let us get on with our business'
1918–1932

Inchape's business concerns – the P&O on the one hand and the closely interconnecting Mackinnon/Inchcape group on the other – now faced totally different economic circumstances than they had experienced before. How did he face the postwar boom, then slump, then continued depression?

As in Chapter Six, Inchcape's handling of his business is best considered within a chronological framework: we are looking at how this great maritime entrepreneur grappled with a series of market shifts and changing conditions, as they happened. In this way, problems may be understood as Inchcape himself faced them, as they occurred, and not with the dubious benefit of hindsight. The focus is principally upon Inchcape's role as chairman of the P&O: this is extensively documented, and is how he is best remembered. Yet his work in building up the enormous and powerful Mackinnon/ Inchcape empire in India, headed by Mackinnon Mackenzie, was equally significant, and this group continued to operate to the overall benefit of the P&O.

According to the published results of the P&O throughout these years, it continued to grow and made handsome profits. But this was by no means the case. The details of Inchcape's management of the P&O in the 1920s emerged only after his death, with a report issued by leading accountants Deloitte, Plender and Griffiths. Commissioned by Alexander Shaw, Inchcape's son-in-law and successor as chairman, it exhaustively analysed the fortunes of the entire P&O group over the previous decade.

Deloitte's saw a powerful shipping company, with large and important subsidiaries and associated companies owning over half a million tons, offering services all over the Indian Ocean and Far

East. Yet its fleets were written down far too conservatively for a major company in the economic conditions of 1932, and the whole group was desperately illiquid. Provision for current and maturing liabilities was inadequate and there was insufficient working capital, much of the reserves having been spent on new tonnage.

During the previous ten years, the 'net results' – all that Inchcape would reveal to shareholders – cannot necessarily be related to the earnings of the P&O fleet itself. Largely without their knowledge, shareholders' dividends were derived from contributions by subsidiaries and by members of the Mackinnon/Inchcape group – including Inchcape's own private money – and benefited from the very liberal depreciation allocations made from the wartime profits.

The 'net results' suggest that the P&O had made aggregate profits of over £11m in the years 1922 to 1931, on which total dividends of £9.3m were paid out. According to Deloitte's investigations, actual profits totalled only £1.8m. £9.4m was contributed from sources outside the P&O itself, and additional sums came from the fleet depreciation fund. Charges for depreciation had amounted to only £23m, but would have exceeded £34m if calculated at the usual rate of five per cent per year on original cost.

The liabilities of the group included the preference stock of £3m, and the deferred stock of £4.6m which had remained static. The £1.5m three and a half per cent debenture stock, issued before 1913, had no expiry date and was not pressing, but in March 1922 Inchcape had issued £3.5m five and a half per cent debentures and in November 1923 £3½m five per cent debentures, and these were due to be redeemed before 1940.

From the profits of the war years, Inchcape had set up a number of special funds which were also used to tide the company over difficulties, such as a special reserve fund standing at £2m, and a Contingency Fund with £1.5m. An Insurance Fund, started by Inchcape in 1917, with Gray Dawes issuing the policies, covered the whole risk of the non-P&O/BI fleets. From 1926, Inchcape merely reinsured the ships on the open market. Thus, the P&O's liaibility for claims were confined to rare cases of insurers being unable to fulfil their commitments, so this was another fund which could be drawn upon for the profit and loss account. In 1921 it had already made a substantial transfer of nearly £400,000, to be followed by further sums in 1923, 1929, 1930 and 1931. By 1930, all the ships of the group were insured in the open market for total loss only, and for written-down book values – so an absolute minimum was being spent on insurance premiums, and replacement cover was entirely inadequate. Inchcape saw the insurance fund as much more useful for the 'net results'. A Provident Good Service Fund had been set up by the P&O founders, Wilcox and Anderson, to pay pensions and grants to employees. This too became a place in which to store extra profits from the war.

A substantial fund of £1.6m was also held in reserve to redeem the debentures, all invested in gild-edged securities – Government stocks such as the War Loan, India bonds and Bank of England stock. This would produce £2.5m by 1940, inadequate for debentures totalling £7m.

The most controversial fund was 'unappropriated balances', nearly all from recovered excess profits duty totalling £1.6m, which made credits to profit and loss, to recondition steamers, of over £½m in 1922–3. This fund had also been used to cover unsuccessful speculations, such as Inchcape's investment of over £11,000 in a coal concession. On Inchcape's final instructions, the balance in this account of nearly £1m was to be used to write off the book value of the fleet.

Besides debentures, the P&O group had several large loans still outstanding, with no provision for repayment. Those secured on gilt-edged investments included £3.2m from a City merchant bank, Cohen, Laming & Hoare, and £2.9m from the P&O Banking Corporation, set up by Inchcape just after the war. The New Zealand Shipping Company had lent £875,000, including £½m advanced in 1924 when Inchcape wrote to the chairman, Hughes, that 'It would be a convenience to us at the moment if the New Zealand could lend us £500,00 of their War loan to serve as a floater. The Bonds would be held by us in safe custody for the NZ'. In September 1931, Inchcape requested and received more advances in war loans – another £355,000 from New Zealand, £300,000 from Federal, £120,500 from Hain and £100,000 from BI.

The Union Company was especially supportive, with a total outstanding at Inchcape's death of £3.5m, at no interest. The first Union loan, of nearly £1m, was provided in 1921. Union was as anxious to offload funds as the P&O was to receive them, to avoid tax difficulties in New Zealand. Rather than the P&O declaring dividends on its New Zealand shares and revealing their profits, New Zealand allowed substantial rebates on trading arrangements.

Inchcape's private help to the P&O included a loan – one of many – of £200,000 from Eastern Traders Ltd, arranged through Mackinnon Mackenzie, repayable in Hong Kong dollars. With fluctuations in the rate of exchange, this liability had increased, and was still outstanding. None of these loans ever appeared in P&O's published balance sheets. Inchcape's private investment holding company, Mackay & Co., bought up the P&O's shares in the Khedivial Mail Company at cost when it was realised that the concern was unlikely to be profitable in the foreseeable future. Deals, including the purchase of Anderson & Green, Hain and Stricks, were another way by which Inchcape privately channelled extra funds into the P&O.

Bills payable, mainly to shipbuilders, were not so pressing as they first appeared. Shipbuilders received bills of exchange renewed every three months which they could discount at the P&O Banking Corporation, which meant that the P&O only had to pay five per cent of its bills every three months, thus taking five years to pay off the cost of a new ship. Inchcape considered this a useful instrument in reducing sudden calls on liquidity.

To a limited extent the P&O called on employees for financial support. Inchcape had started a banking scheme, putting employees' money into gilts and banks, paying them five and a half per cent. Although not strictly liable, the company always made good any deficit between the earnings and five per cent. But this deficit had amounted to a total of only £2,844 since 1915, and was covered with an adequate surplus. In 1925 he started a profit-sharing scheme, paying five per cent on the funds invested by employees of the P&O and its agents. An extra two per cent was paid when the dividend on the deferred stock exceeded five per cent, which it did until 1930. Standing at a balance of £1.4m, Inchcape decided to hold this in reserve and not accept further deposits.

In examining the P&O's tax situation, Deloitte's discovered that the allowance on income tax due to the company for depreciation on the steamers actually exceeded the P&O's trading profits as computed for income tax, and this was offset against investment income. One consolation of this poor performance was that the P&O but rarely found itself liable for income tax at all.

Deloitte's, in examining the P&O group's assets, were especially concerned with the thorny question of depreciation on the fleet, valued in 1931 at £14.7m. The amount put by each year (or not, as the case may be), was never declared to stockholders under Inchcape's chairmanship. It fluctuated annually, supplemented by sums from reserves and exceptional profits. It was broadly interpreted at four per cent on original cost, and included an allowance for obsolescence from the Government of £2.475m in excess profits duty refunds. At this rate, the P&O should have charged profit and loss at least £10m for depreciation in the 1920s, but in fact only £2.7m came from this source. Instead, substantial credits from subsidiaries and from the insurance fund, which never appeared in profit and loss, paid for this.

In allowing for depreciation, Inchcape seems never to have considered obsolescence or the possibility of sudden shrinkages in the value of his vessels, when technological developments in shipbuilding, both in materials and propulsion, could render whole fleets out of date overnight. He regarded his conservative finance policy as sufficient to allow the P&O to face bad times without having to pass the dividend or write down its capital.

Assets also included properties (£1.4m), the BI fleet, written down to £0.7m, the New Zealand ships (£0.9m), and Union (£2.5m). With the Orient shares, the book value of investments in subsidiaries was almost equal to that of the P&O fleet. Besides the transfers already mentioned, Federal had paid P&O £300,000 in 1924 towards group profits; £1m passed to the P&O's dividend account from Union in 1927 and another £½m, the following year.

The General Steam Navigation Company had sold two lots of 40,000 £1 shares to Mackinnon Mackenzie also to help out in 1927 and 1928. The latter held them as a P&O nominee, with no transactions appearing on the books. Mackinnon Mackenzie then made the profits available to P&O, based on £15 *13s 6d* per £1 share. Inchcape was apparently unconcerned with the inconsistency between this share price and the fact that the P&O's remaining holding in General Steam was written down to par at £1 each.

In concluding their report, Deloitte's emphasised the extent of the P&O's liabilities heightened by their lack of cash, and the severe decrease in gross receipts from voyages. In 1929, P&O ships aggregating over 450,000 tons struggled to earn as much as 360,000 tons had earned in 1922, an amount just over £7m. Between 1923 and 1926, earnings had fallen below this amount, especially in 1924 and 1925, and did so again at the end of the period, reaching £5.8m in 1931 on 416,000 tons. This poor performance in 1931 was even worse than it first appeared, as the earnings from the Branch Line – the service to Malta, Port Said, Suez, Aden, Colombo and on to Australia – were included for the first time.

Despite a mail subsidy of £295,000 per year, Inchcape realised that the P&O could no longer maintain its fortnightly service to Australia at a profit, and had to cut out alternate voyages, suffering a loss in their subsidy of £42,500. Income from other sources was maximised, such as sales of wines and tobacco at various ports, and their coal and water services at Aden.

The P&O was helped particularly by rebates from Mackinnon Mackenzie on their commission charges: in the autumn of 1931, these amounted to £100,000. But these and other contributions were not enough to offset the especially heavy losses on P&O voyages which occurred just before Inchcape's death and which mark the real downward turning point. They came at a time when reserves built up in more prosperous times, now remote, were becoming exhausted.

Deloitte's realised this, despite the inconsistent basis of the P&O's profit and loss accounts. As they wrote, 'the methods of accountancy adopted in arriving at the results render difficult a clear view as to how far and to what extent the final net results may be said to represent current or other earnings attributable to each year'. There were three ways by which Inchcape had done this: by supplementing profits by transfers from unappropriated balances, by showing against reserves items in fact charged to revenue, and by omitting items of income as a result of using them to write down assets. Deloitte's findings are summarised in Appendix One (see p.000)

The 'net results' show suspiciously little variation, whereas according to Deloitte's there was a severe decline in P&O profits, concealed each year by transfers from the variety of sources discussed above, with minimal sums paid out to offset depreciation. Inchcape had masterminded a very successful piece of creative accounting, continuing to pay acceptable, if not handsome, dividends when the P&O was actually making a loss, but he was running out of luck by the end.

Thus, the first P&O AGM after Inchcape's death – the first not under his chairmanship for nearly twenty years – revealed much more about the manner of his direction of P&O affairs than those AGMs over which he presided. Shaw showed that Inchcape's policy of preventing shareholder intervention by maintaining the dividend whilst keeping the accounts close to his chest, could not have continued for much longer. The P&O's sparse balance sheet had been meaningless for years.

Therefore, there would be no dividend for the first time since the opening of the Suez Canal. Inchcape's policy of skilled accumulation followed by skilled juggling had enabled him to go on paying a reasonable return, which dipped only from ten per cent in 1931 down to six per cent. Many other shipping lines had had to draw on their reserves to pay their shareholders but, as Shaw declared, 'you will agree that such a policy has limits, and that it ought to cease well short of the point where the inherent strength of a great concern, and therefore, of course, its future earning power, may be prejudiced'.

The revolution in the finances of the P&O was not confined to the non-payment of the dividend. Shaw then introduced the first ever P&O consolidated balance sheet, presenting the accounts in more detail than ever before. There was no provision under the P&O charter to appoint an auditor, but fortunately Lord Plender of Deloitte's was qualified to examine the accounts by virtue of the fact that he was in any case a stockholder, holding at least £1,000 of preference stock.

Shaw revealed what Plender had discovered, that the allied companies had played a substantial part in the P&O's income. Their contributions had been markedly less in 1931 than previously, which accounts for Inchcape reducing the dividend that year from ten to six per cent and for Shaw deciding that paying out of reserves must end and that the dividend payment must be foresaken. Maintaining dividends on the P&O's large debenture issues was a strain on the company and Shaw resolved to try and convert them to stock with a lower rate of interest than five and five and a half per cent. The P&O's gilt-edged investments, retained principally to redeem the debentures, had suffered a decline in value, and had to be bolstered up with £110,000 from sales of other investments.

Providing for depreciation was one of Shaw's greatest worries. The accounts in Inchcape's day – although he must have been one of the first to appreciate this – did not reflect the enormous increase in shipbuilding costs since the war. These were due to higher costs of labour and raw materials, the increasingly stringent Board of Trade regulations, and the need for vessels to be larger and more luxurious, in the case of passenger ships, to compete.

Yet the P&O did survive the 1920s, and Shaw paid tribute to Inchcape's achievement: 'If in the days of shipping prosperity which are now long past we had divided profits up to the hilt we should not have been able to provide for the necessary renewals to the P&O fleet, and consequently our position today would have been very different'. Now, in 1932, 'unless our earnings are very much increased next year it will be necessary to draw upon our reserves to provide for depreciation'.

Through considering the performance of the P&O throughout this decade, year by year, the success – but ultimate failure –of Inchcape's financial management becomes clear. He was able to cope with the P&O's difficulties and maximise on its advantages in a day-to-day sense, but could not overcome the fundamental problems posed by the end of the war. He realised, as he exclaimed at the Shipowners' Parliamentary Committee: 'At no time in the life of the Empire has the mercantile marine proved its value so clearly or been so seriously threatened in its very existence as at the present time'.

The principal problems of the shipping industry, as he saw them in September 1918, included the threat of State control, overall lower profits and the inability of shipping firms to build up reserves, high rate of tax, and increased competition from Scandinavia, the United States, the Netherlands and Japan. The last mentioned were building ships at a third of the price of British yards, and furthermore, as Inchcape pointed out, 'The American people are resolved to have an immense mercantile marine, whatever may be the cost'.

To try and counteract these developments Inchcape, in a series of newspaper articles, called for a 'Shipbuilding Crusade', complaining that the Government was doing nothing to encourage the renewal of British merchant fleets. Whilst the Americans, Japanese and Dutch had expanded their national tonnage, repairs and overhauls of British ships had to be foregone despite urgent need. Whilst others expanded their trading networks, Britain had kept but a tenuous hold on the markets it once dominated.

Yet he undermined his own argument by criticising the Government for neglect whilst in the same breath attacking Government interference. For the previous four years he had demanded 'Let us get on with the war': now he cried 'Let us get on with our business'. He wanted subsidies and mail contracts, insurance and compensation, but when opportunities for profit presented themselves, he wanted to be left alone to make the most of it. In the short postwar boom, the shackles of Government control, relatively patiently endured in wartime, chafed intolerably.

One such area of immediate demand was the passenger trade. In November 1918, the *Daily Mail* reported that the shipping companies were inundated with liner bookings, but had no ships. The P&O had hundreds of bookings to India in the one ship available and a huge demand for passages to Australia, reflecting an understandable desire to leave war-torn Europe for pastures new. But the company could offer no guaranteed service in the foreseeable future. They were not alone. The Union Castle Line had a waiting list of 3,000 for Cape Town and East Africa. The White Star Line had a thirty per cent increase in bookings to New York but could only offer one sailing a week. The Government would not release requisitioned fleets in a hurry, mindful of the relatively low hiring charges it enjoyed which would be difficult to reimpose once the ships were returned.

At least Inchcape succeeded in bringing public attention to this and other problems of the shipping industry. His speech at the 1918 P&O AGM had a profound impact throughout shipping and general commercial circles. He kept his pessimism and despair to himself, and the *Journal of Commerce* saw him as a breath of fresh air, breathing a spirit of progress and renewed hope. The *Westminster Gazette* saw him, while he complained that twenty-two of his ships were still under charter, as 'having the impatience of a strong businessman who sees the trade that he has built up handled by officials who have no direct concern in running a business profitably'. He did not necessarily gain complete sympathy. The editor argued that Government restrictions might well reduce chances for profit, but at least the 'old system of parcelling out the world into spheres of influence for different groups of shipowners' would no longer be tolerated.

In steering the P&O through this minefield, Inchcape's first moves were to conserve funds. So, instead of paying the usual bonus of six per cent on the deferred stock, these amounts were added to the reserve fund, and £200,000 new deferred stock was issued at par. Then he set to work to rebuild his fleet and his business. He reached an agreement, in January 1919, with the shipbuilders R & W Hawthorn Leslie to place two of their berths at the P&O's disposal for ten years. But shipbuilding costs had increased dramatically. As he told shareholders at the 1919 AGM, percentage increases in costs compared with 1913 were like this: wages 130 per cent, canvas 408 per cent, ropes 220 per cent, cargo handling 200 per cent, provisions

150 per cent. He quoted not without envy a foreign shipping company, not liable to such heavy tax and such high costs, which had recently paid 100 per cent dividends. But considerable progress had already been made in restoring the fleets to their normal working strength. Ninety-four ships of 543,540 tons had been lost in the war but by taking over existing fleets and building new, 169 ships of 1,168,298 tons had been added, bringing the total to 427 ships of two and a quarter million tons.

In order to recover and develop his business, Inchcape lobbied for more subsidies. The P&O was still receiving a British Government mail contract worth £40,000 per quarter, but he wanted to renew the Australian postal contract, despite the new Australian Navigation Act and attempts to reserve the Australian trade to locally owned vessels. Australia was already a nightmare to Inchcape. The Commonwealth Government had bought ships before the war and had successfully competed against private lines including the P&O and the BI, and now was in a very strong position.

But in the Australian trade, as in many other services, Inchcape faced two new threats. Firstly, great progress had been made in civil aviation, reducing the journey between London and Calcutta to nine days. Secondly, the Government was considering limiting profits officially on coal to coal producers to 1s 2d per ton, and Inchcape took umbrage at what he saw as the Government wilfully stifling individual initiative, concerned that this rule might be imposed on other industries, and afraid that it would ultimately push up coal prices.

It must have appeared inconsistent to some shareholders that Inchcape complained so much about poor returns in shipping and the massive problems it faced, yet the P&O's mysterious 'net result' remained high, at £614,600 with £115,200 carried over to reserves, even higher than before the war. The chairman claimed that the bulk of the profits had to be paid to the Government, that – bearing in mind the attacks he had suffered in *The Times* from Sir Leo Chiozza Money and others – 'we have not been profiteers. We have made no furtune out of the war'. But, fortunately for shareholders mindful of the continued payment of their dividend, he was not telling the whole truth.

The P&O's finances were certainly enough to continue founding businesses and acquiring shipping lines. At the end of 1918, a 'French P&O' was formed with a capital of 250,000 francs, mainly to raise funds for M. Brenier-Estrine, the P&O's Marseilles agent. Another shipping company was brought into the fold in 1919, the Eastern & Australian Line, as a subsidiary of the AUSN. The 'E&A' provided a profitable service between Sydney, Hong Kong and Kobe with four ships running every three weeks, enjoying a large through-passenger traffic and fair interport trade.

The recent movement towards oil-fired ships made shipbuilding costs higher than ever, so Inchcape looked more and more to his policy of acquiring existing tonnage. For this he needed long-term capital and in January 1920 he launched his plans for the P&O Banking Corporation. The P&O's considerable private banking business had expanded in recent years, offering great convenience to customers at some profit to the P&O. Over £12m was held in London alone. If the corporation were put on a separate footing, Inchcape argued, services could be extended to other ports by opening branches, thus attracting much larger deposits from P&O group companies, other shipping lines and agents, and freight customers and passengers.

Official bank status and public flotation enabled the new P&O Bank to raise money to fund its expansion. Inchcape used his contacts as a director of The National Provincial Bank to persuade them to take up a large block of 50,000 shares, and attracted interest from other bankers, shipowners and P&O stockholders themselves. Only the war, during which the Chancellor of the Exchequer did not welcome new flotations which reduced investments in Government stocks and war bonds and loans, together with a severe shortage of administrative staff, had prevented him from initiating the P&O Bank earlier.

Incorporated on 3 May 1920 with an issued capital of £2m, the P&O Bank opened business in London the following month and simultaneously at Calcutta, Bombay and Madras. By March 1921, a further four branch offices had been established in India, including Karachi. A year later, the P&O Bank was also operating out of China and the Straits. The bank also expanded by acquisition, through a further share issue of £94,161, acquiring a controlling interest in the Allahabad Bank, a northern Indian bank with thirty-four agencies.

The rebuilding of the fleet and Inchcape's personal contacts helped build up the P&O Bank's business in the early 1920s, and by 1927 it had attained a recognised status among Eastern exchange banks.

That same year it affiliated with a major bank, when the Chartered Bank of India, Australia & China took a controlling interest. This bank's Eastern business was such as to make it a natural choice, especially through Inchcape's personal connection as its chairman in the 1890s, and the support of the current chairman, his friend and colleague Sir Montague Turner.

The creation of the P&O Bank fuelled rumours that Inchcape was again on the acquisitions trail, pushing up the P&O deferred stock share price to an all-time high of £700 in the late autumn of 1919. The financial press speculated about a possible amalgamation between the P&O, Cunard and Furness Withy.

Instead, in January 1920, Inchcape announced the purchase of one of Britain's oldest shipping lines, the General Steam Navigation Company. At £5 10s for General Steam's £1 shares, the acquisition brought considerable cash assets, freehold property and, most significantly, twenty-seven steamers, equal to a cost of £1.9m. General Steam had first approached Sir Owen Philipps of the Royal Mail Group, but found his offer of £5 5s per share for the whole or £6 per share for fifty-one per cent of the equity unacceptable. Characteristically, by the time Inchcape made this announcement to his board, he had already secured 93.78 per cent of the shares on behalf of Gray Dawes. However, if the P&O directors so desired, 'then it is theirs without any profit to me or my firm'. So General Steam too joined the group. They welcomed the merger, having lost sixty per cent of their tonnage in the war and now lacking the resources for a major rebuilding programme. A quarter of a century ago, Inchcape had briefly acted as their chairman, so they trusted him.

Rebuilding the P&O also meant employing the fleet as profitably as possible as soon as they were released from requisition. Three voyages to India in 1919 made aggregate net profits of nearly £55,500, and P&O ships successfully completed fifty voyages throughout 1920, to India, Australia and Japan. With so few services for so long, these ships could hardly fail to make money: they earned in aggregate over £1m (the *Kashigar's* voyage to Japan alone making £72,000) against only ten loss-making voyages, producing an overall balance of more than £978,000.

The P&O group seemed to be getting back to normal: ship repair staff who had been seconded to the Ministry of Shipping for service in Italy had been released, and P&O vessels in the Persian Gulf were completing their Government duties, freeing staff to return to work, who were, according to Mackinnon Mackenzie, 'tumbling over each other and clinging onto their jobs'.

Inchcape wrote to the BI agents in East Africa, Smith Mackenzie – run by his nephew, William Mackay Sim – that all efforts should be made to restore services on that coast, even if they did not pay at first. If he could work up a local trade, the service could act as a feeder from the Bombay and London lines. Inchcape suggested not employing the relatively expensively-operated BI ships, but setting up a small separate company, in which Smith Mackenzie should have a substantial holding, 'and it might be worth while to let some of the natives have an interest'. In due course, this materialised with considerable success.

Inchcape was particularly keen to drum up more business in India, to offset the headway made by the Japanese and by the Scindia Line, a locally owned rival. He was also anxious to take advantage of the Persian Gulf trade, again opening up: Inchcape's friend Sir Percy Cox, the local Political Resident, suggested he start up a new shipping service on the Hassa coast.

Final insurance payments on ship losses helped add to the P&O's funds in 1920. Inchcape fought hard for each one. As he wrote to Sir Norman Hill, of the Liverpool and London War Risks Insurance Company, 'the judgement on the *Matiana*'s case is that she was lost by war risk. Will you now send us a cheque for the instalments due on her policy money, or will you notwithstanding your seventeen millions of profit put us to the expense of an appeal?'.

This aided the building of new ships for the group, but in dealing with William Gray of Hartlepool, Inchcape received a taste of his own medicine. In pressing Inchcape for payment on the £40,000 bill, Gray hinted that his customer had made a fortune when the Government Standard Ships policy was introduced, as Inchcape had had a special arrangement with Gray to reserve berths for building P&O and BI ships for which he received compensation when they were taken over. Inchcape was angry: 'I would like to put you right here. I have not made a penny out of it personally, the whole advantage reaped has gone to the P&O and BI'. At the same time, he faced paying out £96,000 for the new *Erinpura*, to be built by Denny, complaining constantly of the increased prices.

Besides acquiring fleets and building new tonnage, Inchcape pressed the Ministry of Shipping for the return of his ships. They had agreed to recondition requisitioned tonnage when it was paid off but, suffering labour troubles in the yards, they wanted Inchcape to waive the strike clause, so that they could not be held responsible for delays. Inchcape lobbied for the return of his ships and a lump sum in lieu of reconditioning, but backed down when he realised that this held up proceedings even more. The Ministry's offer of a number of redundant single-screw patrol boats to the BI was not welcomed – the BI marine superintendent did not think much of them, and nor did Inchcape.

Good income from voyages in 1920 prompted Inchcape to increase the final dividend on the deferred stock from six to nine per cent, a total of fifteen per cent on a declared result of £710,400 (£100,000 higher than the previous year) although he was careful to continue to allocate at least £100,000 to reserves. At the 1920 P&O AGM, he warned that this improvement could not last, that passengers were being carried at less than cost despite the increase in passage money. The main problem was the need to expand exports; he complained bitterly about the overall lack of demand for British goods anywhere. He had identified British shipping's biggest problem, but he had no solutions to offer. In 1920 he worked at making the most of the postwar boom, without yet formulating any detailed strategy for the future.

Alexander Shaw, the future chairman, first became closely involved in P&O administrative and executive work during Inchcape's many absences in 1921. Inchcape thought highly of his son-in-law's abilities. To Bonar Law, in recommending Shaw for Government committee work, Inchcape wrote:

he is exceptionally capable, extremely industrious, he has an economical disposition and I am perfectly certain he would co-ordinate the various departments and carry the different heads with him. I don't know that I can say any more of him than that I have made him a partner in one of my firms and I hope he will succeed in a good many of my enterprises. He is a very promising businessman and at the same time he has made his mark in the House of Commons [Shaw had recently been elected as MP].

Shaw, from this point onwards, was to play a crucial part in P&O affairs, although Inchcape was still responsible for the bottom line. The chairman was torn between welcoming the brilliant young man in taking on part of the burden of work, and fear that he would become too powerful and threaten his own ultimate authority. The older man must have reflected on the parallel between his situation and that of Duncan Mackinnon's final years as chairman of the BI before the outbreak of war. In 1921, tired with increasing responsibilities and depressed about the future, Inchcape was glad at this point to leave for India and trust Shaw.

Shaw was helped and constantly supported by Inchcape's son Kenneth, who became the second Earl, valuing his contribution so highly that he persuaded Inchcape to make him joint deputy chairman. Kenneth was heavily involved in many of the day-to-day activities, looking after the BI and Mackinnons under his father's general supervision. Of a quieter nature than Shaw, his achievements were less obvious, yet it is certain that he did much of the backroom work behind Shaw's reports to fellow directors.

The Government still owed Inchcape a great deal of money from war service, according to his systematically kept accounts, and he and Shaw spent a good deal of time claiming as much as possible. The BI were apparently owed twenty-two lahks of rupees, nearly £150,000, for freight and passage to Bombay alone. It was crucial to Inchcape that he was promptly paid, because the rupee fell heavily from 2*s* 8½*d* in February 1920 to 1*s* 3½*d* in July 1921 and he was losing money with every delay. The Ministry of Shipping had refused to pay him at exchange rates ruling when the agreements were first made, and continued to employ BI ships in trooping at rock-bottom rates.

As in 1920, Inchcape wrote at length, at least every week, to Mackinnon Mackenzie in Calcutta to protect his Indian Ocean business, now struggling to survive. William Currie (later himself a P&O Chairman) who ran the office, was instructed by Inchcape to sell of their holdings in the Bombay Persian Steam Navigation Co. and any other Arab concerns in which the BI had invested, to make more funds available for India.

Besides competition in India, Inchcape now faced increasing rivalry from his fellow shipowners at home. Between July 1919 and July 1921, 11m gross tons of new shipping had been ordered by British owners, when international trade was down to eighty per cent of 1913 levels. Operating costs were three times those ruling before the war, yet freights were about the same as in 1913. With 2m tons of shipping laid up, shipowners were now fighting over the remaining spoils.

Inchcape was particularly upset when Andrew Weir's offered a service to Australia, a direct attack on the P&O, which had recently lost the Australian coastal service. He complained that 'through good times and bad we have kept the berth [to Australia] occupied for 40 years and have given satisfaction in the trade. I look on it as a child of my own as I inaugurated the line when I was a youngster in Calcutta'. Now nearly seventy and appalled at shipping conditions much worse than he could ever imagine, Inchcape was becoming increasingly sentimental and nostalgic.

Labour unrest was another problem which threatened the P&O as never before. In one instance, to avoid a strike and to placate the Stewards' Union, two dishonest stewards caught stealing from passengers were let off lightly; Inchcape's secretary fortunately managed to prevent him from sending a furious letter to *The Times* which would only have made matters worse. But he did publish a general attack.

The unions dictate to the shipowners what men are to go in the ships, with the result that incompetent men of whom nothing is known have often to be taken merely because they have joined the union, while men who have been in the service of the company for years are excluded. One result is that passengers' belongings and enormous quantities of cabin, saloon, and table furnishings are constantly being stolen. On one voyage alone of a P&O steamer, plate and linen to the value of £1,043 were removed from the ship ... the end, of course, will come, and we will get back to a sound working basis, though it may not be quite yet.

This general recovery depended very largely, as Inchcape realised, on the specific recovery of Britain's overseas shipping trade. He was stunned when he read in *The Times* of the growth of the American and Japanese merchant fleets, which had expanded sixfold and more than double respectively. In spite of increased shipbuilding output in Britain and the P&O's attempts to rebuild its fleet, the proportion of British tonnage in world shipping had dropped from $44\frac{1}{2}$ per cent to $35\frac{1}{2}$ per cent, whilst the USA's share had risen from 4.3 to 22.7 per cent.

Another and perhaps even more alarming threat to British shipping which Inchcape apparently chose to ignore at this point was the development of oil fuel. Coal-fired vessels were down to 72.3 per cent from 88.9 per cent, sailing ships had all but disappeared at 5.1 per cent, but oil was now used by 20.6 per cent of ships, and they were paying their way when coalburners were losing.

These factors played an important part in the reduction of the

P&O voyage profits of 1921 to a third of the 1920 figure, despite the
achievement of twice as many total round trips. Takings were only
one-sixth of the previous year, less than £370,000 on 100 voyages.
Profit-making voyages were outnumbered by those making a loss.
There is no clear pattern between profitability and destination, but
many voyages to Bombay lost heavily, although more than £31,000
was earned through Government trooping to this port.

The downward movement in the P&O share price reflects the low
ebb of the shipping industry. From a high in January 1921 of £365 on
the deferred stock, it fell forty-five points on the announcement of
the reduced dividend. Shareholders responded predictably to a fall in
the 'net result' from £710,400 to £623,500. At the AGM, Inchcape
described the year as 'wretched', but shareholders were only
concerned with when their dividend would rise again, questioning the
existence of the £3m insurance fund. It would have been difficult for
Inchcape to take radical new measures, even if he had wanted to. The
need to placate shareholders, especially in view of the lack of
financial detail published, heavily restricted the availability of capital
for building new tonnage and developing new trades.

Inchcape tried to solve this problem the next year with a new stock
issue. The prospectus for £3,500,000 5½ per cent debenture stock,
repayable in 1930–40, priced at £96 10s per £100 stock, was three
times over-subscribed, despite the comparative lack of confidence in
the share price. Inchcape was so delighted by the result that he
decided to go for another £3.5m issue to make a total of £7m, the
maximum he was allowed under the charter. Although the capital
was badly needed, keeping up the interest payments and making
provision ultimately to redeem the debentures was to become a
severe burden upon P&O liquidity in the future.

Problems in running the P&O services fell more and more upon
Shaw, but Inchcape allowed no one to run the BI but himself. Indian
income tax now threatened to eliminate its profits entirely, and he
tried to arrange a new method for Mackinnon Mackenzie to collect
its commission yet avoid tax. He asked Currie to reduce wages all
round as a first measure, offering to give up his half a per cent
director's commission on earnings in solidarity. At the same time,
agitation to preserve Indian coastal waters for Indians was
mounting. 'If the extremists are unfortunately able to force the
passing of a resolution to restrict the Indian coast trade to Indian-

owned vessels, we may have to register the Company in India', he
warned. At this time, in 1922, the BI was the largest single merchant
fleet in the world, with 158 vessels of nearly 1m tons gross.

Inchcape's greatest service to the P&O in this year was persuading
Sir Robert Horne at the Treasury to make grants to all shipowners to
offset the obsolescence of their fleets. This was worth £2,475,000 to
the P&O alone, and it was never revealed to shareholders.

The share price rose on the announcement of the improved 'net
result' of £696,600. But this was mainly due to the Government
hand-out for obsolescence and the income from the debenture issue,
not from the P&O voyage results. Of 145 voyages, eighty-three made
an overall loss. The small balance remaining, of less than £100,000,
was due entirely to earnings from Government trooping to Bombay
and Karachi. The Australian trade was picking up, with the
Narkunda, Naldera and *Mantua* making profits of up to £69,000 per
voyage, but this was wiped out by heavy losses in the Indian Ocean.
Inchcape did not mention this at the AGM, but mysteriously referred
to earnings by the Allied fleets, and added that the P&O's
Government securities, bought for £6.8m, were now worth £7.5m.
Things appeared to be looking up, but in fact they were worse than
ever.

Despite the boost to the P&O finances in 1922, further liquidity was
needed by 1923, which this time came from Inchcape's own pocket.
As well as arranging profitable deals on behalf of the P&O, he was
prepared to take unprofitable investments off their hands. For
instance, he had recommended buying over £½m in shares in the
Khedivial Mail Steamship Company back in 1919, when they looked
to be a promising investment. An arrangement for the interchange of
cargo and passengers with the P&O at Aden had brought some
revenue, but there had been severe unforeseen competition from
highly subsidised Italian lines and it had not paid its way for the last
three years. Inchcape recorded that

feeling myself responsible for an investment which has turned out to be an
unfortunate one I arranged for a small company – Mackay & Co. – of which
I and my family are the sole proprietetors, to take over the shares of what the
P&O paid for them ... I was determined to free the P&O Co. and not to
leave my successor in the Chair with a bad legacy.

The takeover of the Khedivial shares was typical of many smaller

deals Inchcape undertook to offload debts and liabilities from the
P&O. It was highly necessary: the voyage results for 1923, the first
year in which depreciation was allowed, were disastrous. Of 150
voyages, eighty-one made losses, and only sixty-nine made a profit.
Again, the highest earnings were mainly coming from voyages to
Australia, so Inchcape invested heavily in new ships for the
Australian trade. There was no point in putting more money into the
Bombay and Calcutta services, which were losing almost constantly,
despite low operating costs. The year's workings produced a small
balance to profit of £60,854, about two-thirds of the previous year's
profit, but when depreciation was taken into account the loss
approached £500,000.

Inchcape partially offset this poor performance with another
profitable deal on behalf of the P&O group: the Strick Line. To
rebuild the BI's Persian Gulf trade, Gray Dawes had acquired Strick
for £1.6m in 1919 and sold it to Hain in 1923 for a third of this sum.
With a capital of £250,000 and four steamers of 27,040 tons, it earned
profits of £80,000 in its first year under Hain, and continued to make
money.

Reflecting difficult trading conditions overall, the share price of
the deferred stock fell again, to only £270, but picked up at the end of
the year when Inchcape declared a final 'net result' of £1,013,200.
Earnings from subsidiaries and associated companies, and funds
Inchcape had put by during the war, were enough to overcome the
losses on voyages of P&O ships and to pay handsome returns. 1923,
according to Shaw, had been the last relatively successful year,
before things got really disastrous, but 'right from the time shipping
was de-controlled the operations of the P&O Company's ships have
had disappointing results'.

Inchcape's explanation of difficult trading conditions took the
form of an elaborate joke concerning the

safety of the most valuable ship in the fleet, caught without warning in a
terrible typhoon. The skipper, Asquith, with his second officer, George (who
also has an extra master's certificate) both have an intimate knowledge of the
law of storms, and the ship is basically well-found. The ship has not been too
badly damaged, but some of the crew are missing.

The ship's name was not in the company's books but it played an
important part in the company's annals – the *Free Trade*.

Inchcape told the joke partly to offset accusations that he was becoming a protectionist. The P&O and allied fleets, Union, New Zealand and Orient, favoured shipping conferences, seen by many as monopolistic and non-competitive. Inchcape argued that all benefited from an absence of violent fluctuations, and conference rates broadly followed the general level of the freight market. Stability was vital, as shipping lines had goods in transit which would be rendered unprofitable if there was a sudden collapse in the market. Conferences helped ensure punctual services if goods were ready for shipment at an assured price. It avoided starvation of goods in some markets and gluts in others.

At the end of 1923, Inchcape faced press speculation about when he would retire. He refuted the implication that he manipulated the entire fleet of over 2m tons single-handed; and pointed out that his absence for so long in India showed that he was not indispensable. Yet the accusation was not so far from the truth. He would never give up the reins of power. He wrote praising fellow directors 'who carried on in my absence just as if I had been here. They kept me in touch by telegram on all matters of importance, they sent me regularly my weekly bag, and I turned up in Leadenhall Street after six months' absence with as full a knowledge of the affairs of the P&O and our Allied Companies as if I had never been away'. His particular brand of 'hands-on' management, as he became aware of the growing crisis facing the P&O, did not allow him to delegate any major decisions, let alone to stand down.

Inchcape's viscountcy, marking his achievements in public life, was only a partial compensation for the new disappointments suffered by his business interests in 1924. The P&O 'net result' of £1,346,900 which he announced at the end of the year really concealed a tiny profit, according to Deloitte's, of only £137,003. The P&O voyage accounts were the worst ever: 162 voyages, only thirty-eight making a profit, with an overall loss of £655,471, rising to a staggering £1,263,758 including depreciation. Despite more losses in earnings in the Indian trade, Inchcape restored the prewar service connecting the Australian mail steamers with Bombay via Aden with the new *Razmak* which replaced the *Salsette*. Trooping work was limited now, and could not be relied on as a ready source of income.

The pressure upon Inchcape to make the P&O appear prosperous and successful came not just from shareholders. As Britain's premier shipping line – a national institution more than a commercial organisation – it had to seem unaffected by collapsing markets and falling freights. As such, Inchcape went to great lengths to accommodate royalty and leading politicians, such as the Duke and Duchess of York and their entourage on board the *Mashobra* to Mombasa.

He became obsessed with maintaining standards and keeping a close eye on the smallest detail of operating the fleet. For example, he wrote to *The Pioneer*, a newspaper published in Allahabad, after seeing a complaint in its pages of irregularity in delivery of P&O baggage. 'I instituted a weekly report from the Company's agents, Messrs. Mackinnon Mackenzie', Inchcape wrote, 'which I have got regularly ever since, and I find that from January 1923 to date 91 steamers have arrived in Bombay from Europe with 13,254 passengers, and the only missing packages have been 44, out of which 19 were traced and sent to their owners' and only one item had been lost in the last eight months. He passed on a complaint by 'a passenger of note', that the pen he was using in the writing room of the *Naldera* was 'vile', to the superintendent purser at the docks.

In announcing an unchanged dividend of twelve per cent. Inchcape warned shareholders that the P&O's investments and allied lines were primarily responsible for profits now. Freights were low, the new mail service to Australia was suffering by the recent labour troubles there, and Continental firms were undercutting the P&O all along the line. At the end of the AGM, a shareholder suggested that he would accept a lower dividend until the situation improved. This gave Inchcape some confidence in finally taking the decision to reduce the dividend in 1925.

1924 had been seen as a bad year, but Inchcape declared that 1925 'has been the worst which shipping has ever experienced'. The P&O share price fell to its lowest recorded level of £235 on the announcement of the cut in dividend to ten per cent. The 'net result' of £1,273,500 hid another very bad year of trading losses, the 1925 voyage accounts almost identical to those of 1924. The Australian service was still unreliable, with one voyage making £47,000 and another losing £19,000. Bombay voyages were also up and down, with profits of £8,000 one time and losses of £31,000 another.

As a further method of raising funds, Inchcape started a profit-sharing scheme for employees, paying five per cent on their deposits and an extra two per cent when the dividend on the deferred stock exceeded five per cent. By 1932 this fund had accumulated £1.4m.

Inchcape now felt that he had completed much of his postwar rebuilding plan, especially with the launch of the famous *Rawalpindi,* the first oil-burning P&O liner. But, with increasing building costs, strikes in Australia and South Africa, the disruption of China trade and agitation in India and the Dominions against imports of foreign goods, the P&O fleet could not profitably employ its ships.

Perhaps this explains why he did not take advantage of the Trade Facilities Acts, by which the Government advanced money to build ships, enabling fleets such as Kylsant's Royal Mail Group to grow. He pointed out that there was already an oversupply of tonnage, and agreed with the Prime Minister that direct subsidies for shipping would not be the answer. Real recovery would come only with increased employment.

1926 was the first year in which the P&O made a net loss, of £306,237, but a 'net result' of £1,196,000 profit was nevertheless declared. The share price continued to fall and the loss on voyages was heavier than ever, so Inchcape decided to stop charging depreciation. Of 172 voyages, only thirty-six made a profit. Three voyages to Australia earned over £15,000, but the loss incurred by the *Cathay's* maiden voyage, expected to be a great success, was a serious disappointment. Four other round trips to Australia lost over £20,000 each, two of them nearer £30,000. The only profits came in the summer months of June and July, the peak of the cruising season; otherwise the year was disastrous.

But for a rebate on marine insurance of over £500,000, the mail contract subsidy of £294,944, and interest from a profit-sharing scheme run by the Suez Canal Company, the situation would have been even worse. Inchcape further revealed that cash deposits of over £5m from the allied companies had played a vital part in keeping the year's results high, paying the dividend and maintaining the fleet.

Inchcape saw it as imperative that the P&O's standards, especially in the luxury liner business, should be as high as possible. His gifted, intelligent and attractive daughter Elsie, who in many ways inherited more of his flair for business opportunities and zest for life and travel than any of his other children, made a valuable input into ensuring that P&O liners were in a class by themselves. Her interior designs and fittings were acclaimed by several journalists and the most sophisticated travellers. But customers who could afford these truly magnificent services were relatively few and far between and insufficient to offset losses.

The General Strike added to the P&O's problems. The *Kaiser-I-Hind* had to leave for Bombay without an ounce of cargo on board. The price of coal rocketed, and that available was poor quality stuff, leading to greater consumption. Fortunately, despite Inchcape's early reluctance and suspicion about the use of oil rather than coal, nine of the P&O's mail steamers were oil-fired by 1926. Only the P&O's fleet of forty-nine tramp steamers were able to pay their way, but in this respect they were far from typical of British tramp shipping as a whole.

1927 saw slight improvements, but Inchcape was far from sure if this was the light at the end of the tunnel. According to Deloitte's adjustments, the P&O profit was about £½m (the 'net result' was £1,200,000). The share price began to rise again, and topped the £300 mark at more rumours, in May, of a possible merger deal with Cunard.

Passenger earnings were up one quarter of a million pounds, especially in the new cruise services offered. A tour around the Greek Islands, with a call at Constantinople in the *Ranchi* made a profit of £8,000. Services to Bombay, previously heavily loss-making, were now profitable, the popular *Rawalpindi* and *Kaiser-i-Hind* making an average of £13,000 each trip. Despite the political problems in China of which Inchcape complained at the AGM, the *Karmala's* voyage to China made £22,000. The Australian trade was as unprofitable as ever, with each round trip losing up to £41,000. Emigration was less popular, with many businesses begun by emigrants having failed. Through losses in the Australian trade, together with the increase in coaling costs of £241,000 due to the coal strike, the 1927 voyage accounts show a debit balance of over £800,000.

Fortunately the BI, which achieved consistently higher earnings than the P&O, was able to help considerably with group profits; for the six months ending in December 1926 its steamers earned net profits worth nearly £200,000 which could be remitted home without problems. Inchcape wrote to Sir John Bell, who had taken over from Currie, that 'it is gratifying to see this improvement in the working results'. He then praised the BI's repair facility, the Mazagon Dock, which apparently enjoyed a monopoly of non-Indian steamer repair work in Bombay, for making over £5,000 in January 1927 alone, mainly due to Government work. These profits were to be sustained: BI steamers earnings equalled nearly £600,000 in the year ending June 1927.

Working in the Indian Ocean trades, the BI offered a much less sophisticated and luxurious service in comparison with the P&O. BI steamers on the Bombay coastal emigrant service accommodated passengers four to a cabin in the preferred class, allowing them fifteen square feet per head. Running water was not supplied, according to Inchcape, because 'if fresh water taps were fitted in all preferred cabins and wash-houses, owing to the wastage through carelessness of passengers, it is doubtful if the ship could carry sufficient fresh water for voyage requirements'. This was not unreasonable, Inchcape maintained, because 'such fittings are not supplied in ordinary emigrant ships. The general comfort and sanitary condition of the cabins could not be maintained if passengers of this class were allowed to wash in their cabins'.

Besides passengers, BI steamers trading out of Bombay also profited from carrying gold from Durban. The BI Malabar coast service from Karachi made profits considerably in excess of the rival Scindia line. Carrying pilgrims to Jeddah was also worthwhile, the *Takada* making the equivalent of well over £3,000 in one voyage. The Mogul line was trying to break into this market, but Inchcape doubted if they could meet the cost of at least £125,000 for the necessary new steamer. Thus the BI was keeping its head above water.

This gave Inchcape some grounds for optimism at the 1927 AGM, and enabled him to finance the building of a revolutionary new turboelectric ship, much more economical than internal combustion: the future *Viceroy of India*. He argued that the P&O fares, although not cheap, continued to offer excellent value for money when compared with the average hotel bill and charges by GWR and the other railway companies. Another healthy growth area was the P&O Banking Corporation, whose £10 shares now fetched double their face value.

Yet he found himself, unusually, up against doubting and questioning shareholders. One demanded to know the exact nature of the P&O's investments, especially the associated companies, and another criticised the management for its lack of a chartered accountant. Inchcape brushed them all aside, insisting that it was not to the advantage of the company to have such details bandied around, and received his usual applause when he declared that the other shareholders had confidence in the board. As far as their immediate dividends were concerned, they felt justified in leaving everything to Inchcape.

Inchcape continued to defend his policy of what Deloitte's were to refer to as conservative finance. He explained that he had generously set aside money for depreciation in the war years, instead of making a larger distribution to shareholders. He had written down the book values of each of the 324 steamers of the P&O fleet, so that a smaller sum could be left for depreciation now, providing £1m for the *Viceroy of India* and other new vessels. The P&O paid minimal tax and allowed a four per cent reduction for depreciation and obsolescence. The previous year's improvement in results had been maintained, so he felt justified in restoring the deferred dividend to twelve per cent in 1928.

The low stock market value of P&O shares continued to worry Inchcape. However, the price rose to 61*s* by the end of the year, a substantial rise, through attracting a large number of new small investors. Inchcape's words seem familiar today: 'the more so-called capitalists there are in the country the better will it be for all concerned'. The same attitude lay behind the P&O profit-sharing scheme, which had reached £864,000. This idea apparently came to Inchcape whilst he was travelling by sleeping car to Scotland one night and, characteristically, by the time the train pulled into the final stop, all the details had been worked out.

While the loss on steamer services in 1928 was half that of the previous year, there was no sustained improvement in performance, and earnings from the BI fell sharply to only £60,000 on the half year ending January 1928. Even this could not last: prospects of major difficulties in India for the BI arose with the Indian Coastal Shipping Bill, which proposed to prohibit the trading of any ships on the coasts of India and Burma not owned by Indians.

Thus 1928 saw the introduction of an extensive economy drive. This was in keeping with the work of the National Maritime Board in reducing wages, and J. H. Thomas's similar policy relating to the severe fall in railway traffic which resulted in wage cuts of two and a half per cent. Inchcape presided over the first P&O Economy Committee meeting, which set out its plan to scrutinise every aspect of group expenditure. Running costs were helped in any case by the reduction of 4s a ton in the price of fuel oil, saving P&O £600,000 per year, but the costs of repair work and labour as a whole were still too high.

Staff pay packets and allowances bore the brunt of the cuts, as they had risen more steeply than other costs. Inchcape calculated that total P&O salaries had increased from £82,697 in 1913 to £158,135 by 1928, for 9,591 employees of the P&O and all the agencies at home and abroad. Cargo ships were to carry only three officers instead of four; victualling rates generally were reduced, from 3s to 2s 6d per day for European crews, to 1s 3d for deck and engine crews from Bombay and China. Calcutta crews were the cheapest of all, subsisting on only 1s a day, and at Inchcape's request they replaced other crews whenever possible. The BI traditionally employed Calcutta crews, incurring lower operating costs than the P&O.

Rationalising the mail services also saved money. The P&O and Orient lines now ran alternate weeks to Australia covering passenger requirements in fourteen to eighteen voyages per year rather than twenty-six saving £300,000 without jeopardising the luxury end of P&O cruising services.

Most of the work of the committee over the next three years was carried out by Shaw. But Inchcape's authority was needed to enforce the recommendations. He wrote the necessary letters, such as those informing captains that their pay would be reduced by ten per cent. This financial analysis was an essential preliminary to the real streamlining of the P&O under Shaw.

Despite 1929's heavy net loss, an estimated £105,847, Inchcape still maintained the twelve per cent dividend and declared the same 'net result' as the previous two years. He spoke confidently of the solid assets behind the P&O, of the 318 steamers worth £47m and property worth £½m. The share price continued stable, and the profit-sharing scheme now exceeded £1m.

The economy drive was still absolutely necessary, however, as lossmaking voyages, although only half as bad as 1928, were still all too common. Thanks to a marine insurance rebate, an increase in the mail subsidy and by not charging depreciation, the balance on the voyage accounts of over £500,000 was higher than any year since 1920. The *Rawalpindi* made a particularly successful run of voyages to Bombay and, with the Australian trade continuing to pick up slightly, Inchcape ordered two new vessels for the Australian run.

The P&O group still relied heavily on the allied companies – the Federal, New Zealand, Union, BI, Hain and Nourse – who had contributed substantially to the results of the decade. Yet their earnings were now threatened by the Indian Coastal Shipping Bill, the interruption of trade by the civil war in China, and the possibility of the 'Eight-hour Sea Day' proposed by the International Maritime Labour Conference in Geneva.

Inchcape refused to accept that the changes over the last decade were of a long-term nature. He still harked back to the prewar days, regarding them as the normal state of affairs, and this is reflected in his handling of the P&O in a day-to-day, make do and mend fashion.

Although 1930 represented a real improvement in the performance of the P&O itself, with the highest net profit since 1923, because of declining profitability among the subsidiaries and associated companies, Inchcape decided to reduce the dividend to ten per cent again. The share price promptly fell to 36*s*, half the previous year's high.

The voyage accounts appeared healthy, with an overall profit balance only slightly down on 1929. The *Viceroy of India* alone earned over £50,000 in three voyages, and Far Eastern services improved, despite heavy Japanese competition. Yet with depreciation, which had been excluded far too frequently in the past, the accounts were transformed to a huge deficit of over £1m.

But the shareholders did not know this. Instead, their chairman boasted that the P&O was still paying an acceptable dividend even though trade with India, Australia and China was bad, and that 368 British ships, of over a million aggregate tons, were laid up. The passenger trade had fallen off by 50,000 passengers and 80,000 animals. The P&O was forging ahead, building six new oil-fired steamers.

Otherwise, Inchcape's remarks at the AGM were totally uninformative. He compared the changes in ship design since the 1870s; he described the improvements in P&O bills of fare since the 1860s. He was getting increasingly out of touch.

There could not have been a greater contrast between the AGMs of 1930 and 1931. In Inchcape's absence, Shaw read his speech, but then hinted at the need for a thorough financial investigation. Shaw was already considering asking Deloitte's to undertake this survey, which was underway by February 1932.

A total restructuring of the management of the P&O was on the cards for two reasons: Inchcape's increasing age and declining health, and the fact that 1931 was by far the worst year the P&O had ever faced. The P&O fleet lost £1m including depreciation, and total net losses exceeded £800,000. The dividend was cut drastically to six per cent reflecting a sudden collapse of the P&O's lifeline, the earnings of its subsidiary and associated companies. Income from the group's investments was meanwhile heavily devalued with the abandonment of the gold standard. Inchcape worried that the P&O could not redeem the £7m debenture stock, now falling due. The share price fell below par to only 19s.

Inchcape had tried to maintain shareholders' morale in the speech which Shaw read, by enthusing over the fabulous new P&O *Strathnaver's* record 1,416 passengers, the improvements in cargo handling at the Port of London, the ten per cent reduction in Suez Canal dues, and the reduction in fuel oil price which he had negotiated with the Anglo-Persian Oil Co. in Egypt. But he could not escape the fact that even those ships not laid up sailed with thousands of tons worth of unoccupied space. The P&O was now in the grip of the worst ever shipping depression. It had been in dire peril for much of the previous decade and had been kept going but it was not adequately prepared to weather the storm which now broke over it – as Shaw was to reveal.

There is no doubt that Shaw was highly competent and cared deeply about the P&O. Wilfrid Mizen highly praises his administrative and executive skills in steering the P&O through the 1930s and safely into better times. That he was perhaps a better chairman in the 1930s than Inchcape does not mean that he could have maximised the P&O's business and prosperity in the war years as his predecessor had done. In early 1932, with Inchcape suffering increasingly long bouts of ill health, Shaw was the man for the moment. Inchcape realised this and, depressed by illness, tried unsuccessfully to remove Shaw not only from the seat of power at the P&O, but as a beneficiary of his will. The latter decision was never effected as Inchcape died whilst the solicitors were redrawing a new codicil.

As acting chairman, Shaw pointed to the fact that Inchcape had handled all matters of high finance, and that most directors and managers had no idea how the accounts were compiled. Shaw quickly discovered that, contrary to the accusations of many that the late chairman had been feathering his nest, Inchcape had put a great deal of his own money into the P&O. Furthermore, he had obtained favourable loans at below market rates and without securities from trusting friends. Shaw exclaimed that the board would be amazed if it realised the extent of Inchcape's personal money in the P&O's coffers, and the significance of his contribution from his own pocket in the rebuilding of the P&O fleet, which cost at least £25m.

Of Inchcape's chairmanship, Shaw suggested that 'the more the facts were examined, the more clearly shone out of his generosity and self-sacrifice'. Yet Shaw had found it extremely difficult to try to manage the company from London whilst all the official mail was redirected to Inchcape's yacht, the *Rover*, moored in Monte Carlo, the directors being afraid to contradict Inchcape's directives. Shaw had offered his resignation several times over this issue.

Shaw's plans for the future, implemented on Inchcape's death in May 1932, were in many ways extensions of what his predecessor had already set in motion: reducing expenditure without making the passenger liners less attractive, rationalising the entire P&O group by coordinating services more closely, and expanding the existing holiday cruising business.

But there were three features of the Inchcape administration to which he objected, and which quickly disappeared. The first of these was the secrecy surrounding the accounts. The juggling of funds behind the scenes was replaced by detailed published information. Although the trial of Lord Kylsant following the collapse of the Royal Mail Group favoured such a development, Inchcape had not necessarily been criticised for following what was common practice at the time. Wilfrid Mizen attests to how many people then felt sorry for Kylsant, that he was unlucky in being caught when he was not alone in creative accounting and cross-shareholding. Before the Companies Acts were changed in the later 1930s, there was no statutory regulation concerning company reports and accounts to inhibit Inchcape's approach. Shaw decided secondly to suspend the dividend entirely, and thirdly to address the problem of depreciation.

Shaw inherited a shipping line suffering from the problems of British shipping as a whole, which Inchcape had not been able to offset. Rising nations, keen to develop their own resources and their

own fleets, took Britain's markets and carrying trade, helped by
subsidies, tariffs and lower operating costs, whilst British ships were
largely unassisted by the Government until the mid-1930s. British
exports fell sharply whilst imports rose, destroying tramp
profitability and hitting the liner trade hard, especially with the
parallel decline in emigration.

But why was Britain the only country besides Germany to
experience a net tonnage decrease in the period 1914–38, whilst
United States tonnage quadrupled, Japanese tonnage trebled and the
fleets of Norway, Italy and Greece expanded by at least 100 per cent?
There are four main reasons, and Inchcape did little to combat them,
although there were signs in each case that he was prepared to make
changes. Unfortunately, these were implemented all too slowly.

Firstly, the company structure of British shipping was strictly
divided into tramps, liners and tankers, whilst foreign shipping
companies were much more flexible and often owned all three types.
The P&O was strictly a liner company, but with Hain and Nourse,
Inchcape showed he was willing to diversify into tramps, and these
vessels were more successful than many other tramp fleets in this
period. Secondly, British ships remained of the traditional prewar
type, without enough appeciation of technical change, although
Inchcape's final ships, such as the turboelectric *Viceroy of India,
Strathaird* and *Strathnaver*, show signs of progress. British
shipbuilding stagnated technologically through its reliance on
conservative British shipowners and its failure to establish markets
overseas. Thirdly, British shipping was hidebound by its adhesion to
the conference system, which tried to make trade safe and reliable for
the shipowners, without trying to break into new markets. Inchcape
nearly always supported shipping conferences and was the first to
attack those trading outside them.

Finally, British shipping in the 1920s did not take full advantage of
the great new fuel of the twentieth century, oil: if only the British fleet
had had more oil-fired ships, and if only it had made greater
headway in the oil carrying trade. As the modern shipping economist
Sturmey comments, 'if enough British owners had responded in this
way no decline in the position of the British fleet in the interwar years
need have occurred'. And he was thinking particularly of Inchcape,
the outstanding British shipowner of this period.

But Inchcape was by no means just a shipowner. He saw himself as a merchant, and in the postwar years, Inchcape's merchant interests – referred to here as the Mackinnon/Inchcape group, some parts linked to the P&O, others not – expanded to form the basis of not only his family's investments but also what was to become the Inchcape group. Many were important companies in their own right, such as Binny's, in which Inchcape provided considerable executive guidance.

These interests are listed in Appendix Two (see p.000) which, for the sake of brevity, includes only the larger holdings, and those of which Inchcape was director, partner or chairman. They were in shipping, oil, insurance, tea, communications, railways and harbours, coal, banks, textile mills, refrigerated meat, and in general merchant partnerships with a variety of functions, such as Gray Dawes and Macdonald Hamilton.

The expansion of the Mackinnon/Inchcape group in this period was funded mainly by the reinvestment of its dividends which, except for those of the BI, were largely retained in India. This included a major reconstruction of Binny's in 1920, incorporating companies in India and London, and consolidating the textile mills into The Buckingham and Carnatic Company Ltd, with a paid-up capital of Rs 1 crore, or about £½m. Profits reached Rs 12 lakhs p.a. (about £80,000) in the mid-1920s, thanks to the abolition of the countervailing cotton goods excise duty. The Bangalore Mill was doing equally well. In all, he ploughed Rs 66½ lakhs (nearly £400,000) into the company, including setting up an engineering department. Binny (Madras) Ltd paid Inchcape the equivalent of £60,000 in deposit interest by 1928, but this was subject to heavy income tax.

The Joint Steamer Companies also required income for rehabilitation after the war. Despite a destructive cyclone and a series of strikes, the companies expanded to take advantage of the trade boom of 1923–8, when a severe depression necessitated drastic economies.

Mackinnon Mackenzie, Binny's and his other Indian holdings were severely threatened by the Indian Coastal Shipping Bill, which Inchcape saw ultimately leading to the expropriation of all other manifestations of British commerce in the subcontinent. At his last P&O AGM, he spoke sadly of the commercial contribution of the British Raj to India – the increase in railway mileage from 6,000 to 42,000, the huge number of jute, woollen, cotton, paper and rice mills, the coal, gold, iron and steel mines and works, the coffee and tea estates, and the banking, insurance and river steamer companies. Now the Congress Party was advocating its boycott, unless at least seventy-five per cent of the capital was held by Indians and two-thirds of the directors were Indians. Developments in India greatly added to Inchcape's pessimism in his final years.

Inchcape's many interests in Australia also came under attack from nationalist groups. The Australasian United Steam Navigation Company, a prominent coastal shipping company, made record earnings of nearly £120,000 at the end of the war, but declined steadily after 1925 with the loss of the mail contract and the building of the Townsville–Cairns railway. He had already diversified the AUSN's business with the acquisition, in 1920, of the Eastern and Australian Steamship Company, which traded with Far Eastern ports. A debenture issue in 1927 raised fresh capital, but by 1930 the directors described commercial conditions on the Australian coast as 'deplorable' and meagre profits were maintained only by dint of non-shipping investments.

Gray Dawes in London, by contrast, could be generally relied upon for steady profits. In 1919–20, Inchcape's forty-one per cent almost doubled his 1920 income from the P&O. Mackay & Co. had also handled Inchcape's dealings with the Strick Line, which had been bought by Gray Dawes on Inchcape's behalf and sold to Hain & Co. in 1923 for £½m. Half of the interest in the company was sold back to Strick in 1927, but not before Hain had made a profit of nearly £250,000. In this instance, Inchcape passed over to the P&O the chance to make profits, as he also did in the case of the William Cory shares he purchased on the P&O's behalf, which increased in value by over £2m. He was also prepared to take back losers, as he did with the Khedivial Mail.

The Gray Dawes accounts survive only up to 1926, but give an idea of the magnitude of Inchcape's private dealings, especially as they represent only one of his businesses. In 1925 his sixty-seven per cent share brought him over £80,000, with an additional £5,863 interest on his account, which always stood at £100,000 or more. That year alone includes payments to the BI of £84,000 and receipts of £24,000, and a further £25,000 from Calcutta. In 1926 he received £71,875 as his share of the profits, and paid nearly £20,000 into this account from the P&O Banking Corporation, the Yokohama Specie Bank and miscellaneous holdings in Calcutta. By 1930, even Gray

Dawes was needing money, and Inchcape advanced over £25,000 to them by selling off stocks from his wife's accounts and from her marriage trust.

A substantial element of the earnings of Mackinnon Mackenzie in Calcutta, among many other agencies and holdings, was derived from commissions from the P&O. Over the period of Deloitte's report, 1922–1931, these payments totalled £1,446,954, with Mackinnon Mackenzie in Bombay alone earning nearly £½m, Calcutta more than £150,000 and Shanghai more than £133,000. A loss on the agencies in Japan of £16,754 was borne by P&O, and Macdonald Hamilton, the P&O agents in Australia, received another £½m, with over £200,000 going to Melbourne alone. Wilfrid Mizen attests to Inchcape's preference of BI and Mackinnon Mackenzie interests, and his efforts to maximise their business, even at some cost to the P&O; but this was certainly offset by rebates which Mackinnon Mackenzie made to the P&O in the late 1920s.

Inchcape's vice-presidency of the Suez Canal Company was not necessarily directly remunerative, but it did bring opportunities. Noticing the old-fashioned and expensive water boats supplying steamers at Suez and Port Said in 1924 on one of his many visits to Egypt, he initiated the Egyptian Water Co., and he also had substantial interests in the Middle East oil industry. The Euphrates & Tigris Steam Navigation Company, which joined with fellow river steamer company Lynch Brothers in 1919 to form the Mesopotamia Persia Corporation, handled nearly all the foreign shipping agency work at Busreh in 1919. We have already seen how Inchcape's contacts through his membership of the board of the Anglo-Persian Oil Co. helped him to lobby to reduce the price of oil to P&O liners.

Inchcape's chairmanship of the P&O and BI may be the business role in which he is most familiar, but it was only one aspect of his affairs. The Mackinnon/Inchcape group was of greater importance to him, as his inheritance from Mackinnon, and as the business in which he had spent his formative years. It has been impossible to separate its activities from those of the P&O, and the exact nature of their symbiotic relationship was never made clear. At the end of Inchcape's life, his commercial empire in and around the Indian Ocean was still immensely powerful, and its paramount position, although threatened, was not yet seriously undermined. It continued to expand, and as this biography goes to press, the Inchcape group declared profits before tax of over £86m. Its foundation and growth since going public in 1958 would have been impossible without the First Earl's strategic investments of the 1920s, and their subsequent development by the second Earl in the 1930s and the Third Earl since the Second World War.

8

Retrenchment and disillusionment
Public life, 1918–1932

In the aftermath of war, Inchcape's work on Government committees increased to a level which far outweighed the time he spent with his businesses. Admittedly, his commercial interests were well established, and much of the routine work was entrusted to experienced staff. But his public work was motivated, not by a lack of stimulus from business, but by a growing obsession with preventing continued encroachment of Government regulation and control of trade and industry. Aged sixty-six by 1918, he had grown up in the prewar period, which to him was the normal state of affairs, and saw the war as a dangerous (although for him, profitable) interlude. Like many of his contemporaries, he sought a rapid return to prewar conditions, especially in terms of *laissez-faire* politics and the low profile of Government in private business.

The part played by Inchcape in the Government's postwar economic policy may be divided into five principal areas:

1. His contribution to the ironing out of immediate postwar problems, settlement of disputes and rationalising of administrative entanglements which had emerged during the hostilities,
2. His work in the restoration of Britain's currency, monetary and banking systems,
3. His help in cutbacks in public spending on the Geddes Committee during the economic doldrums of the early 1920s,
4. His involvement in the encouragement and development of a new industry which had been stimulated by war, embryonic commerical aviation, and
5. His efforts in respect of Britain's imperial commitments in India, the Middle East and on the Imperial Shipping Committee.

Why was Inchcape so enthusiastic to undertake often tedious and certainly time-consuming committee work and why was he so frequently chosen to serve? He saw his contribution as a duty and a privilege, and took part out of a genuine conviction that he really knew what the country needed. It is less clear why he was appointed – especially to committees involved in topics of which his practical knowledge must have been limited, such as the Aviation Advisory Committee, where he was in a minority of one in not having a post or rank connected with the industry or the RAF. Certainly, the Government favoured the appointment of businessmen generally and Inchcape, a keen Lloyd George supporter until 1926, was well known for his commitment to economy and minimising the role of Government in business and everyday life.

In the immediate postwar years, in the breathing space which lasted to the spring of 1919 and the boom which peaked and fell after the summer of 1920, Inchcape served on a bewildering range of committees. He jumped at the chance to join these committees through his growing hatred of the proliferating state bureaucracy. He was fond of repeating the *Punch* joke: 'Why are men in Government offices like the fountains in Trafalgar Square? Because they play from 10 till 4'. Inchcape believed that his way of running a business was the only way to manage any enterprise efficiently, and was amazed that Government departments, lacking his approach, failed to share his conviction. Whilst serving on the Committee on Contracts in 1919, Inchcape recommended that the Ministry of Supply should supervise all stocks and stores from one central point, receiving the support of Lloyd George against the separate establishment of each of the armed forces who wanted to manage their supplies separately.

Inchcape's hatred of Government supervision of business meant that, in a sense, he was an inappropriate choice for an investigation of 1919 into possible corruption and profiteering by the British Cellulose Company, which monopolised the production of 'dope' for strengthening aircraft wings during the war. With a nominal capital of only £4,000 in sixpence shares, it had received over £900,000 from the Ministry of Munitions by the end of 1918. The supply of 'dope' had been inconsistent in quality and quantity, and the British Government were charged up to £190 a ton, whilst the French paid only £50 a ton to their producers. There had been no objections from Sir Harry McGowan and his fellow businessmen on the 'Explosives Syndicate' who had put up the initial capital, or from the banks, who constantly advanced more funding. Despite calling in leading accountants W.B. Peat & Company, the conclusion that there was no evidence of illegal practices was accepted by the Government with reservations.

In seventeen sittings, thirty-two witnesses from various Government departments and the chemicals industry were examined. The need for a British manufacturer of 'dope' had been uppermost, with the only other manufacturers being Bayer of Germany and Usines du Rhône of France, but there had only been one application for the War Office tender. Public outcry in the press continued, with a feeling that there could be no smoke without fire, especially as it was known that Inchcape was sympathetic to fellow businessmen in the face of Government investigation.

On a tribunal looking into the alleged destruction of documents relating to wartime contracts made by the Ministry of Munitions, Inchcape represented all businessmen who had had occasion to enjoy Government contracts in wartime. He was thus acting as a watchdog in the interests of economy and efficiency when, in the administrative confusion accompanying the end of hostilities, these might be overlooked. By the mere fact of holding the tribunal, the Government showed that it was willing to undergo investigation, and that the increased part it played in business life did not mean it was above the law.

At the Ministry of Munitions in 1919, a reduced staff faced 57,949 outstanding contractor's bills. A powerful six-member committee was appointed within the ministry – the Accounts Liquidation Committee – to agree quickly to lump sum payments, to avoid the expense of maintaining a large staff, and to keep Exchequer and Audit involvement to a minimum to prevent the whole process continuing indefinitely. The problem arose when an over-zealous senior ministry official, on instructing his ledger investigators, suggested that the various working papers used to prepare the final payment in each case should be 'lost', either temporarily or permanently. This was interpreted as an order to destroy documents, and as such was passed on to the assistants. There was a good deal of confusion among all who gave evidence, especially relating to the fact that the Exchequer and Audit knew of the existence of the working papers and would inevitably ask about them at some point. Ledger clerks were told that the Exchequer and Audit had no jurisdiction over working papers and they were to refer them to their superiors.

In fact, no documents were actually destroyed, and the defaulting official was exonerated. Inchcape was just concerned that the businessmen wanting to be paid finally received their money.

When the need arose to dispose of Government standard ships, ex-enemy and prize vessels, it was inconceivable that anyone other than Inchcape, the unchallenged leader of the shipping industry, should be called upon. In total, he sold over 400 ships, exceeding 2½m tons, raising nearly £80m for the Treasury. He savoured every deal, seeing himself as making much-needed money for the Government and distributing the fruits of Britain's victory to his fellow shipowners. But he was later to admit the inferior quality of many of these vessels, which in effect contributed to the reduced demand for tonnage from British yards. With hindsight, Inchcape would have done greater service in scrapping them all.

Yet it is not fair to criticise Inchcape in this way. At the time, he saw it as one of his greatest achievements. Early in 1919, on behalf of the Ministry of Shipping, he sold 156 steamers of over a million tons – this raised £24m for the Treasury. A further forty of nearly 350,000 tons followed, bringing total revenue to £35m, at a cost of only £850. All this was achieved by individual private sales, of which no details were ever recorded. Inchcape, who had in effect sold a fleet as large as his own P&O group, reckoned he had negotiated double the prices which an auction would have raised.

But the British shipping industry found itself flooded with obsolete foreign tonnage which, especially in terms of the passenger ships, were in Inchcape's words, 'as a rule not a patch on ours'. Despite heavy expenditure, 'they fall far short of our own ships' and 'the shipbuilders and shipowners of this country so far as I can see have nothing to learn from Germany in ship construction.' Yet in the immediate postwar years, the demand for tonnage, when Britain's mercantile marine had lost a fifth of its 1914 fleet was such as to negate other considerations.

Inchcape's responsibility for this task was the result of Sir Joseph Maclay's anxiety to wind up the work of the Wartime Shipping Committee in 1922. As Maclay wrote to Lloyd George on his departure:

Lord Inchcape has agreed without renumeration to dispose of all Government owned or controlled craft of any kind as well as remaining enemy ships which remain to be sold during the current year. I have told

Lord Inchcape this is agreeable to me, and I am sure will also be agreeable to you.

Surviving Treasury papers reveal further controversies surrounding Inchcape's work on the sale of ex-enemy shipping. His enthusiasm for making the best possible deal and selling to the highest bidder meant that he would consider any purchaser, when Maclay wanted British shipowners to have first choice. Maclay had spent a long time convincing the Prime Minister of the 'iniquity' of allowing the Germans to come in at the bottom end of the market, and had so far kept them out. He was outraged at Inchcape, who had announced an open sale without consulting Maclay. But in opening the sale to all bidders, Inchcape received the support of many shipowners, including Ellerman, who pointed out that it was difficult to justify a lower price to avoid selling abroad, especially as the taxpayer would ultimately suffer. Overall, Inchcape's decision was understandable in the circumstances, but his long experience in public life by 1921 had not made him tactful or diplomatic. He finally completed his Government ship sales work in 1927, realising a further £75,000 through the disposal of prize vessels.

In all, Inchcape worked extremely hard for the Ministry of Shipping, shown by the voluminous correspondence it generated, more than on any other single committee or departmental project, ranging over every aspect of foreign and coastal trade. One of his chief priorities was to scrap the Board of Trade's wartime import licences and priority permits. He quoted his own example of how time-consuming and inefficient these were: to import a bundle of carpets from India required a document signed before a Commissioner for Oaths with a half-crown stamp declaring one's previous business in the article in the years 1911, 1912, 1913 and 1914.

Other concerns of the Ministry in which Inchcape was closely involved included the repatriation of British Territorials from India and German POWs from Australia, postwar commercial uses of military wharves on the Suez Canal, delays in cable messages to India, the Far East and Australia due to continued official censorship, the removal of a prohibition order on supplying propeller shafts other than for naval and Government use, the development of British merchant shipping at the port of Antwerp to take full advantage of the withdrawal of competing German lines, the return of German steamers being employed on Government account in India and Australia, the increased costs of shipbuilding contracts owing to Government intervention, the imposition of new rules concerning the certification of officers aboard river steamers in India, which favoured Europeans against natives because of an English language requirement, the charging of excess profits duty on sales of outdated British ships overseas, which Inchcape strongly opposed, and last but not least, the planning of a peace celebration for all the schoolchildren of London on the Thames embankment.

The scope of the Ministry's work is apparent from a special dinner hosted by the liner companies for Ministry officials. Every name in British –and some overseas – merchant shipping was represented: Vestey, Weir, Lamport & Holt, the Royal Mail Steam Packet Company, MacIver, H. & W. Nelson, the Prince Line, Donaldson Bros, the Ocean Steamship Co., China Mutual, the Glen Line, Thomson's of Leith, the Aberdeen Line, Shaw Savill & Albion, Commonwealth & Dominion, Turnbull Martin, Trinder Anderson, Ellerman & Bucknall, White Star Line, Clan Line, Cunard, Pacific Steam Navigation Co., Gulf Line, Union Castle, Harrison's, Bibby Line, Anchor Line, Elder Dempster, Canadian Pacific and many Australian lines, not to mention all the companies and lines of the P&O group. Officials attended from every branch: the Shipping Control Committee, the Ship Requisitions Branch, the Home Trade Branch, the Naval Sea Transport Branch, the Technical Branch, the Military Sea Transport Branch, the Finance Branch, the Commercial Branch, the Ship Management Branch, the Legal Branch and the Overseas Ship Purchase Branch – fifty altogether, and only a small part of this huge bureaucratic proliferation which Inchcape was glad to see finally disbanded at the end of the 1920s.

Sir Joseph Maclay wrote to Bonar Law that all these 'transactions have reflected the greatest credit possible on Lord Inchcape'. He did not know the whole story. The recent memoirs of a Greek shipowner, now based in New York, Manuel Kulukundis, describe a meeting with Inchcape in 1927. He had bought ex-enemy ships from Inchcape five times between 1921 and 1924, and on hearing of the release of the last few in 1927, put in a bid. He was asked to make a personal visit:

I was 28 years old and with some trepidation I went to see the Great Man. He received me very graciously but as I sat down he said to me, 'Mr Kulukundis, I cannot accept your offer – you must improve it, otherwise I will get the Hain Company to purchase them'. Though I knew Hain was his own company, I answered, 'My Lord, they will not buy them!' Lord Inchcape, surprised at my answer said, 'Why?' – 'Because the ships are not their meat. They cannot make any money with them!' He was silent for a minute and then said to me, 'All right – you can have them'.

Did Maclay realise that Inchcape was favouring his own companies in selling the vessels, or at least threatening to do so in order to raise the price to others?

Despite the plethora of administrative work connected with postwar problems, Inchcape found time to serve on a little-known committee concerned with the decasualisation of dock labour after the war, appointed by the Ministry of Labour, in November 1918. Inchcape felt strongly that casual labour should be discouraged, and that workers should be 'regular wage earners and respectable members of society, instead of living from hand to mouth and knocking off work as soon as they have earned a few shillings'. He does not seem to have realised that many did not have a choice.

Inchcape chaired the committee, which brought together such characters as Broodbank of the Port of London Authority and leaders of all the dock unions, including Ben Tillett of the Dock, Wharf and Riverside General Workers' Union, and introduced regular working practices to the port for the first time.

The second of the five principal areas in to which we may divide Inchcape's public life after the war was currency and banking. In 1918, he took part in three committees concerned with putting Britain's monetary problems on a more even keel, principally as a result of his early experience with India's currency back in the 1890s, and through his presidency of the Institute of Bankers in 1914–16.

His role as deputy chairman of Lord Cunliffe's Committee on Currency and Foreign Exchanges after the war was one of the most difficult and perplexing he had ever undertaken. First meeting in February 1918, fourteen bankers and Treasury officials led by Cunliffe, the Governor of the Bank of England, considered what steps should be taken after the war to restore 'normal conditions', especially in relation to the Bank Act of 1844.

The workings of the 1844 Act, which formalised a currency of gold and subsidiary coin and notes with no restrictions on gold imports or exports, had the effect of providing no means of increasing legal tender except by importing gold from abroad, and there was no way it could be reduced, except by exporting bullion or sovereigns. It did not take account of the more recent development of the cheque system. Gold was being bought and sold by cheque according to fluctuations in the rate of exchange, and the bank's ratio of reserve to liabilities often fell sharply, which could only be checked by raising the rate of discount.

The worry was that in the case of a long-term adverse trade balance this policy would be inadequate. Any large-scale indebtedness to foreign countries would be disastrous to Britain's credit. A trade imbalance would hinder new enterprise, shorten the supply of capital goods, lead to a fall in demand for consumer goods, with a resultant slackening in employment, and collapse of prices with the weak market. This is what actually happened as the postwar boom ended in 1921.

In wartime, to increase the supply of money, the Bank of England had raised its discount rate to prevent a fall in the proportion on reserve. The refusal of the Government to extend State insurance to cover bullion cargoes meant that movements of gold in wartime were limited, and the 1844 Act had had to be suspended. The Currency and Bank Notes Act of 1914 authorised the Treasury to issue £1 and 10*s* notes as legal tender.

Total deposits at banks in Britain rose from £1.1 billion in December 1913 to £1.7 billion by December 1917, but the growth in demand for legal tender currency was even larger. The demand was such that the Government began to increase the issue of notes backed not by gold, but by Government securities. Of £382.7m in circulation by 1918, £230.4m was not covered by gold. For practical purposes the gold standard had ceased to be effective.

The members of the committee, particularly Inchcape and future P&O director, Sir Charles Addis of the Hong Kong & Shanghai Banking Corporation, were enthusiastic supporters of the restoration of conditions to maintain the gold standard. They argued that it was of paramount importance to restrict the expansion of credit and the drain of gold overseas, which would undermine Britain's international trade. Government borrowings after the war must cease, and the shortage of capital must be made good by genuine savings. It was vital to increase British exports, and not continue to rely on borrowing from the USA.

The responsibility for note issue was to be controlled by the Bank of England, which would keep all gold and allow unrestricted imports of gold. Gold would be exported when necessary in exchange for notes, allowing a temporary issue of notes over the legal limit, but fixing an absolute point below which the central gold reserve should not be allowed to fall. In the first instance, a central gold reserve of £150m was recommended, with a policy of reducing the uncovered note issue to this amount.

Inchcape expressed his support for London remaining a free market for gold, arguing that one can only sell overseas if one can buy overseas, and that if Britain were to increase her exports, she needed to export gold to pay for imports of raw materials. Even with a sound money policy, he felt it would take between ten and fifteen years to get back to the position of 1913. As the only shipowner on the panel, Inchcape was seen by the witnesses and other members of the committee as uniquely wealthy and not affected by many of the problems they discussed. He made evasive statements and showed signs, like many of his colleagues, of being out of his depth.

Yet he turned up to the majority of the sessions. He was particularly concerned with the matter of detailed publication of banks' balance sheets, anxious that this would not be imposed on his own banking interests, such as the P&O Bank and the National Provincial Bank. He considered the joint stock banks most irresponsible, opposed local note issues, and maintained that anyone should be allowed to convert gold if they so desired. Inchcape's questions augmented the conservatism of the committee's conclusions, without suggesting anything revolutionary.

The report was welcomed by the City, eager for financial stability and anxious to restore London's financial supremacy. It was less popular with many small bankers, who objected to handing over their gold reserves to the Bank of England, and by many politicians who feared that this would mean a lack of credit for postwar reconstruction. The *Daily Telegraph* represented many in its realistic view that the conclusions were just too conservative, and were appropriate only for a creditor nation. Inchcape – and he was not alone – could not see Britain as anything else.

Closely linked to his work on the Cunliffe Committee was Inchcape's membership of another Treasury committee, on gold production, to: 'consider the effect of the war upon the gold production of the British

Empire with reference more particularly to the treatment of low grade ores and how far it may be of importance to national interests to secure the continuance of the treatment of such ores and generally how to stimulate the production of gold'. Gold in South Africa – the Committee's main area of attention – had become more expensive to mine during the war, mainly due to a decrease in native labour and increased cost of explosives and stores, but the gold was now needed more than ever. So new interest was taken in mines regarded as on the margin of profitability, which earned less than 4s profit per ton of ore produced.

Yet the Gold Producers' Committee, when petitioning the Chancellor for a subsidy, were not successful, despite the overall decline in gold production in the British Empire, at least half of which came from South Africa. From £51m in 1910, Empire output had risen to £59.5m in 1916, but fell sharply to £56m in 1917. The committee argued that once wartime constraints on labour were removed, production would again increase, without financial intervention on their part.

Inchcape in particular stood out against subsidising gold production. He argued that when new gold reserves were located at a low cost and brought into the market, the price of commodities would rise, and when the new gold supply was exhausted, prices would fall again. Thus, subsidising gold production would lead to commodity price rises. As he had done in the Cunliffe Committee, Inchcape supported the idea of a free market in gold, and agreed with the conclusion that 'if we want gold and cannot produce it at a profit, we must depend on our capacity to render services and to produce at a profit the commodities wanted elsewhere by the holders of gold, and to do so we must adjust our prices to world prices'.

Many British businessmen took a more practical viewpoint, fearing the effects of a sudden fall in prices after the war, and representatives of the London Chamber of Commerce recommended stimulating gold production, even at the expense of the taxpayer. The committee, including Inchcape, refused to entertain the idea, arguing that 'to give more for an ounce of gold than it is worth in currency appears to us out of the question, except on the supposition that we want gold for the purpose of keeping it locked up and unavailable for export. We cannot, however, see any use in acquiring gold for such a purpose'. They concluded that, even though gold production had fallen, it was still higher than at the beginning of the war and the British Empire still produced sixty-two per cent of the world's gold output. Before the collapse of the postwar boom, Inchcape was satisfied that Britain's monetary policy was sound. He appears not to have appreciated the full deflationary implications of returning to gold at prewar parity.

Inchcape took part in a third committee in 1918 discussing financial and monetary matters: a Treasury committee on banking amalgamations. In this instance, he served as a witness, in his capacity as a director of the National Provincial and Union Bank of England Limited, usually known simply as the National Provincial. As the chairman of the National Provincial, Inchcape had been instrumental in completing the last of the great banking amalgamations: the merger between this bank with the Union Bank of London and Smith's. This was part of the process which led to the emergence after the Second World War of the big five clearing banks.

He was also asked, in May 1918, by Bonar Law, to advise the Government on this subject. It seems strange that the Government, concerned about the implications for fair competition in the proliferation of bank mergers, would ask one so much in favour of this development to advise them.

Inchcape was among twenty-two witnesses, including Edward Holden of the Midland Bank, Charles Addis again, Gordon Selfridge, representatives of the leading merchant banks and Sidney Webb. The committee reported that at least 300 banking amalgamations had taken place in Britain since the beginning of the nineteenth century. This phenomenon had gathered momentum in recent years and now the number of private banks had fallen from thirty-seven to only six. Since 1891, joint stock banks in England had declined from 106 to 34.

Adverse criticism of mergers had been aroused by not only their increased number but change in nature. Rather than a small local bank being taken over by a larger and more widely spread joint stock bank, large banks were joining other large banks, both already with large funds and branches over a wide area. Arguments which could justify the former could not justify the latter. Many of the most recent amalgamations did not lead to the bank expanding its catchment area, but to it increasing its share of the banking market in an existing town or city. This was seen as reducing competition, and leading to the monopolisation of banking business into fewer and fewer hands. For example, the National Provincial itself, when it took over the Union Bank of London and Smith's, added thirty-one London branches to its existing twenty-six. Its total of 567 branches meant that it frequently had more than one banking office in many localities. There were 27 such cases, including most major provincial cities.

Inchcape argued that banks must grow to keep pace with the size of their customers, and be able to deal with a company's trade both throughout Britain and abroad. This was why some large businesses had dealings with more than one bank, as single banks could not meet all their requirements. The committee were not wholly convinced. They examined the resources of the leading banks in 1913 compared with 1917, and maintained that they were already substantial, and the mergers could not be justified on grounds of the need to expand reserves. In 1913, the National Provincial's reserves totalled £118.9m, and its merger with Union and Smith's brought them up to £185.2m. It was second only to the London County & Westminster, which boasted reserves of £143m in 1913 increased to £228m by 1917. Inchcape's reply was to point out that most of this capital was increasingly made up of deposits. The proportion of paid-up capital and reserves to deposits had decreased from eighteen to only six per cent between 1890 and 1917. There was, therefore, a need to increase reserves.

The committee hesitated to restrain amalgamations: 'it is a serious step to interfere with the natural developments of trade'. What really worried them was this decrease in capital – that substantial benefits had accrued to shareholders when their banks were taken over, at the expense of security for depositors. They also feared that a lack of competition would lead to a dearth of cheap money and unwilling-ness to allow overdrafts, with banks becoming heavy-handed towards their customers.

The Stock Exchange also had grounds for concern: that London's worldwide fame as a money market before the war, which was based on the freedom with which London bills could be negotiated and the ease with which discount houses could obtain funds, would be undermined by a reduction in competition between banks. The few banks would become more and more powerful, and would inevitably put the interests of shareholders above those of depositors, eventually threatening the standing of the Bank of England and its ability to regulate the money market. This, the City lobby suggested, would be a menace to the public.

Despite Inchcape's strong denials of the existence of a 'money trust', the committee felt that although some of the dangers from banking amalgamations were remote and problematical, they were enough to outweigh arguments against Government interference. They recommended that Government approval should be obtained before a merger was announced. If the proposed amalgamation would secure important new facilities for the public or a really considerable and material extension of the area or sphere of activity for the larger of the two banks in question, the merger would probably be approved. But if, on the other hand, it would just lead to a greater overlap of branches without advantages, it would be rejected.

Inchcape's support of commercial freedom and Government non-intervention would appear to have been unsuccessful in this instance, but he was not to suffer restrictions as far as the National Provincial and his later banking interests, including the P&O Bank, were concerned.

Inchcape's interest in Britain's general financial conditions moved him to address the House of Lords on the matter, in July 1918. He spoke in debates comparatively rarely, preferring to air his views at P&O AGMs or in letters to *The Times*; but when he did, much thought and preparation went into what he said. So in this instance he sought Bonar Law's advice in advance.

Inchcape opened with an attack on increasing levels of taxation, especially the new super tax on unearned income. He accepted the imposition of a massive 12s 6d in the pound tax on incomes of over £100,000. But he argued that the rate of tax was far too high for more modest earnings. For example, a judge with a responsible salary of £5,000 would find himself with only £3,212. The danger, Inchcape maintained, was that the best men would be tempted away to more remunerative but less public-spirited appointments. 'There are many others in the same boat such as Bishops and Civil Servants', he went on, struggling to drum up sympathy for those more used to abuse. 'There are also country squires in many cases saddled with large houses and dependents ... being wiped out by the hundred. The case of many professional men and many shopkeepers is also deplorable.'

The main reason why Inchcape opposed the tax so vehemently was the way it reduced incentive for profit. He argued the case of an individual entrepreneur whose business makes £10,000 a year. After income tax and super tax, this is reduced to £5,834. If he had made £10,000 profit before the war but in 1918 his profits were £12,000 he would have to pay £1,440 in excess profits duty on the extra £2,000, and tax on the remainder of 8s 4d in the pound or £231. 'There is not much in this' Inchcape complained, 'to scorn delight, live laborious days and develop their business. It is no incentive to effort.'

So where were businessmen putting their capital, if not into heavily taxed new business? In Government securities, Inchcape suggested, such as war loans and bonds, treasury bills and exchequer bonds. One day, these would have to be paid back, and meanwhile the interest payments were pouring out of the Government's purse.

Bonar Law wrote a supportive, uncritical and congratulatory note to Inchcape, but privately, he confided to a cabinet colleague that 'his [Inchcape's] intentions are wholly good but the danger is that he will scare the very people – the lenders instead of the spenders – and do more harm than good'. But they hesitated to point this out to him. Did they fear losing his much needed committee services? Were they concerned that they could lose the support of the shipping industry? Or were they not worried that the speech would have a great impact?

Inchcape's opinion was undoubtedly valued at the highest level on financial matters. In November 1918, he was summoned to advise the Chancellor on future Government borrowing policy as a representative of the banking community. In 1919, he stood out against tentative backbench proposals to introduce decimal coinage. Two years later, he was a prominent signatory of 'An Appeal by Bankers of the United Kingdom' to reduce taxation by reducing national expenditure, and was joined by directors of banks holding £1.6bn of the total £2bn deposited. The Government was not helping, the bankers maintained, by interfering with natural economic laws and disrupting foreign trade by introducing protectionist measures.

In 1923, Asquith records a visit to the Bank of England 'to discuss rather abstruse questions of finance with the Governors and Lord Inchcape and other City pundits'. Montagu Norman was seeking Inchcape's advice on that occasion to draw up a series of recommendations for the Bank of England. It was decided that at least £100m should be invested by the Bank in America, in US bonds, to be available for contingencies. If Britain's gold reserves had to be called upon to make the transfer, they should never be reduced below twenty-five per cent of the outstanding legal tender notes: the return to the gold standard was then high on the agenda. The Export Control Act was to be continued until a gold reserve of at least £150m had been held under favourable exchange conditions for two consecutive years. Inchape's attachment to conservative finance was well known through his management of the P&O, and his opinion could be relied upon in this instance. His note to the editor of *The Spectator* at that time confirms this.

The sooner we get back to our real gold standard the better it will be for the country ... I think it would be better to disassociate the Government altogether from the issue of currency and hand it over to the Bank of England. It will be a long and painful process getting rid of the paper issue but I think it should be faced. It can only be done by the Government exercising the strictest economy and by seeing that the revenue is fifty millions or so a year in excess of the expenditure ... if we went on borrowing to meet our expenditure ... we should be living in a fool's paradise of rising prices and would never get out of the quagmire in which we have been landed by the war.

It was natural, from the views he expressed on currency, banking and finance, that Inchcape would be chosen to help wield the great Geddes Axe in 1922. When the postwar boom peaked and fell, the Government turned to the old remedy of public economy. As A.J.P. Taylor (1962) put it, 'Heavy taxation was regarded as the root of all evil. The anti-waste campaign against squander-mania and against the two mythical civil servants, Dilly and Dally, swept all before it.' Few public figures were known to loathe taxation, waste and civil service bureaucracy more than Inchcape, and he was joined by four kindred souls who, incidentally but perhaps deliberately, were also fellow Scots. Geddes himself was embittered by the sacrifice of his railway modernisation schemes in the first round of cuts. Sir Joseph Maclay, Inchcape's old colleague on the Ministry of Shipping, had had his fiil of Government departments, especially related to the armed services. Lord Faringdon and Sir Guy Granet were similarly disillusioned and ready to tighten the national belt.

Their brief was:

to make recommendations to the Chancellor of the Exchequer for effecting forthwith all possible reductions in the National Expenditure on Supply Services, having regard especially to the present and prospective position of the Revenue. In so far as questions of policy are involved in the expenditure

under discussion, these will remain for the exclusive consideration of the
Cabinet; but it will be open to the Committee to review the expenditure and
to indicate the economies which might be effected if particular policies were
either adopted, abandoned or modified.

The Geddes Axe was more than just a committee to cut back
expenditure; it signalled the end of high hopes of reconstruction and
put paid to the creation of a 'land fit for heroes'.

The final report of February 1922 recommended a return to
Treasury control of departmental expenditure as exercised before the
war – which operated from a baseline of the previous year's
expenditure – to save £70m in the first instance. The report
advocated the concept, later turned down by the Government, of a
Ministry of Defence to coordinate economy of £21m in the naval
estimates, irrespective of the savings which might result from the
Washington conference. £20m had to be saved from army
expenditure, and £5.5m in the air force.

Spending on the social services which, due to inflation and the
pressures of war, had increased from £86.5m in 1913–14 to £243.5m
by 1922–3, suffered the most savage cuts of all. The lower age limit
for free education was raised to six years, and secondary education
was 'confined to children whose mental calibre justifies it' with a
drastic reduction of teachers' salaries. At this point, Geddes and his
colleagues were most certainly tackling a question of policy,
although the full implications were not necessarily appreciated at the
time.

Similarly, the committee saw Local Authority Housing Schemes
simply as a drain upon the taxpayer – of a hefty £60m annually – and
argued that as many as possible of the houses should be sold.
National health insurance should be transferred to private insurance
associations. The public health service budget should not exceed the
previous year. These departments should make economies of £22.1m,
not including the sale of council houses.

The findings were immediately attacked from a variety of
directions. For example, an official report by the Admiralty stated
that

the Committee's main recommendations are based on so serious a
misconception of the character and requirements of our Naval Organisation
that the practical value of their suggestions is greatly diminished ... the

Admiralty have the best grounds for questioning the Committee's accuracy and judgement.

Why were Geddes, Inchcape *et al.* chosen and what was Inchcape's contribution in particular? The Exchequer papers recording a Cabinet meeting to discuss the formation of the committee reveal that a response such as that expected from the Admiralty, cited above, maintaining that only they could decide on their own cuts, was exactly what the Chancellor was trying to avoid. Instead of piecemeal savings here and there, he wanted 'a bird's eye view of the situation', to prevent different departments trying to steal a march on each other, and to see the exercise as one of obtaining equilibrium in income and spending as a whole. Therefore there must be no departmental heads on the committee, and no MPs.

Violent criticism was voiced in opposition to the Committee's view, arguing that 'it might please the so-called Anti-Waste press for a time but, in fact, it was impossible to substitute irresponsible outside businessmen for responsible Ministers, or even effectively to supplement their activities'. This opposition was stifled by the insistence that the committee had no executive function and was only acting in an advisory capacity and in any case the principal ministers were already suffering from enormous pressure of work. The committee was appointed on the strict proviso that its findings would be kept secret – a requirement which Inchcape was later tactlessly to overlook – and many ministers registered their dissent, especially Winston Churchill, then Secretary of State for the Colonies.

The Secretary of State for India, Montagu, despite his friendship with Inchcape, was stunned.

I see it stated on the one hand that the Committee is going to make recommendations as to policy, either directly or indirectly, and is going to advise the Government as to the abandonment of particular functions or services. This is surely incredible. Can it be right that a committee of businessmen should tell us whether capital ships are good or bad things; whether we ought, or ought not, retain a mandate for Mesopotamia or Palestine; whether we should, or should not, substitute air squadrons for cavalry squadrons, or how many infantry battalions are necessary in Ireland, or what is the most economical method of tackling tuberculosis?

The formation of the Committee was thus a real sign of the times: that as the slump deepened, saving money became paramount, and tough businessmen who could run a tight ship came to the fore. It enabled the Government to renege on election promises, safely distancing themselves through the device of this strictly extra-Governmental enquiry whose sole view of policies and commitments was whether or not they could be afforded.

Sir Robert Horne, the Chancellor, announced in a speech in the Commons in March 1922 that the Geddes Committee had saved £86.75m, destined to reach £100m after the navy cuts laid down at the Washington conference. About three-fifths of the savings were from defence, followed by education, war pensions, health and the Post Office. The Government, much to Inchcape's chagrin but not to his surprise, refused to accept the recommendations *en bloc*, and pointed out that even if they did, they could not expect to accrue the saving until the beginning of the next financial year. They challenged the validity of all the committee's conclusions because of their unfamiliarity with department-specific problems. Horne to a certain extent realised that this was inevitable, and blamed the departments for being so uncooperative.

The committee's suggestions of the formation of a Ministry of Defence, the transferring of the Ministry of Transport to the Board of Trade, abolition of the Department of Overseas Trade and the abandonment of afforestation schemes were ignored. The Government welcomed the committee's 'spirit of economy', but it was not always in the right direction and, moreover, a further £175m needed to be saved.

Yet now the Chancellor had 'a clear view of the whole expenditure of the country' and immediately enforced the proposed cuts in education, housing, national insurance and the Ministry of Labour. In the first draft of his Commons speech, Horne alluded to his fears of increasing Labour Party support in the country by these measures. He crossed it out of his notes, but he did not remove the threat. Horne also thought better of promising to reduce taxation; he knew he could not afford to.

Inchcape's role on the Geddes Axe was controversial rather than constructive. In the first instance, he frequently provided hospitality to committee members at his castle at Glenapp, where many of the sessions were held. Surviving correspondence reveals a major gaffe on his part which outraged H.A.L. Fisher, the academic drafted in to improve education. Fisher wrote from the Board of Education in December 1921 to the Prime Minister that he had read in *The Times* a violent attack on the 'wild cat schemes' of the Government by Lord Inchcape:

> It appears to me to be the most improper that a member of the Committee should use the information which he has acquired from members of the Government in a confidential enquiry to make a public attack in denunciation of Government extravagance before the Committee's report has been submitted to the Cabinet. Lord Inchcape should either withdraw from the Committee and denounce us, or remain in the Committee and hold his tongue. His present course of conduct seems to me to be intolerable.

Inchcape particularly supported the heavy cuts in teachers' salaries, on the grounds that he was personally none the worse for having received but little formal education. A member of the deputation of schoolteachers who lobbied the Prime Minister subsequently wrote to Fisher that violent opposition and disillusionment had been provoked among his constitutents and 'for that temper, no man is more responsible than Lord Inchcape'.

The Geddes Committee experiment was a 'once and for all' accounting exercise which was not repeated. The image of wealthy businessmen trying to run the nation like one of their giant corporations was greeted with incredulity or fear. Baldwin joked that when he was ushered into one of the committee's sessions, he surveyed Maclay and Inchcape with a smile and remarked 'I feel as if I have come to arrange an overdraft with my bankers. I expect you are good for a million, aren't you? Upon which they each one buttoned up his trouser pocket'.

There was no humour in the situation for the Rt Hon. Christopher Addison, who wrote that the Geddes report

> is perhaps a classic as an example of the merits and of the defects of the businessman in Government. As a businesslike examination of expenditure it has, perhaps, not been equalled, but as an expression of sound policy, it displayed a lamentable failure to recognise the real need of people, in education, in social and industrial opportunity and in their home life. It provides, perhaps, as fine as text as any that has ever been forthcoming for those who seek to discover the causes of the growth of the Labour Party in recent years. The spirit and aspirations of common people have no great recognition in this document, but it was nevertheless, a great and valuable piece of work as a capable, if cold-blooded, examination of national expenditure. It has the influence of that great and capable businessman, Lord Inchcape, written all over it ... it certainly put to shame the fiddling proceedings of the Public Accounts Committee.

Inchcape, was, overall, dissatisfied at the outcome, that the nation did not fully appreciate his efforts. Perhaps it needed a more powerful force to impress upon it the need for economics. Four years later, Inchcape wrote to *The Times* that perhaps the best person to introduce real Government economy was Mussolini.

Inchcape was in his element in the Geddes Committee, but was at times out of his depth on the Advisory Committee on Civil Aviation in 1919 and 1920. It was a curious appointment but, as the Secretary of State for Air, Winston Churchill, wrote to him, 'We are, I am afraid, a long way off serious competition with ships, and I am not apprehensive of becoming embarrassed by any prejudicial views you may hold as to the superiority of sea transport'.

Most of the other committee members had close links with aviation: it was headed by Lord Weir of Eastwood, previously Secretary of State for the Royal Air Force, and included many representatives of the Society of British Aircraft Constructors and the Air Ministry. Inchcape, along with the chairman of Lloyds, were the token outsiders.

In discussing air routes, top priority was given to speeding up communications between parts of the Empire, to link up Egypt, South Africa, India and Australasia, and also Canada and Newfoundland. If the main trunk lines could be established, then local lines would follow.

The main problem was the lack of available financial help from the Government. Such a new industry needed an input of capital to help it, literally, get off the ground, so that flights could begin on a paying basis. The nature of the industry was not yet fully understood, there were no precedents to fall back on, but at least there were no vested interests either. The lack of data made policy statements difficult, but a service from the UK to India was seen as a first step. Yet how could it be encouraged without heavy demands on the public purse?

The committee considered giving RAF stations the task of carrying passengers and mails as far as their service duties would permit, or allowing them to increase their formations to take in civil aviation. But, Inchcape point out, private enterprise would object to a state monopoly of aviation, and in any case, commerical air requirements would be quite different. But it might be possible for both sectors to share aerodromes and wireless and meteorological facilities.

Much as he disliked Government intervention in business, Inchcape accepted that it would be almost impossible to establish an aviation industry, with so many unknown factors, without State aid. The crucial future significance of air travel was such that the Government must make some form of undertaking. A State monopoly was not acceptable, so it boiled down to a choice between a chartered company combining State and private capital, or a private industry with some State support.

The advantages of a chartered company would include formal representation of all the various interests – aircraft constructors, shipping companies, Departments of State and the Post Office – and would ensure a uniform development of policy and co-ordination of effort, standardisation of material and yet, by involving all aspects of the industry, would avoid accusations of monopoly. Inchcape did not like the scheme, and nor did many of the others. The industry should be open to new ideas, and this arrangement might have a narrowing tendency likely to jeopardise success. It would inevitably be bureaucratic and inefficient. Inchcape was reminded of the problems of the standard ships policy: too much weight could be attached to arguments for standardisation.

So the committee turned to the idea of providing State support for private industry, seen as more in the tradition of British trade and industry. State aid must be limited to an amount enough to ensure success, but not enough to appear protective or to stifle competitiveness. The State was prepared to provide much of the infrastructure, such as wireless and meteorological services and air ports (not as this stage referred to as airports). Such facilities would be an enormous and crippling burden on a new industry. When the industry took off and became profitable, the State could then charge them for the use of their facilities. This would prevent operating firms from becoming too powerful.

The War Cabinet had already approved the building of an aerodrome for the Egypt/India route to meet service needs and provide one civil flight each way per week. The service would mean much greater speed – three and a half days rather than nine – so the committee must agree some concrete means by which it could be assisted. This is where Inchcape came in: he was asked, in his capacity of P&O chairman, to draw up a tender for an air mail contract, to service Egypt, Karachi and Bombay. It would fit in with the existing ocean mail contract. Meanwhile, surplus RAF aeroplanes could be made available for a civilian company in Britain or in the colonies, though so far local pioneers' aviation work in India and Egypt had been prevented by various Government regulations, which must be removed.

No one yet knew how much any of this would cost, but the committee concluded that 'these modest recommendations are made on the assumption that the State intends to maintain flying supremacy by supporting the service side at a level that will ensure the safety of the position'.

A year later, the committee produced another report, considering the aerial transport services which had evolved since the Armistice to form a nucleus for future growth of services and manufacturing, but they warned that 'no action on the part of the State which we should regard as justifiable, nor any development of private enterprise which is yet within sight, can save the industry from great reduction from its wartime magnitude'.

Inchcape again emphasised that the function of Government was to encourage and assist, not operate or initiate, especially in the circumstances in which it found itself at the end of the postwar boom. Nevertheless, all agreed that 'British prestige in air development won during the war should not be lost', skilled aircraft manufacturers must be kept at work, and all efforts must be concentrated on the most important routes, i.e. to Egypt and India. Air travel had to be faster than any other service, despite the fact that at this stage it was not safe enough to fly at night, when ships and express sleeper trains could run at any time. So far, the service to Paris by Aircraft Transport & Travel Co. had been most successful, although it had attracted little in the way of mails.

The actual operation of the subsidy on Continental flights was then discussed. It was agreed that grants should be paid only on useful work performed, so they were made conditional on regularity of service and proportional to the income received from the public using the service. Meanwhile, the relationship with the Post Office must be strictly commercial to avoid confusion between State assistance and payment for work done.

Direct assistance was finally agreed, to a maximum of £250,000 for the financial years 1920–1 and 1921–2, equal to twenty-five per cent of the total certified gross revenue of each company, earned by the carriage of passengers, freight and mails, and to be exclusive of the mail subsidy. The aircraft had to be of British manufacture with

British engines, with a maximum time between London and Paris or Brussels of four hours.

Inchcape signed the report with the other members of the committee, but made a separate written statement: 'In the present state of the Country's finances I am not in favour of subsidising any aviation Company'. Having made this stand, he was not appointed to a committee the following year to discuss commercial airships. This later enquiry bemoaned the fact that the United States had bought Britain's latest airship, the R38, the last word in aviation, and was threatening the trade between Britain and the Dominions. Fortunately the airship never became commercially viable on a large scale, but many felt that the attitude of businessmen like Inchcape enabled the Americans to take a lead, which apparently explained Britain's failure to maintain her competitive advantages in this exciting new business.

During this final period of his public life, Inchcape spent much time and energy preoccupied with overseas problems, involving long absences from P&O meetings and his public duties in Britain. But he tackled them with more enthusiasm, and generally with more constructive results than the committees dealing with solely home matters. They fall into three areas: India, the Middle East and imperial shipping policy.

India was always of utmost importance to Inchcape, and he was seen as an authority on the subcontinent from the days of his membership of the Viceroy's Legislative Council back in the 1890s. So, immediately after the war, Inchcape was called upon by Montagu at the India Office to join a committee 'to consider the organisation and composition of the India Office'. As Montagu said, 'your long experience on the Council of this Office together with your deep knowledge of all things Indian would make your presence on the Committee a real source of strength ...'. He made relatively few changes, reinforcing the power of the viceroy, but did agree enthusiastically to allowing a larger proportion of Indian staff.

He was less inclined to help in a committee of 1919 discussing Indian currency problems. He made a brief statement on the need for stability above all. The rupee had risen in value to 2s, and was to reach 2s 8½d in February 1920. During Inchcape's final years in India, it had been fixed at 1s 4d. It was to fall back to this point by July 1921. Inchcape suggested that a 2s rupee might lead to a fall in prices in India, which would be good for business.

Inchcape's most outstanding service for the subcontinent in this period was the committee which bore his name of 1922–3, which sought, with rather more success, to be a Geddes Axe for India. The establishment costs of the British administration had expanded uncontrollably, while the home country could hardly afford to maintain its own institutions, let along those of the Empire.

Inchcape arrived in Delhi at the beginning of November and met the other members of the Committee – three prominent Indian leaders, including Sir Rajendra Mookerjee KCIE, and two longstanding British administrators, Sir Thomas Catto and Sir Alexander Robertson Murray. Inchcape discussed the results of the questionnaires he had prepared for the various departments of the Government of India, which had been despatched in advance. While waiting for all the replies, he set an example for economy by staying with his wife and staff in very modest quarters.

The original brief had been to make recommendations to reduce the expenditure of the central Government, under a wide range of headings: military, railways, posts and telegraphs, irrigation, general administration, the political establishment, the civil jurisdiction, scientific bodies, education, medical affairs, agriculture, industry, civil aviation, commercial intelligence, joint stock companies, revenue collection, forestry, famine relief and frontier defence.

In 1913, India's total expenditure was sixty-nine crores of rupees (about £40m) against sixty-five crores of revenue. In 1921, expenditure had soared to 143 crores (around £84m) with income at only 114 crores. Inchcape's projected savings, which were implemented with some success, raised revenue to 133 crores and reduced expenditure to 142 crores, still a deficit but more manageable. He reduced the total revenue payable by India to England by more than half – £1m compared with £3m – and increased Britain's support of India to nearly £90m by 1922–3. He saved more than twelve crores of rupees (over £8m) and effectively balanced the budget.

In his report, Inchcape argued, as he did in Britain, that no further tax burdens could be tolerated, so that stringent economies were needed. The loss-making railways were one of his greatest problems and he initiated a complete review of railway management. The military and civil administration bore the brunt of the cuts. Irrigation schemes were slashed at the very time when they were most needed, but such facilities are always reduced first simply for administrative ease. The post of Inspector of Irrigation was abolished.

It would take some time to implement the economies, especially in the army which was to be reduced to a reservist force only. The air force, however, was to be supported, in view of its greater speed and efficiency. Britain was to give 100 aeroplanes to the Government of India and the cost of running an air service between Cairo and Karachi would be shared between them. The navy received the heaviest service cuts of all, with sales of troop ships and the turning over of the dockyards to commercial use. As in the Geddes Report, the military and administration suffered drastic reductions but so did many useful and creative projects, such as the founding of Delhi University, a grant for medical research and the School of Mining.

Inchcape recorded his views on the future of India at this time in many periodicals, including the French *Journal des Débats*. In a letter to the editor of *The Spectator*, for whom he frequently wrote, he expressed his belief that it was inevitable that Indians would increasingly seek self expression, and Britain must 'help India towards the fulfilment of her destiny among the peoples of the world. It must be recognised that 99% of India is mute, while the over-articulate part is not wholly wise'. He considered that India was in its infancy politically, and that it must continue to look to its British administrators and more enlightened princes.

He attacked those who tried to impose heavy import duties on British goods, emphasising the crucial importance of commodity exchange to the Indian economy in the international scene. He was particularly thinking of the role of his ships in this, and the increased competition they now suffered.

During his stay in India, Inchcape faced much criticism from the Indian press, but received much praise from the Indian Government, not only for the work of the committee but also in his tours of frontiers and his support for the viceroy during a growing constitutional crisis. He argued that a strong British Government in India was needed more than ever.

There will always be hotheads endeavouring to stir up strife ... India's security ... will for many generations continue to be dependent on the Central Government with, at its head, the Viceroy representing the Sovereign of Great Britain. Sensible Indians recognise this and realise that anything else would spell anarchy, chaos and bloodshed throughout the country.

By July 1930, writing to the then Prime Minister, Ramsay
MacDonald, in the wake of increasing anti-British disturbances,
Inchcape was more worried than ever.

We have pandered to native agitators in a way that has given them the idea
that the more trouble they make the more chance there is of getting rid of the
British. The only way to govern an Asiatic country is by a benevolent
autocracy. The trouble in India was started by Montagu who said that he
wanted India to be freed from the British Yoke. The British Yoke has meant
freedom, justice and protection for all India under the British Crown ... all
attempts to destroy law and order must be put down with a firm hand ... the
trade with India and in India has been brought practically to a standstill by
the boycotts now instituted. This will have a disastrous effect on the revenue
not only of India but of Britain ... I hope the loss of India to the British
Crown will not come about while you hold the reins.

Inchcape's depression about the future of this land and people that
he undoubtedly sincerely loved for most of his adult life was
exceeded only by his concern over the desperate condition of British
shipping.

Two years before his work on retrenchment in India, Inchcape had
been posted to the subcontinent for quite a different task, which also
drew him into Middle East affairs: the sale of the wartime
Mesopotamian River Fleet. He was already well accomplished as the
Government's own shipbroker, and this undertaking was to realise
another £1,080,000 for 360 vessels, to be added to the £35m he had
gained from the sale of the standard ships and the £20m for ex-
enemy tonnage. This sale was to be much more difficult than those
he had handled before.

Inchcape's original brief of January 1920 was vague, and left much
to his initiative. He could decide whether to sell the vessels, many of
which were held in India, by auction, tender or private treaty as long
as competition for them was maximised, although he was to exclude
would-be purchasers who were regarded as politically undesirable.
The Government would pay for them to be delivered to purchasers in
Basrah and, for a price, to Mesopotamia itself. He was to sell them
for cash only as far as possible, and to try and dispose of all of them,
breaking up those which were completely unsaleable. Everything was
left to his discretion. Inchcape was specifically excluded from giving
preference to his own companies in the sale; as we have seen, this was

not the case in his earlier transactions, when Hain certainly took up several vessels.

His report, written on board the *Devanha* off Port Said, described the problems he had encountered in this two-month task. He argued that towage to all delivery points should be undertaken by the Government who could then charge the purchasers for this service, and that repairs should be carried out to make the vessels seaworthy to their destinations and nothing more. This added to Government revenue considerably. He made sure that the whole fleet was widely advertised in Bombay, Calcutta and Mesopotamia. His companies may have been precluded from buying the ships, but Mackinnon Mackenzie handled the enquiries generated by the advertisements.

The commissioners in India and in the Middle East showed a remarkable ability to misunderstand their instructions, so Inchcape travelled to Delhi to make clear that the sale would not be carried out by open auction but by sealed tender, so that Indian bidders could not increase offers to outbid Mesopotamians. The Government of India was afraid that the vessels might be run on the Tigris and Euphrates and upset their monopoly on those waters, so Inchcape had to undertake only to accept offers from firms and individuals subject to Government approval for the vessels' intended use. Officials in Delhi complained constantly of

the hole and corner manner in which the question had been handled by the Ministry of Munitions which have made it almost impossible for Inchcape and representatives in Mesopotamia to come to a working agreement or indeed give practical effect to any arrangements for the sale of the fleet.

In the middle of everything, the authorities in Baghdad started to have second thoughts as to exactly how many vessels were surplus to requirements, and how many they should keep.

The Anglo-Persian Oil Company were interested in the vessels, and Inchcape asked if they could be permitted to purchase some. He was told that the company had been informed that they might by letter, but it never reached them. The eventual purchase by this company of an undisclosed number took months to go through. Inchcape finally sold the fleet under the two general conditions that the ships would be subject to various navigation rules which the Government might lay down, and that delivery would only be made when the authorities in Mesopotamia agreed to release the vessel. With these conditions, it is amazing that Inchcape was able to sell any of the fleet at all, let alone at such a profit. It reveals not only his abilities as a negotiator and salesman, but the great shortage of tonnage in this region at a time when trade was booming.

Instead of elation, Inchcape felt great disappointment that the Mesopotamian authorities had retained so many vessels, which he considered were in excess of the necessary reserve, and continued as a drain on the taxpayer, when services on the Tigris and Euphrates could be maintained with a much more modest fleet.

His thirty-four page report, including the name of every tenderer and the prices received, shows his attention for detail, determination to stick to the exact letter of his instructions and immense patience. He saw this and his other ship sales – mammoth, time-consuming, largely thankless tasks involving hours of haggling and arguing – as his greatest achievements. Unfortunately, in his excitement to make the best deals, he saw them only in the short term, rather than in the context of British shipping generally. Although the majority of the vessels were sold to British firms, at least a third went to fuel the competitive advantage enjoyed by many local firms, who were soon to increase their edge even further.

Inchcape's overseas duties in this period also included service on the Imperial Shipping Committee, which had been set up by Lloyd George as part of the Imperial War Conference of 1918. As chairman of the General Council for British Shipping – twice – he was an obvious choice. In 1923 Inchcape, on behalf of the Board of Trade, helped investigate complaints from the Government of Australia about the deferred rebate system and its operation in the outward trade to Australia. They claimed that it operated against the interests of the Commonwealth and Government Line, in favour of conference members. Witnesses were drawn from every sphere of Australian trade, and they were questioned by Inchcape together with Sir Alan Anderson of the Orient Line, Sir Percy Pates, the deputy chairman of Cunard, P.D. Holt of Alfred Holt and Sir Ernest Glover representing tramp shipping.

All the shippers complained of exceptionally high freights and profits for the shipping lines, due to offering deferred rebates to shippers keeping within the conference system, a method by which conference loyalty was maintained and rewarded. The shipowners countered each charge of profiteering and keeping freights unduly high by claiming the existence of additional factors. For example,

British freights rates were much higher than Continental charges, but this was due to exceptional competition between the foreign lines which had brought the Continental rates below their true economic value. Conference rates kept freights at parity, not higher than justified, they explained.

The shipowners united in pointing out that they did not enjoy a monopoly. There were great limitations to their power, and shippers were quite free to go out of the conference if they were willing to forfeit their accrued rebates, which worked out at up to ten per cent of their freight business over nine months or more. Only the large bulk shippers had a lot to lose by going elsewhere.

As in several P&O AGMs, Inchcape spoke of the advantages of the conference system in steadying freights, which could be passed on to their customers through the use of deferred rebates. Services could thus be maintained with greater regularity, frequency and efficiency, to everyone's benefit. The shipowners could think of no alternative to the deferred rebate which would tie the shipper and provide stability. But as the Australian trade declined with reduced emigration, and local coastal services faced heavy competition from the railways, the whole controversy passed.

In these fourteen years, Inchcape's public work covered an immense variety of assignments, indicative of his range of interests and expertise, and his willingness to undertake almost any mission. These tasks also show the plethora of problems which the British Government faced in the 1920s, both at home and overseas, that British political and economic life was in a state of flux, and that the future of the Empire was already in considerable doubt.

As in his public duties before and after the war, Inchcape displayed a remarkable consistency of attitude: protecting private enterprise and restricting government intervention to a minimum. Seeing politicians as commercially ignorant and naive, he was glad to take tasks such as ship sales off their hands, and to mount investigations into Government departments when economies were needed. His greatest pride in working for the Government and his fascination with the insight he was thus given into the workings of state were his blind spots: rushing into the work, he did not stop to think out the full implications of his policies, and he made many tactless public utterances, especially in the press.

His public work was grist to his journalistic mill. He wrote on shipping, India, wages, prices, and all aspects of Britain's trade – often unhelpfully, as he spoke with the authority of a man walking the corridors of power, but without the responsibility of a cabinet post or even a seat in the Commons. He could not discreetly offer advice without subsequently drawing attention, in public, to the weaknesses which he had revealed at the Ministries of Supply, Munitions, Shipping and Labour.

As a businessman – shipowner, banker and merchant – he was predictable in voicing conservatism, stability and restraint without thinking of the long-term future, because he was still preoccupied with a return to pre-1913 conditions. His obsession with freeing business from the shackles of politics conflicted with his complaints of the lack of Government support for economic revival. The attitudes he displayed on the Geddes Committee revealed all these features and more; a disturbing lack of tolerance and concern for the weak and unfortunate.

As Britain's postwar breathing space blossomed into a short boom and then faded into a long decline, Inchcape's political sympathies moved from Liberalism to Conservatism, and his outlook was tinged with increasing disillusionment. Any chance that the infant aviation industry had of state subsidy faded as the boom collapsed, and so did India's hopes of more support. He tried to stand up for Britain's flagging status overseas but realised that time, and money, were running out.

From 1928 onwards, with the death of his beloved daughter Elsie in her attempt to be the first women to cross the Atlantic by air, Inchcape retreated more and more from public life, spending increasing time at his Scottish estates. His lengthy and regular press correspondence was not, however, reduced; he wrote more than ever, especially on India's problems.

Although a desire for honours and titles, especially to raise his wife's status in the snobbish social environment of expatriate India in the 1880s and 1890s, had influenced the early years of his public life, this was not the case in the 1920s. His viscountcy and GCSI in 1924, and his earldom in 1929, were some comfort that his efforts had not gone unappreciated, but the main reason was that he felt too involved by then to be able to stand aside.

At a time when the Government was increasingly interfering in all aspects of economic life, especially shipping, he spoke out more than any other single businessman for freedom of trade and business.

When Government expenditure threatened to get out of control, he played a prominent part in its reduction. And in a period when the future of India was in the melting-pot, he did more than any other influential old India hand to try and keep her in the Empire. The fact that he was ultimately unsuccessful in all these tasks does not detract from his endeavours at the time, which were seen as duties discharged in the best interests of Britain generally. He was from the prewar generation and, together with the majority of his contemporaries, saw the future in prewar terms, and he liked it less and less.

9

Conclusion

In the early afternoon of 23 May 1932, when news reached London from Inchcape's yacht *Rover* in Monte Carlo that the shipping magnate, in his eightieth year, had peacefully passed away, it was like the end of an era. Despite his age and the fact that Shaw had taken over much of the P&O management and other deputies, especially the second Earl, had been helping run Mackinnon Mackenzie and the rest of the Mackinnon/Inchcape empire for a number of years, and regardless of the severe depression and stagnation in British shipping and trading, the City was shocked. The news of Inchcape's death was deliberately withheld until the Stock Exchange closed; when it reopened on 24 May, P&O £1 deferred stock nosedived to only 11s, and the whole market fell noticeably. Immediate reaction came not only from the commercial world: Lady Inchcape had her family were swamped by official telegrams expressing condolences from every Government department.

The sheer volume of newsprint expended on Inchcape's life and contribution shows the enormity of his impact on both business and public life in Britain and the Empire. Much of it showed more than a hint of graveside deference, and most writers dwelt on the high points of the Earl's career, but a substantial minority introduced disquieting angles and interpretations.

For instance, the majority viewed Inchcape's role in business as that expressed by the shipping interest: the Chamber of Shipping saw him as 'a man of outstanding eminence in British and world trade who enjoyed universal respect and admiration', and *Fairplay* wrote that he was 'farseeing, thorough, shrewd, a tireless worker and capable of inspiring others with his own indefatigable energy ... an acknowledged authority in high finance, Eastern politics and economics, he was a man of affairs in the best sense of the term'.

The more conservative British national newspapers also spoke highly of Inchcape's business acumen. *The Times*, striking a general note, described Inchcape as possessing 'shrewd judgement of men and things', and the *Daily Mail* wrote that 'Lord Inchcape's death is a heavy blow to British shipping at a time when his counsel and influence are most needed'. Remarks in the international press included evaluations of Inchcape as 'a Napoleon of Commerce' and many agreed that 'he had more experience and more knowledge of Oriental trade than any living man'.

Yet an American writer in the New York based *Journal of Commerce*, with the benefit of transatlantic detachment, saw Inchcape – and by implication the British shipping industry as a whole – somewhat pejoratively as 'the last survivor of Britain's feudal shipowners, who always acted as though the companies he headed were his own private property'. The British *News Chronicle* echoed these sentiments: he was 'one of the few remaining men who actually rule giant businesses, modern conditions making the emergence of such figures more and more difficult'. The official organ of the Labour Party, the *Daily Herald*, said the same. Inchcape was 'the last autocrat in the shipping world'. The *Daily Mirror* described him as so overbearing that no shareholder would dare ask questions at AGMs.

Many Australian newspapers, who had frequently attacked Inchcape in the past, took a similar line, but were not always sure of their facts, as when the *Adelaide Chronicle* described him as 'Britain's richest shipping magnate'. Inchcape's active promotion of the shipping lines he controlled led the *Bombay Chronicle* to complain that he 'successfully thwarted all endeavours of Indians, including even the efforts of such an able and resourceful captain of industry as Sir Jamsedji Tata to build up an Indian merchant navy during the last half century'.

Inchcape's public life was applauded in his obituary in *The Times*, which declared that 'probably no civilian outside the Cabinet discharged during the War a greater range of administrative activities'. Overseas newspapers paid tribute to the fact that 'there are few men who have sat on so many Royal Commissions, mostly as chairman, and still fewer who have saved the State so much money'. He was 'the world's best ship salesman'. At the same time, perhaps paradoxically, many remembered Inchcape best as 'a lifelong opponent of Government interference' and because 'he fought strenuously for private enterprise to be left severely alone'. His public generosity was frequently acknowledged (two bequests to the Treasury, £2½m just before his death, and £½m representing the assets held by his beloved daughter Elsie on her tragic attempt to cross the Atlantic by air in 1928): 'unfortunately the Lord Inchcapes of this world are all too rare in this grasping age'.

Although great praise of Inchcape's work in India followed the announcement of his death, defiantly nationalistic Indian news-papers inevitably took a different line. The *Bombay Chronicle* wrote of how Inchcape 'exploited India's resources' and questioned whether or not he served Indian interests at all when he joined Lord Lansdowne's Council in India, and subsequently the India Council in England. The *Bombay Chronicle* suggested that many Indians felt resentment at Inchcape's attitude to their national aspirations and his bitter opposition to Gandhi. The *Daily Mirror* drew attention to Inchcape's extreme views, that the payment of dole to the unemployed was 'a sin against the country', that the Labour Party were 'agents of Bolshevism' and that education 'would make the workers unhappy'.

Yet what was Inchcape really like as a businessmen and as a public servant? And what was he like outside his working life?

In Chapters Two, Four, Six and Seven, Inchcape emerges as a businessman who was very lucky, but who capitalised on every stroke of luck to the full. He was supremely fortunate in the firm he worked for, not only in that Mackinnon Mackenzie enjoyed such prominence in British India, but also because he faced relatively little competition in his climb to the top of the organisation, and in ultimately taking over its leadership. He was lucky with his first big break in Bombay, and unusually fortunate in the robust good health he enjoyed for most of his twenty years in India.

He returned to London at an ideal time, when both the BI and P&O needed new blood at the top. The outbreak of the First World War meant that his first few years as chairman of the merged P&O/BI group were extremely profitable, and he was lucky in his choice of acquisitions, especially in terms of their subsequent high earnings. The Mackinnon/Inchcape empire in India was fortunate in the temporary collapse of attempts to reserve Indian coastal shipping for Indians only, and in the failure of local or other foreign concerns seriously to undermine their position for most of the period of

Inchcape's leadership.

Others had the same luck and did nothing with it. The future Lord Inchcape rose to the top of the Mackinnon group only through great ambition and hard work. He was certainly a workaholic: he often said that 'in my experience there is no greater pleasure than that which was derived from work, and work is the cheapest form of amusement, and idleness the most expensive'. Only Inchcape's extensive knowledge of day-to-day matters of shipping and trading enabled him to make the most of his opportunities. This had been gained through decades of spadework of literally getting his hands dirty at docks and warehouses all over the Indian Ocean, of great attention to every rupee of expenditure and every detail of Mackinnon Mackenzie's operations, of taking the trouble to learn Hindi and getting to know as many native businessmen as possible.

The profits which the First World War brought could easily have been squandered in large dividends and bonuses, as happened in several cases, rather than being carefully husbanded for the future. The acquisitions which appeared such good buys at the time could have turned out to be unsuitable. Inchcape always did his homework. Contemporaries saw him as methodical and precise in manner: 'he never hurried, and one seldom saw an unanswered paper on his desk'. As he said in response to a request for the formula of his success: 'I never fail to keep my work and I always clear up my desk at night'. The survival and continued prominence of the Mackinnon/Inchcape empire in India was by no means accidental. It owed much to Inchcape's constant lobbying of the Government against discrimination; his support of local merchants, even to the extent of guaranteeing their credit with banks; and making freight and profit-sharing deals with competitors.

Inchcape was also a successful troubleshooter and turnaround man. At Bombay, he transformed the BI agency from bankruptcy to annual net profit for remittance home of £32,000 in less than five years, whilst other businesses were falling by the wayside. Back in London, he raised the BI's profitability with new routes and services, before his epic rescue of the AUSN. By judicious hiring and firing, bargaining with competitors and ruthlessly sifting through years of accounts, the AUSN operated on a secure, businesslike and largely profitable footing until its *raison d'être* was undermined by new rail services. Especially in his prewar days, Inchcape was innovatory and radical in business; he never lost an opportunity. Taking on a camel-

carrying contract when he had no steamers at his disposal, employing
sailing ships with plenty of sand ballast, was typical.

Inchcape's commitment to his companies' interests – both the
Mackinnon/Inchcape group and the P&O – was total, like a religion.
With shipbuilders, he used the leverage of his almost unlimited good-
customer potential to minimise costs and maximise quality and speed
of delivery. With the Government, he exerted his position as a leader
of the shipping industry and his long record of official service to gain
the best compensation packages (such as on the *Ballarat*), insurance
and freight deals, and a crucial Treasury grant to the P&O of £2.5m
for obsolesence costs, at a time when funds were desperately needed.
With the Suez Canal Company and other outside directorships, he
advanced his companies' trading opportunities and upheld their
global status. With fellow bankers, he raised funds for the P&O and
helped keep interest rates low, using his prestige from the National
Provincial and his establishment of the P&O Bank. With the General
Council for British Shipping, he protected his fleets' interests
nationally and internationally.

This commitment is reflected in his willingness to redirect his own
private funds and the reserves of the Mackinnon/Inchcape group in
order to keep public confidence in the P&O – and thus the P&O's
share price – high. The P&O needed glamorous, modern new liners
to compete and survive. But, as we have seen, working costs rose and
voyage profits fell throughout the economic storms and troughs of
the 1920s. Meanwhile, the investments of the Mackinnon/Inchcape
group in India, which had accounted for most of the young Mackay's
disposable income (to a greater extent than any other of the
Mackinnon Mackenzie partners) were less and less accessible for
remission home in the 1920s, and in any case Inchcape had always
favoured ploughing back profits where they were most needed.
Inchcape cannot personally be accused of contributing to the 'drain'
of wealth from India; on the contrary, he foresook more profitable
ventures to invest in India.

By skilful accounting, Mackinnon Mackenzie, Gray Dawes,
Binny's, the BI and other outposts of the Mackinnon/Inchcape
empire which enjoyed greater profitability than the hard pressed
P&O were able to come to its aid financially even at a risk to their
own reserves; they had already long provided managerial help and
many commercial opportunities, such as Gray Dawes' sale of Strick
to Hain. This consideration largely offsets contemporary accusations

that Mackinnon Mackenzie and the BI were the greatest beneficiaries from the merger. Although P&O staff sometimes resented the fact that their chairman originally came from another shipping line which was now included in the group fleet, Mackinnon Mackenzie partners in Calcutta were none too happy at instructions from Inchcape that every box of tea and bale of gunny then had to go by the P&O, often displacing their own interests.

Additionally, through private family companies such as Mackay & Co., Inchcape was able to personally support the P&O by taking over the burden of unprofitable investments such as the Khedivial Mail. With income from the subsidiary and associated companies, especially the Union and New Zealand companies, Inchcape was able to turn the P&O's aggregate profits of the 1920s from £1.8m into £11m and maintain the dividend. Thus Shaw paid tribute, on taking up the reins of power, to Inchcape's 'generosity and self-sacrifice'. The P&O and Mackinnon/Inchcape flag flew high, whilst many other shipping and trading concerns, such as the Royal Mail Group, despite generous Trade Facilities Act loans, were going under.

Yet Inchcape's policy of conservative finance and mutual support could not fundamentally solve the deep-rooted problems of British shipping in the interwar years. His principal weakness as a businessman – and this is fully understandable in the context – stemmed from the fact that the bulk of his commercial career belonged to the prewar era, and he could not escape from a commonly held assumption that sooner or later everything would get back to normal: normal being defined as the situation in 1913. Thus he clung to traditional Empire trades in the face of a falling demand for British goods and anti-British feeling in Australia; he made but inadequate attempts to offset the dramatic increase in competition from the United States and Japan; and he invested much of the P&O's cash assets in securities, which were severely undermined when Britain was forced to abandon the gold standard. When the subsidiary and associated companies started to lose too, an economy drive, primarily based on wage cutting, was inadequate in offsetting the effects of particularly heavy losses in 1930 and 1931.

Shaw, from a different generation, was inevitably more forward-looking, and initiated radical policies long avoided by his predecessor. He revealed the whole picture, published the full accounts, addressed the problems of depreciation and liquidity, and suspended the dividend, knowing full well that the P&O's market price would plummet. His long-term plan for the P&O's recovery was ultimately more successful than Inchcape's constant patching and repairing – the P&O ship needed completely new fabric, not just another jury-rig. Undoubtedly, Inchcape held on to power too tightly and too long, but only in the very last few years. Then, less attractive sides of his nature became exaggerated, aggravated by his disillusionment with the British shipping industy and the future of India, and the loss of his beloved daughter, which deprived him of his zest for life. He could be intolerant, extreme, overbearing and secretive; miserly with his power, he tried to frustrate the attempts of the able deputies he had wisely selected to run the companies effectively.

Inchcape's last few years should not detract from his achievements. His leadership, transformation and development of the Mackinnon group not only laid the foundations for present-day Inchcape PLC; it produced a prototype of an Eastern commercial empire which became a forerunner of even more successful and powerful Indian commercial groups such as the Tatas and Birlas. Inchcape would have welcomed both developments, particularly the latter. Although he is perhaps best known as a British shipowner, he was always an India merchant first.

In his public, as opposed to his business life, Inchcape invariably prefaced each political remark with the words 'I am no politician but ...'; yet he played as important a part in public life as was possible without actually holding elected office. Although his motives for venturing into public service were initially to gain honours and public recognition, his approach was honest, open and not self-seeking. His anger against bureaucracy and his concern for India were never mere gestures. He pragmatically considered the issues put before him as a businessman first, interpreting issues in terms of a simple cost–benefit analysis rather than diplomatic or moral considerations.

He worked his way up in public life from the very bottom to the very top, from Chamber of Commerce and Port Trust committee work in Bombay and Calcutta to advising prime ministers. Lloyd George saw him as one of his best 'finds' of the war years; had he actually gained the proferred viceroyalty, he would have devoted the rest of his life to public service. In India he was best remembered for his fight against taxes on commercial profits, the opium question, the Factory Acts and the Currency Commission: but these issues were the culmination of many years' graft with the minutiae of local politics.

Before winning the confidence of leading politicians at home and receiving his peerage, Mackay was often unrealistic and undiplomatic; if he felt strongly about an issue, he spoke his mind, whatever the consequences. Thus he stood out in support of a gold standard for India at all costs, although he had not grasped all that was involved, and was not supported by British merchants trading to India from home. Even after many years' experience in the highest political circles, he was just the same, as in the case of his outspoken remarks on education in the midst of the Geddes Axe investigations, before the report was published.

Despite occasional *naïveté* and indiscretion, Inchcape's energy and enthusiasm for public service were prodigious and declined only in his very last few years. Thus he served for four terms as president of the Bengal Chamber of Commerce, despite a plethora of other activities in India, and thus he served as Chairman of the General Council for British Shipping, and on seventeen committees in the twenty years between his return to Britain and the outbreak of the First World War. He took on an enormous burden of responsibilities during the war, in addition to managing the nation's largest shipping conglomerate.

Combined with this energy was an astonishing degree of patience, which was but rarely exhibited in Inchcape's business life. The year he spent in China on behalf of the British Government, much of it in frustrating idleness, would never have been expended on a business venture whose success was as problematical. Inchcape willingly put aside his personal felings, never questioning the ultimate value of the tasks he took on and practically never refusing such calls. He had a great capacity for committee work, despite its time-consuming and tedious qualities, which gained him the ear of ministers who felt considerably indebted to him as a result.

Although Inchcape's work in public life spanned almost half a century, his attitude remained remarkably consistent. He always opposed government intervention in business – such as on the Commercial Information Committee – yet did not see this as contradicting his constant lobbying for increases in mail contracts, as in the case of the mail service to East Africa to subsidise P&O group routes. He favoured reducing Government factories and workshops to a minimum and handing over military support contracts to private firms: like the majority of his contemporaries, he could not envisage the extent of the demands for wartime supplies in an unprecedented global conflict, but Geddes always said that Inchcape was one of the first men he knew to appreciate the likely duration of the war.

Inchcape's work for the Ministry of Shipping during and after the war was geared towards winding down this massively proliferating bueaucracy as soon as possible and freeing commerce completely, yet at the same time he accepted that Government intervention was necessary to consolidate the national war effort. His own work on the problems of the home production of food and the efficiency of British ports made a substantial contribution to this end, but he promoted such intervention only on the grounds of helping the national emergency, never seeing this role of the state as desirable in the long term, least of all permanently.

His contributions to postwar committees showed an even greater obsession than before with freeing business from the strictures of Government. Thus he would accept no prosecution of the profiteering British Cellulose Company; thus he eagerly fell upon the task of selling Government standard ships and prize vessels to private shipowners; and thus he would not support state financing of the infant aviation industry. His decisions, which carried considerable weight, were not necessarily appropriate in any of these instances.

The consistency of Inchcape's stand broke down in only one instance, when he moved dramatically from free trade to protection in 1931. Free trade had always been one of his favourite causes, and kept him in the Liberal ranks of the House of Lords, despite his increasing disilusionment with Lloyd George in the mid-1920s. After the war, he had been one of the first to argue that trade should be reopened with Germany and with Soviet Russia, and was in frequent correspondence with the famous free-trader Sir Hugh Bell. Yet he accepted that import duties were crucial to the revenue of many countries, and that in the postwar world completely free trade without any embargoes was impossible.

By 1923 he expressed anxiety about the future of Britain's free trade policies in the light of the poor performance of British industry and about demands in India for the unrestricted development of its own trade, well aware of the difficulties of British shipping trying to compete with low wages and subsidies in foreign shipping. Although not fully relinquishing free trade until 1931, he joined the Conservatives in September 1926. He did not expect immediate

election to the Carlton Club: 'in view of my free trade propensities ...
I shall probably be blackballed', but the Tories were naturally glad to
welcome any defectors from the Liberals. Lloyd George pretended
not to care, agreeing with Beauchamp that 'he has never been much
use to us in the Lords', but he realised that the loss of such a
previously loyal and stalwart supporter was symptomatic of his
party's decay.

Inchcape may have veered from free trade to protection, but he
never stopped seeing politics with a businessman's eye. In this respect
he frequently acted as the Government's official business watchdog,
such as the time he gained Lloyd George's support for his plans to
centralise military supplies for all services; this culminated in his
service on the Geddes Committee, the greatest opportunity a
businessman such as Inchcape ever had to run the ship of State like
one of his own fleet. His and his colleagues' recommendations so
went against the grain of the postwar social and economic ideology –
despite the slump and the strong anti-waste lobby – that such a
committee was never repeated.

His attitude to postwar monetary problems also reflects his vision
of the national economy as one big corporate balance sheet and, as in
his management of the P&O and Mackinnon/Inchcape group, he
saw the prewar era as the normal and desirable state of affairs, and
the 1920s as a painful yet, he hoped, a temporary aberration. He
expressed no real fears of Britain successfully returning to the gold
standard when he gave evidence on the Gold Production Committee,
and welcomed a series of broad principles to protect London as a free
market for gold, mindful of his banking interests. Understandably,
he believed that a secure monetary framework would help Britain to
recover and grow, but mistakenly saw the successful working of the
gold standard as a prerequisite of monetary stability, not as a
by-product.

Inchcape's postwar outlook in all national issues was shaped by
the First World War, which took an enormous toll on his optimism.
It brought with it a fear of social instability, especially influenced by
the Bolshevik Revolution, and abhorrence of nationalisation plans.
Few reacted as strongly as Inchcape, who was convinced that
nationalisation of coal mines would be disastrous to that industry
and therefore to the British economy as a whole. The implications for
other industries filled him with horror.

Inchcape was also profoundly unsettled by the increasing power of trade unions, especially incidences of striking without ballots and the compulsory political levy. He then became convinced, and he was not alone, that trade unions were evil and working against the wishes of many of their members. By 1930 he strongly believed that trade union restrictions were largely responsible for the 1½ million people on the dole. In recounting his career and his achievements and the low salary he was paid in his first job, Inchcape commented wryly, 'had the dole then been in existence I might have got no further'.

Inchcape cut a familiar figure in British political life in the wartime years and the 1920s. His opinion was obviously respected, as in 1923 when Geddes inaugurated a series of regular discussions between top businessmen and politicians to discuss broad policy issues at least eight times a year. Inchcape joined Balfour, Sir Guy Granet, Sir Robert Horne and Lord Inverforth on several occasions.

Yet he moved from active support of Lloyd George, from wanting him as Prime Minister in 1922, to regarding him as wrecking the Liberal Party by 1926. His attitudes to Baldwin and Ramsay MacDonald changed in the opposite direction. Inchcape considered the former to be mediocre, but later commended Baldwin's financial policies to reduce the national debt and support retrenchment.

When he first met Ramsay MacDonald, Inchcape saw him as a wild man, out to nationalise everything in sight. In January 1924, he wrote with disbelief that 'here we are with a Socialist Government ... we must do our best to keep them from wrecking the country and the Empire'. But only six months later, on closer acquaintance, he saw MacDonald as surprisingly reasonable, looking on him as a modern-day Whig. 'If we could only get two parties in the country, Whigs and Tories as in the old days, what a blessing it would be!' MacDonald, like many other politicians, was favoured with special treatment on P&O steamers, but he never became a close friend. Instead, Inchcape looked to Asquith, Reading and Kilbracken as those he could really trust; they truly appreciated his dedication to public office and shared his outlook. The rising generation of politicians, such as MacDonald, Snowden and Churchill, tolerated Inchcape when they needed his support and his tireless committee work, but saw him as more of a relic from a bygone age than a force for the future. Inchcape, on the other hand, saw them as doing nothing to restore his faith in Britain for the decades to come.

As the First World War coloured Inchcape's attitude to home affairs it inevitably underlay his outlook overseas, especially in relation to India. He could not cope with the increasingly nationalist and anti-British attitudes current in India, and was frustrated by Britain's decreasing ability to do anything about the situation. If only he had been viceroy, he would never have 'kowtowed' to Gandhi the way that Irwin did. Inchcape was accused by prominent nationalist Indian politicians of denying India the right to free choice and of paying lip service to the idea of Dominion status, when proposals were announced to debar British subjects from doing business in India. But Inchcape's work on Indian railways and retrenchment attracted great praise in the subcontinent and at home, where traders in Indian goods saw him as a champion.

The only official position overseas which Inchcape had ever wanted was the viceroyalty. It never came his way again, but in 1921 he had another, rather bizarre, opportunity to make a greater impact abroad: he was offered the throne of Albania, when that country finally threw off the Turkish yoke. With several palaces, a cabinet of ministers and complete economic and political power over an underdeveloped Muslim country, he was asked to accept responsibility for building railways, schools and public buildings and exploiting the country's natural riches. But Inchcape dismissed it in a sentence: 'It is a great compliment to be offered the Crown of Albania but it is not in my line!'.

With such growing disillusionment in his business and public life, Inchcape retreated more and more into his private home and family circle, which had always been a source of great comfort and, until the death of his favourite and most talented daughter Elsie, a source of great joy.

He particularly relished life as a Laird of Glenapp and its 13,000-acre estate Castle. He was much fonder of this than any of his other residences, especially because of the grouse and pheasant shooting. Glenapp was favoured over his native Arbroath because Inchcape was still concerned about local gossip relating to Christina Mackay and his illegitimate antecedents. A now-retired estate worker spoke of his friendliness and caring attitude, and of his large and charming family and circle of friends, particularly Elsie. Yet the family were demanding employers, expecting minute attention to detail and very high standards: for instance, the Earl and Countess did not wish to see any branches or leaves on the roads when they enjoyed their daily drive round Glenapp and its environs. When in residence, helped by a staff of 17, they entertained several leading Scottish and Indian families.

Few staff complained, as Inchcape paid more than surrounding estates: £2 10*s* a week in 1924 for the lodgekeeper was five shillings more than at a nearby estate, and all were provided with a rent-free house, free coal, potatoes, milk and the products of the shooting and fishing expeditions in which Inchcape and his guests delighted. The Inchcapes treated servants and employees well; in the context of the time, it would be unfair to criticise him for not allowing them greater equality. For instance, it was acceptable in the late 1920s for his Lordship to travel by first-class sleeper whilst his butler went third class.

The Inchcapes were popular local hosts, but their prosperity was occasionally sneered at by resentful members of older and more distinguished Scottish families who had fallen on hard times; not that this stopped such critics from hoping to share the largesse. Perhaps those with more grounds for complaint were the Kennedys, on the nearby estate of Finnarts who, finding themselves in financial difficulties, decided to cut their losses and emigrate to Australia. They hung out for a good price for years but eventually accepted the market rate for their property from Inchcape. Adjoining landowners were horrified when Inchcape then promptly demolished Finnarts House, well known in the locality as of great architectural merit, and one of the oldest inhabited houses in Ayrshire. But it was badly affected by dry rot and too costly to preserve.

The great Christmas parties which were provided for all in the heyday of the estate were fondly remembered. Inchcape was not religiously devout, often critical of the Church's influence in society and politics. He openly opposed the restrictions of the Scottish sabbath, and would not conform: but he was careful to go fishing out of sight of the road on Sundays, where he would sit for hours smoking very strong Egyptian cigarettes, which he enjoyed in great number with no ill effects. But life at Glenapp was by no means all leisure; he never stopped working. Every day before breakfast, whatever was happening, he received a huge mailbag from London and overseas, and expected his secretaries to work as hard as he did.

Inchcape's yacht the *Rover* – of over 700 tons, nearly 300 feet long and over 40 feet wide, with a crew of more than thirty and accommodation for fourteen guests – was used mainly for humble mackerel fishing when not carrying the Earl and his family and friends – often other local landowners – around the Mediterranean. It was especially large to reduce the effects of seasickness, from which the Countess suffered. Even royalty were entertained on board.

But everything changed with Elsie's death in her pioneering transatlantic air bid. The Countess's health deteriorated so as to render her a constant invalid, needing the daily attendance of doctors, and Inchcape then spent as much time with her as possible, taking comfort from the tranquil surroundings. His other children did not mean so much to him as Elsie had done. Kenneth, the Second Earl, served his time for five years before the war in the Mackinnon/Inchcape businesses, including learning the ropes with Mackinnon Mackenzie in Calcutta and ultimately rose to become deputy chairman of the P&O. He was a man of great modesty who was never able to get out of the shadow of his father. His death as early as 1939 was seen as tragic in the family, the P&O and the firms, especially Gray Dawes. He had not wanted to join the Firms, but would otherwise have been cut out of his father's will.

Inchcape was more as ease with the younger generation. His great nephew, Sir Hugh Mackay Tallack, later deputy chairman of Inchcape PLC, remembers a meal at the Negresco Hotel in Nice, when Inchcape was visiting Monte Carlo in the *Rover*. The fourteen-year-old was asked by his illustrious great-uncle to help check the bill; on discovering that, not uncharacteristically, the millionaire shipping magnate had been overcharged, he was warned to take this as a lesson for the future. A grandson, the Hon. Alan Mackay, saw him as charming, sympathetic and caring, especially to young, old and poor people.

Those who knew Inchcape's home life – his estate workers and family – saw a completely different man from those who came into contact with him at work. The insight provided by Wilfrid Mizen at the P&O (already referred to in Chapters Six and Seven) gives a picture of a tough and ruthless businessman, intolerant of weaker subordinates, never indulging in small talk, who was permanently poker-faced, apparently without humour but who never shouted and never lost his temper. He was highly respected as the leader of the shipping industry, constantly receiving calls from prominent ship-owners. His authority at AGMs and handling of shareholders was unchallengeable.

Sir Andrew Crichton, a veteran of Gray Dawes, Mackinnon Mackenzie and the P&O, added that he was regarded with great awe in the office as a lofty personage from another world. Lord Simon, the son of Inchcape's old friend Sir John Simon, who was provided with an attractive position in Mackinnon Mackenzie, spoke of the enormous prestige of this firm in India, especially with Binny's, and the status which Inchcape enjoyed as a result. There was no strictly structured relationship between the P&O and the Mackinnon/Inchcape group, but Inchcape closely supervised every aspect of both activities: too closely for the likes of Shaw and Sir Philip Browne, a leading partner at Mackinnon Mackenzie in Calcutta at this time.

Yet Inchcape occasionally wished he could enjoy the anonymity of life among the junior ranks of his employees. Sachin Chaudhury, who became India's Finance Minister in the mid-1960s, met Inchcape on board the P&O *Dongola* on her return to the breakers' yard in 1921. The young law student, on his way to Cambridge, was one of the few passengers who liked watching the sea and never got seasick: another was a man of seventy who looked more like sixty, apparently a member of the crew on account of his great knowledge of seamanship, the company and world trade, although his nautical attire gave no indication of rank. It was only when, some weeks later, the young man was specially invited to dine with the captain that he realised who his daily companion really was. Inchcape later made several efforts to keep in touch. He could be very human, although the majority of his employees would never appreciate this.

Individual success in business and society is very often measured in personal wealth. Just how much money did Inchcape make? It is almost impossible to judge his overall income due to the variety of its sources, but it must have been very large. Sir Andrew Crichton recalled that the arrival of bullion from P&O ships to the company vault was referred to, only half-jokingly, as the delivery of Lord Inchcape's salary as chairman. Contemporary newspapers estimated at least £600,000. In 1914 Inchcape had received £5,000 p.a. salary as Managing Director and two and a half per cent commission on the net earnings of the P&O, including indemnification against income tax. This totalled £306,103 for the war years. His earnings from the P&O were by no means as large as they could have been, since he decided to forsake his commission entirely to help the company in the mid-1920s. He could have earned a total of £786,785, but collected just over half of this. His earnings from his partnerships are totally unquantifiable but were probably more.

Yet he left comparatively little in terms of real cash. His total estate, severely undermined to a quarter of its original worth by inflation and the decline of the pound, was valued at only £2,124,707, of which £1,027,447 was paid in death duties. This was, of course, additional to the sums already given away to the Exchequer, such as Elsie's bequest. Much of it was bequeathed to staff: every estate worker at Glenapp was given a year's wages; several P&O and BI captains received a thousand pounds each; all officers on the active list received between £100 and £50; and staff of the agency firms in Britain and overseas received a month's salary. He left Glenapp Castle, his London residence in Seamore Place, his yacht *Rover*, and generous sums to his family.

But these are small amounts indeed compared with the estate of fellow shipowner Sir John Ellerman, who left £36,685,000 on his death in 1933: nearly three times the estate of Edward Guinness, Lord Iveagh, and much more than the Rothschilds or the Wills' or Coates'. Inchcape undoubtedly handled enormous sums in the course of his life, and could easily have concentrated on building up a huge family fortune. Instead, he put all his wealth, and efforts, into the two institutions which dominated his life and about which he cared most: the P&O and Mackinnon/Inchcape groups and the British Government.

Appendix 1

P&O 'net results' compared with profit calculated by Deloitte's by taking into account depreciation at five per cent on cost, and by excluding special credits and dividends and bonuses from subsidiaries, Deloitte's presented the real picture of the P&O in the 1920s:

Year	'Net Result'	Carried over	Dividends Pref.	Dividends Def.	Deloitte's adjusted
	£	£	%	%	£
1922	696,600	101,700	5	12	125,506
1923	1,013,200	101,800	5	12	1,017,244
1924	1,346,900	101,000	5	12	137,003
1925	1,273,500	142,100	5	10	345,141
1926	1,196,000	133,000	5	10	-306,237 (loss)
1927	1,200,000	118,000	5	10	513,591
1928	1,200,000	121,000	5	12	371,437
1929	1,200,000	120,000	5	12	-105,847 (loss)
1930	1,165,000	115,000	5	10	916,730
1931	947,800	115,000	5	6	-830,817 (loss)
Totals	£11,309,971				£2,183,751

Source: National Maritime Museum, P&O papers, See Note on sources (p.000).

Appendix 2

Inchcape's business interests: major holdings and positions held by 1929

Director
    Bakhtiari Oil Co. Ltd (appt. by HM Gov)
    N. Persian Oils Ltd (appt. by HM Govt)
    D'Arcy Exploration Co. Ltd
    First Exploration Co. Ltd
    Scottish Oils Ltd
    Tanker Insurance Ltd
    Anglo-Persian Oil Co. Ltd (appt. by HM Govt)
    Anderson Green & Co. Ltd
    Atlas Assurance Co. Ltd
    Burns Philip & Co. Ltd
    Ceylon Steamship Co. Ltd
    Cyprus Asbestos Co. Ltd
    Doodputtee Tea Co. Ltd
    Eastern Extension, Australasian & China Telegraph Co. Ltd
    Eastern Telegraph Co. Ltd
    Euphrates & Tigris Steam Navg. Co. Ltd
    Fishguard & Rosslare Rlys & Harbour Co.
    GWR Co.
    Lloyds & Nat. Prov. Foreign Bank Ltd
    Nat. Pro. Bank Ltd
    Rivers Steam Navg. Co. Ltd
    Royal Bank of Scotland (extraordinary director)
    Salonah Tea Co. Ltd
    Steamship-owners' Coal Assoc. Ltd

Vice-President Suez Canal Co.

Member of Council of Corporation of Foreign Bondholders

Senior partner
    Mackinnon, Mackenzie & Co.
    Macdonald Hamilton & Co.
    Macneill & Co. of Calcutta
    Gray Dawes & Co.
    J.B. Barry & Sons
    Duncan Macneill & Co.

Chairman
    Australasian USN Co. Ltd (& managing director)
    Binny & Co. Ltd
    British ISN Co. (& managing director)
    Bulloch Bros & Co. Ltd
    Central Queensland Meat Export Co. Ltd
    Ceylon Wharfgea Co. Ltd
    E. & Australian Steamship Co. Ltd
    Eastern Coal Co. Ltd
    English Coaling Co. Ltd
    Middle East Development Corporation Ltd
    P&O Banking Corporation Ltd
    Walker Bros (London) Ltd
    P&O SN Co. (& joint managing director)

A note on sources

Only a brief indication of principal sources is given here. Detailed information is available from the archivists and catalogues of the institutions listed.

Inchcape family papers

Miscellaneous letters, press cuttings, photographs, diaries and material relating to properties: privately kept by the Third Earl of Inchcape, and not accessible to the public

Archives of Inchcape PLC

Letters of Sir William Mackinnon and references to the AUSN, BI, Assam Company, Binny's, etc, as listed in *TWO CENTURIES OF OVERSEAS TRADING*. Much material has been passed to the Guildhall Library, Aldermanbury, London. Notebooks and letterbooks of Mackinnon Mackenzie and Gray Dawes, *c.* 1850s–1920s, and unpublished manuscript history of Mackinnon Mackenzie by George Blake, *c.* 1958, passed to the Third Earl of Inchcape's private collection

National Maritime Museum
Romney Road, Greenwich, London.

P&O, BI and associated papers: correspondence, minutes, voyage results, acquisitions, reports and accounts, handbooks, war loss reports, agreements with shipbuilders. Listed in museum catalogue, and see Knight, R.J.B., *Guide to the Manuscripts in the National Maritime Museum,* London, 1980.

Guildhall Library and Museum

Lloyd's Collection, including Lloyd's List, Lloyd's Weekly Shipping Index and Lloyd's Captains' Register.

India Office Library and Records
197 Blackfriars Road, London.

Census information and guides and directories of Calcutta and Bombay
Chamber of Commerce reports, Port Trust reports, administration reports,
Viceroy's Legislative Council proceedings, papers of Lansdowne and
Reading, reports of Indian Retrenchment Committee. See notes of related
archives in India by Martin Moir in the newsletter of the IOL, No. 10, May
1977.

Public Record Office
Ruskin Avenue, Kew, Richmond, Surrey.

Foreign Office, Colonial Office, Home Office, Treasury, Cabinet, Board of
Trade, Ministry of Shipping and other working papers in connection with
Inchcape's committee work.

British Library
Great Russell Street, London.

Secondary source material and Parliamentary Papers, especially on the
Indian Currency Committee (PP LXV 1893–4); dissemination of
commercial information (PP XXXIII 1898); constitution of the Consular
Service (PP LXXVIII 1902 and LV 1903); new Chinese customs tariff (PP
XCVII 1902); Board of Trade and Local Government Board (PP LV 1903
and LXXVIII 1904); Railway Rates (PP LV 1906); Government factories
and workshops (PP X 1907); Indian railways (PP LXXV 1908); war risks
of shipping (PP LX 1908 and LVIII 1908); insurance of British shipping in
time of war (PP LXX 1914); production of food in England & Wales (PP
V 1914–16); banking amalgamations (PP VI 1918); Committee on
Currency and Foreign Exchange after the war (PP VII 1918); gold
production (PP XXII 1919); Advisory Committee on Civil Aviation (PP X
1919); British Cellulose Company (PP XI 1919); Ministry of Munitions,
alleged destruction of documents (PP XV 1921); national expenditure (PP
IX 1922); Imperial Shipping Committee (PP XII 1923).

British Library
Newspaper Library, Colindale Avenue, London.

Inchcape's letters to *The Times, The Spectator*, etc and obituary notices;
some Indian newspapers, *The Times of India* and *Capital*.

House of Lords Record Office
Westminster, London.

Papers of Lloyd George, Asquith and Bonar Law.

Baring Bros. Archives
8 Bishopsgate, London

Letters from Alexander Shaw to the Governor.

Arbroath Museum
Signal Tower, Arboath, Angus.

Contemporary writings, artefacts and illustrations of life in Arbroath, and in Arbroath Public Library, yearbooks, guides, back issues of the *Arbroath Guide* and the *Arbroath Herald*.

Murray, Beith & Murray
Solicitors, Castle Street, Edinburgh.

Correspondence between Mackay and his guardian, Mackay's marriage trust and contract 1888, his final will of 1932.

University of Glasgow Archives
Adam Smith Building, University of Glasgow.

Records of Clyde shipbuilders, including Stephen, Denny, Barclay Curle, John Brown, Russell/Lithgow.

National Archives of India
Janpath, New Delhi.

'B' proceedings – Government records not available at India Office Library, on the BI and the opium trade, opening of the Karun, Mackay in China, the Ottoman Company, East Africa mail service, etc.

Nehru Memorial Museum and Library
Teen Murti House, New Delhi.

Records transferred from Bombay Chamber of Commerce, and large collection of Indian newspapers on microfilm.

Bengal Chamber of Commerce
Royal Exchange, 6 Netaji Subhas Road, Calcutta.

Minutes of Chamber proceedings from 1854 and reports of affiliated organisations. See the Chamber's centenary supplement, February 1953.

National Library
Belvedere, Calcutta.

Secondary sources and newspapers.

Bengal Club
1 Russell Street, Calcutta.

Club minute books and secondary sources.

West Bengal State Archives
Historical Section, 6 Bhowani Dutta Lane, Calcutta.

Records of Marine Branch, Finance Department, Port Trust Department,
Customs and Excise, mail contracts.

British Deputy High Commission
Calcutta.

Papers of the European and Anglo-Indian Defence Association.

University of Western Australia Archives
Nedlands, Western Australia.

Erulkar Collection of material relating to shipping and commerce of British
India, especially competition between the BI and Scindia line and the
Indian Coastal Reservation Bill, with statistics of companies, 1870s–1930s.

University of Melbourne Archives
Parkville, Victoria.

Records of the AUSN and competing Australian coastal shipping
companies.

Mitchell Library
Sydney, NSW 2000.

Letters between Australian and London partners of AUSN, BI&QA and
Macdonald Hamilton, 1900–1930s.

Miscellaneous

Registers of Provincial Museum of Nova Scotia, 1810s–1870s.
Park Street Cemetery Records, Calcutta.
BBC radio transcript, 'The shipwreck of the Juno', Radio 3, 14 March
1973.
Paterson H. 'The Ambrose, Paterson and Highlands Families', unpublished
genealogical study, *c.* 1976.
Elgin Academy Former Pupils Association and magazine *The Academical.*
Speech by Lord Inchcape, 23 June 1919, Imperial Commercial Association,
'The dangers of nationalisation'.

Guide to further reading

Allen C., *Plain Tales from the Raj,* London, 1975.

Armstrong, J. and Jones, S., *Business Documents: Their Origins, Sources and Uses in Historical Research,* London 1987.

Binny & Co. Ltd, *The House of Binny,* London, 1969.

Blake G., *BI Centenary,* London, 1956.

Gellatly's, 1862–1962, London, 1962.

Bolitho, H., *James Lyle Mackay: First Earl of Inchcape,* London, 1936.

Branson N., *Britain in the 1920s,* London, 1975.

Brock, M. and E., *H. H. Asquith: Letters to Venetia Stanley,* Oxford, 1982.

Broeze, F., 'Underdevelopment and dependency: Maritime India during the Raj', *Modern Asian Studies* Vol. 18, 3, 1984.

Buckley, K., and Klugman K., *The History of Burns Philip: The Australian Company in the South Pacific,* Sydney, 1981.

'*The Australian Presence in the Pacific': Burns Philip, 1914–1946,* Sydney, 1983.

Cable, B., *A Hundrd Year History of the P&O,* London, 1937.

Cage, B., *The Scots Abroad: Labour, Capital and Enterprise,* London, 1985.

Cain, P.J., *Economic Foundations of British Overseas Trade, 1815–1914,* London, 1980.

Charlesworth, N., *British Rule and the Indian Economy, 1800–1914* London, 1982.

Cross, C., *Philip Snowden,* London, 1966.

DICTIONARY OF BUSINESS BIOGRAPHY, London, completed 1987.

DICTIONARY OF SCOTTISH BUSINESS BIOGRAPHY, Glasgow, completed 1988.

Farnie, D.A., *The English Cotton Industry and the World Market, 1815–1896,* Oxford, 1979.

Foreman-Peck, J., 'Some measures of foreign investment and exploitation for Britain and India before 1914', paper presented to the Economic History Society Conference, Cheltenham, 1986.

Green E. and Moss, M. *A Business of National Importance: The Royal Mail Shipping Group, 1902–1937,* London, 1982.

Griffiths, P.J., *A History of the Inchcape Group,* London, 1977.

A History of the Joint Steamer Companies, London, 1978.

Harcourt, F., 'The P&O Company: flagships of imperialism', in S. Palmer and G. Williams (eds), *Charted and Uncharted Waters: Proceedings of a Conference on the Study of Maritime History,* London 1982.

Hyde, H., *Lord Reading: The Life of Rufus Isaacs,* London. 1963.

Howarth D. and S., *The Story of P&O,* London, 1986.

Inchcape Lord, 'Shipowners and Shipbuilders', *Brasseys Naval Annual,* London 1923.

Jones, S., 'The decline of British maritime enterprise in Australia: the example of the AUSN Co., 1887–1961', *BUSINESS HISTORY,* Vol. 27, 1985.

'British India steamers and the trade of the Persian Gulf, 1862–1914', *The Great Circle, The Journal of the Australian Association for Maritime History,* Vol. 7, 1985.

Two Centuries of Overseas Trading: The Origins and Growth of the Inchcape Group, London, 1986.

'British mercantile enterprise overseas in the nineteenth century: the example of James Lyle Mackay, first Earl of Inchcape', in Stephen Fisher (ed.) *Studies in British Privateering, Trading, Enterprise and Seamen's Welfare, 1775–1900,* Exeter, 1987.

Kipling, R., *Departmental Ditties,* London, 1898.

Kirkaldy, A. W., *British Shipping,* London, 1914.

Maber, J., *North Star to Southern Cross: The Story of the Australasian Seaways,* Prescot, 1967.

McCormick, R., *The Mark of Merlin: A Critical Study of David Lloyd George,* London, 1963.

McKellar, N. L., *From Derby Round to Burketown: The AUSN Story,* Queensland, 1977.

Morgan, K. O., *Concensus And Disunity: The Lloyd George Coalition Government, 1918–1922,* Oxford, 1979.

Muir, A. and Davies. M., *A Victorian Shipowner: Cayzer,* London, 1978.

Munro, J., 'Clydeside, the Indian Ocean and the City: the Mackinnon investment group, 1847–1893', unpublished paper presented to the 'City and Empire' seminar at the Institute of Commonwealth Studies, October 1985.

'Scottish business imperialism: Sir William Mackinnon and the development of trade and shipping in the Indian Ocean', ESRC Report BOO/23/0049.

Pemberton, B. *Australian Costal Shipping,* Melbourne, 1979.

Taylor, A.J.P., *English History, 1914–1915,* Harmondsworth, 1962

Index

Notes

1. Most references are to the life and activities of James Lyle Mackay, and to shipping and trade, unless otherwise stated.
2. Most sub-entries are arranged in chronological order.
3. The following abbreviations are used: Co. = Company; M = James Lyle Mackay.

Aberdeen, William 6
Abhona (ship) 66
Accounts Liquidation Committee 157
Acts of Parliament *see* legislation
Adamson, Sir William 91
Addis, Sir Charles 162, 165
Addison, Christopher 173
Adelaide Chronicle 187
Adelaide Co. 58
Agriculture & Fisheries, Board of 115–17
Agriculture, Board of 81–2
Aircraft Transport and Travel Co. 176
Albania, M offered throne of 197
Alexander, W. P. 16, 17, 19, 25
Allahabad Bank 131
Allen, F. C. 105
Ambrose, Margaret, 6, 8
American Oceanic Steamship Co. 66
Anchor Line 51, 160
Anderson, Sir Alan 182
Anderson, Arthur 67, 123

Anderson & Green (company) 111, 124
Anglo-Persian Oil Co. 100, 108, 148, 153, 181, 203
Apcar Line 54, 68
Arbuthnot & Co. 60
Argyll, Duke of 69
Armstrong (Sir W.) & Co. 38
Asia *see* China; Far East; India; Japan
Asia (ship) 6–7, 8
Asiatic Co. 51, 54
Asquith, H. H. 86, 139, 168, 196
Assam 25, 26, 61–2
Assam Co. 26
Assam Railways and Trading Co. 26
Australasian United Steam Navigation Co. Ltd (AUSN) 25–6, 204
    1894–1914 56–60, 62–7
    1914–1918 93, 96, 102, 103, 119
    1918–1932 152, 189
Australia 6, 28, 191
    1894–1914 49, 50, 56–67 *passim*

1914–1918 92, 96, 97, 100, 102, 103, 111, 119
1918–1932 126, 129–32, 135–6, 138, 140–3, 146–7, 152, 159–60, 174, 182, 187, 189
aviation 130, 155, 156–7, 174–7
Aviation Advisory Commitee 156, 174–7

Baldwin, Stanley 173, 196
Balfour, Lord 196
Ballarat (ship) 110, 190
Ballin (of Hamburg Amerika) 118
Bank Act 1844 161
banks 61
  British 155, 161–3, 165–7, 168–9
  collapses 20, 24, 42
  see also P & O Banking
Barbara (ship) 3, 6
Barbour, Sir David 42
Barclay Curle (company) 63, 100, 112
Baring Brothers 24, 61
Barnes (of AUSN) 58
Bayer (company) 157
Beauchamp, Lord 195
Begg Dunlop (company) 16
Bell, Sir Hugh 194
Bell, Sir John 143
Bell, William 23
Bell (Messrs William) & Co. 5, 23
Bengal Central Railways 26
Bengal Chamber of Commerce 11, 17–18, 31, 33–40, 42, 46, 193
BI & QA *see* British India & Queensland Agency
BI *see* British India Steam Navigation Co.
Binny & Co. 26, 28, 60–1, 113, 151, 190, 204
Birla family 192
Black Ball Line 6
Bland (of AUSN) 57–8, 59
Blue Anchor Line, 68, 97
Board of Agriculture 81–2, 115–17
Board of Trade 159, 172, 182
  Commercial Information Committee 73–5, 193

Bolitho, H. 23
Bombay 188, 189, 192
  1874–1894 20–5, 31–3, 40, 47
  1894–1914 51, 52
  1914–1918 92, 100, 106
  1918–1932 131, 135, 138–9, 143–4, 146, 153, 181
Bombay Chamber of Commerce 31, 32–3, 40, 47, 192
Bombay Chronicle 187, 188
Bombay and Persia Steam Navigation Co. 55, 135
Bombay Steam Navigation Co. 21
Bonar Law, Andrew 75, 76, 106, 117, 134, 161, 165, 168
Booth, Alfred 114
Bradbury, Sir John 117
Branch Line 126
Brenier-Estrine, M. 131
Britain, M in
  1874–1894 9, 31, 43, 48
  1894–1914 49–52, 59–72, 73–7, 80–8
  1914–1918 89–120
  1918–1932 121–85 *passim*, 188, 196–9
Britannia (ship) 59
British Cellulose Co. 156, 194
British India & Queensland Agency 56, 57, 60
British India Steam Navigation Co. 9, 204
  1874–1894 12–13, 18, 20–3, 26–8, 32, 35, 38–40, 46
  1894–1914 50, 52–6, 59–67, 74, 76, 84–5, 87
  merger with P & O 49, 67–72, 90, 188
  1914–1918 89–113 *passim*, 119
  1918–1932 122, 125, 130, 133–9, 143–7, 151–3, 188–91, 201
Broodbank (of Port of London) 161
Browne, Sir Philip 200
Buckingham and Carnatic Co. Ltd 151
Buick (car manufacturer) 5
Burns, James 59
Burns Philp (company) 58

business life of M
  in India (1874–1894) 11–30
  as shipowner and empire builder
    (1894–1914) 49–72
  during First World War (1914–
    1918) 89–120
  postwar (1918–1932) 121–54
Byron, Lord 3

Calcutta
  1874–1894 10, 11–20, 31, 33, 37–
    8, 46–7
  1894–1914 50–1, 52, 54
  1914–1918 92, 94, 99
  1918–1932 131, 139, 146, 152–3,
    181
Calcutta and Burmah Steam
    Navigation Co. (*later* BI) 13
Calcutta Chamber of Commerce
    192
Calcutta Port Trust 31, 37–8, 46
Calcutta Royal Exchange 46
Cammell Laird (company) 100
Canada 2–3, 4, 5, 66, 96, 102, 174
Canadian Northern Railway 66
Canadian Pacific 114, 160
Canadian-Australian Line 96, 102
Capital (newspaper) 38–9, 42, 44, 45
Cathay (ship) 142
Catto, Sir Thomas 178
Chalmers, James 5
Chang Chi-tang 78–9
Chapel family 5
character *see under* Mackay, James
    Lyle
Chartered Bank of India, Australia
    & China 132
Chaudbury, Sachin 200
Chepstow Shipbuilding Co. 111
children of M *see* Mackay: Elsie,
    Margaret, *and* Kenneth
Chilkana (ship) 90
China 17, 21, 131, 142–3, 146–7,
    153
  M visits 77–80, 193
Chingstee Toung 79
Chiozza Money, Sir Leo 130
'Chitty' 55

Churchill, Winston 95, 119, 171,
    174, 176
City of Glasgow Bank 14, 20
City Line 51
Clan Line 97, 113, 160
Clansman (ship) 7
climate of India 29–30
coal mining 48
Cohen, Laming & Hoare
    (company) 123
Commonwealth and Dominion
    Line 97, 160
Commonwealth and Government
    Line 182
Companies Act 149
compensation for losses of ships in
    wartime 109–10, 120, 135
conference system 150
Consular Service enquiry, M on
    75–6
Contracts, Committee on 156
Cook (Thomas) & Sons 34, 51
Corsar, D. 5
Cory (William) (company) 152
Council of India 76–7
Cox, Sir Percy 133
Crichton, Sir Andrew 199–200
Cunard, Samuel & Edward 3
Cunard Line 114, 132, 160, 182
Cunliffe Lord and Committee on
    Currency & Foreign
    Exchanges 100, 161–4
currency
  British 100, 155, 161–5, 195
  Indian 18, 31, 41–6, 47–8, 73,
    161, 177–8, 192
Currency and Bank Notes Act 1914
    162
Currie, Captain Archibald 54, 59
Currie, Donald 9
Currie, Rivers 30
Currie, William 19, 25, 30, 135
Currie Line 59, 68, 137, 143
Curwen, Mr 23
Cutty Sark (ship) 9

Daily Herald 187
Daily Mail 129, 187

Daily Mirror 187, 188
Daily Telegraph 163
Dalhousie family 5
Dalhousie Institute 46
Dawes, Edwyn Sandys 12, 13, 60,
    96
death
    of M 148–9, 186
    see also disease and death
Defence, Imperial Committee on
    81, 85–6
Defence, Ministry of 170
Defence of the Realm Act 114
Deloitte, Plender & Griffiths
    (company) 121–2, 124–7,
    140, 143, 145, 148, 153, 202
Denny, Peter 102
Denny (company) 25, 63, 133
depreciation 122, 125, 127, 139, 145,
    147–8
    see also losses
Deutsche Bank 118
Devanka (ship) 181
disease and death 148–9
    1874–1894 12, 13, 29–30
    epidemics 33, 37
    1814–1914 79–80
Disraeli, B. 37
Dongola (ship) 200
DORA (Defence of the Realm Act)
    114
Dufferin, Frederick, Lord 73
Dunbar, Duncan 9

earnings *see* profits
East Africa
    1874–1894 19, 28, 39, 50
    1894–1914 76–7, 87
    1918–1932 129, 133
East India Co. 4, 80, 96
East Indian Railways 93
Eastern & Australian Line 131
Eastern & Australian Steamship
    Co. 152, 204
Eastern Shipping Co. 54
Eastern Traders Ltd 124
Education, Board of 172
Egypt 39, 148, 153, 174, 175–6

Egyptian Water Co. 153
El Dorado (ship) 6
Ellenga (ship) 66
Ellerman, Sir John 98, 114, 201
Elliot (ship) 7
Ellora (ship) 66
Enden (ship) 90
England *see* Britain
Erinpura (ship) 133
Euphrates & Tigris Steam
    Navigation Co. 153, 203
    see also Tigris
European and Anglo-Indian
    Defence Association 35
Exchequer and Audit 157
expenditure cuts *see* Geddes
Export Control Act 169

Factory Acts (India) 33, 40, 46, 192
Fairplay (journal) 50, 103, 186–7
famine 41
Far East
    1874–1894 17, 21, 45
    1894–1914 49, 50, 52, 61
    1914–1918 92, 102, 104–5, 113,
        119
    1918–1932 121–2, 126, 131–2,
        142, 146–7, 153, 159
    see also China; Japan
Faringdon, Lord 169–70
Federal Line
    1914–1918 96–7, 98, 109, 111, 119
    1918–1932 123, 125, 147
Finlay (James) (company) 113
Finlay Muir & Co. 16, 18, 62
Fisher, H. A. L. 172–3
Flying Cloud (ship) 4
Flying Horse Line 5
food: home production in wartime
    115–17
Foreman-Peck, J. 28
France 34, 45, 50, 76, 78, 130, 92
Fraser (Douglas) & Sons 5
Free Trade (joke ship) 139
Freshfields (company) 69, 71
Furness Withy (company) 132

Gandhi 188, 197

Geddes, Sir Eric and Axe 112, 114, 155, 169–74, 178–9, 184, 193, 195–6
Gellatly, Edward 9
Gellatly, Hankey, Sewell & Co. 9, 12
General Council for British Shipping 182, 190, 193
General Steam Navigation Co. 125, 132
Germany 194, 45, 50, 53
  1894–1914 73, 76, 78, 85, 87
  1918–1932 158–9, 159–60
  see also War, First World
Glenapp, laird of, M as 197–8
Glover, Sir Ernest 182
Glover Bros. 105
Godley (Under-Secretary) 86
Golconda (ship) 109
gold
  sale and production 162–5, 195
  standard 41–6, 47, 163, 195
Gold Producers' Committee 164, 195
government regulation, M's attitude to *see* public life
Government Standard Ships policy 133
Granet, Sir Guy 169–70, 196
Gray, Archibald 12, 60
Gray, William 110, 133
Gray Dawes (company)
  1874–1894 12, 19, 21
  1894–1914 49, 53, 60
  1914–1918 97, 104, 112
  1918–1932 122, 132, 139, 151–3, 190, 199, 204
Gray Mackenzie & Co. 18
Gray Paul & C. 18, 53
Gray's of Hartlepool 64, 100, 133
Great Northern Railway 82
Great Western Railway 119, 144, 203
Greece 150, 160
Green (R. H.) (company) 110
Grey, Sir Edward 55, 85
Guinness, Edward 201
Gwinner (of Deutsche Bank) 118

Hain, Sir Edward 104
Hain Steamship Co.
  1914–1918 101, 103–4, 105, 110
  1918–1932 123, 124, 139, 147, 150, 152, 190
Hakki Pasha 85
Hall, James McAlister 14, 28, 30, 50, 92
Hamburg Amerika Line 118
Hamilton, David 57, 59, 60
Hamilton, Lord George 61
Hamilton (Secretary of State) 73, 78
Hansa Co. 118
Harland & Wolff (company) 100, 108
Harlington (ship) 90
Hawthorn Leslie (R. & W.) (company) 129
Henniken (of Norddeutscher) 118
Herschell, Lord and Committee on Indian currency 31, 43, 48
'Higgins, Aunt' 6, 8
Hill, Sir Norman 133
Holden, Edward 165
Holt, P. D. 182
Holt, Richard 114
Holt (Alfred) (company) 182
Hong Kong & Shanghai Banking Corporation 162
Hook, F. A. 107
Horne, Sir Robert 138, 172, 196
Howard Smiths (company) 58
Huddart, James 102
Huddart Parker (company) 58
Hughes (of New Zealand Shipping) 123

illness *see* disease
Imperial British East Africa Co. 39
Imperial Shipping Committee, M on 155, 182–3
Imperial War Conference 182
Inchcape, First Earl *see* Mackay, James Lyle
Inchcape, Second Earl *see* Mackay, Kenneth (son)

Inchcape, Third Earl 53, 154
Inchcape PLC 192, 199
   see also Mackinnon/Inchcape
income *see* profits
income tax
   Britain 99, 107, 109, 124, 152,
      167–8
   India 19, 33–6, 41, 45, 47–8, 137,
      178
   New Zealand 123
India 2, 3–4, 7, 9–10, 186, 188–9,
      190–2, 200
   1874–1894
      M's business life 11–30
      M's public life 31–48
   1894–1914 49–56, 60–1, 67, 70–7
      passim
   1914–1918 90, 92, 94, 95, 98–100,
      103, 106–7, 113, 119, 197
   1918–1932 121, 124–6, 129, 131–
      47 *passim*, 151–3, 155, 159–
      60, 171, 174–81
India (ship) 91
India Council in England 188
India General (company) 61
Indian Coastal Shipping Bill 145,
      147, 151
Indian Currency Commission 42–3,
      46
Indian Merchandise Marks Act 34
Indian Merchant Shipping Act 1880
      40
Indian Ocean 45, 48, 105, 113, 189
   1918–1932 121, 135, 138, 144
Indo-China Steam Navigation Co.
      92
Indus Flotilla Co. 21
industry
   infant, protection for 18, 41
   new, in Britain 155, 175–7
Institute of Bankers 161
insurance for shipping 81, 85–6,
      122–3, 142, 146
International Bulkhead Committee
      99
International Maritime Labour
      Conference 147
Inverforth, Lord 196

investment by Inchcape
   1874–1894 25–6, 27–8, 38, 47–8
   1894–1914 61, 66, 85
   1914–1918 90, 93, 99–101, 103,
      106, 110
   1918–1932 123, 125, 132, 154
   see also profits
investment by Britain in India, lack
      of 28, 43–4, 48
Irrawaddy Flotilla Co. 39
Irwin 197
Italy 50, 150
Iveagh, lord 201

Japan 45, 54–5, 191
   1918–1932 128, 131–3, 136, 153
Jardine Matheson (company) 92
Jardine Skinner (company) 16
Jones, Stephanie 12, 60
Journal of Commerce 129, 187
Journal des Débats 179
Juno (ship) 3–4, 7, 10

Kaiser-I-Hind (ship) 143
Karmala (ship) 143
Karoa (ship) 93
Kashigar (ship) 132
Kennedy family 198
Kersey, Martland 114
Keynes, J. M. 42
Khedivial Mail Co. 124, 138, 152,
      191
Kilbracken, Lord 71, 94, 110, 196
Kipling, Rudyard 29
Kitchener, Lord 93, 114
Kuiating Coal Concession 123
Kulukundis, Manual 160–1
Kurachee Line 23
Kylsant, Lord 149

Labour, Ministry of 161, 172, 184
labour unrest *see* strikes
languages, Indian 18, 24, 34, 189
Lansdowne, Henry, Lord (Viceroy
      of India) 2, 39, 40–1, 43, 73,
      80, 188
Law, Bonar *see* Bonar law
Law, Raga Doorga Churn 36

law *see* legislation
Lawrence, Sir Walter 68
legislation
  banking 161–2
  companies 149
  factory 33, 40, 46, 192
  India 33–4, 40, 46, 145, 147, 151
  shipping and navigation 40, 75,
    130, 145, 147, 151
  trade 34, 142, 169, 191
  wartime 114
Leresche (of AUSN) 58
Levuka (ship) 65
likin duty 77–80
Liverpool & London War Risks
  Insurance Co. 133
Liverpool Steamship Owners'
  Association 85
Lloyd George, David 83, 106, 119,
  156, 158, 182, 192, 194–6
Lloyd's 9, 85, 174
loans 123–4
Local Authority Housing Schemes
  170
London *see* Britain
London Chamber of Commerce
  164
London County & Westminster
  bank 166
Lorara (ship) 90
losses
  and illiquidity (1918–1932) 139–
    42, 146, 148, 202
  see also depreciation
  of ships in wartime 90, 91, 101,
    114, 130, 132
  compensation for 109–10, 120,
    135
Lusitania (ship) 94
Lyle, Alexander 2–3, 5, 10
Lyle, Deborah *see* Mackay,
  Deborah
Lyle, James 4, 6
Lynch, H. F. B. 84, 85
Lynch Bros. 153

Macdonald, B. W. 57, 59–60
Macdonald, Ramsay 180, 196

Macdonald Hamilton & Co. 60,
  151, 153, 204
McGowan, Sir Harry 156
McIllwraith McEachern 58
McIver Line 51
Mackay, Alan (grandson) 199
Mackay, Christina 4, 6, 197
Mackay, Deborah (mother of M,
  neé Lyle) 2, 5, 7, 8
Mackay, Donald, 4, 10
Mackay, Elsie (daughter of M) 142,
  184, 188, 197, 198
Mackay, Captain James (father of
  M) 3, 4–5, 6–7, 8
Mackay, James Lyle (Lord
  Inchcape)
  character 14–20 *passim*, 23–4, 31,
    193, 197–8, 199–200
  early life (1852–1874) 1–10
  becomes Inchcape 54, 86–7, 184
  death 148–9, 186
  see also business life; public life
  and also preliminary note to
    index
Mackay, Jamie (son of M) 30
Mackay, Jeannie (wife, *née* Jane
  Shanks)
  1874–1894 6, 23, 26, 29–33
  1894–1914 59, 78, 79, 80, 86
  1918–1932 153, 184, 186, 197, 199
Mackay, Kenneth (grandson of M)
  53, 154
Mackay, Kenneth (son of M) 53,
  54–5, 89, 135, 199
Mackay, Margaret (daughter of M)
  78, 79
Mackay, Captain William (d. 1804)
  3–4, 10
Mackay, Captain William
  Aberdeen (brother of M) 6, 7
Mackay & Co. 124, 138, 152
Mackenzie, George 21, 61
Mackenzie, Robert 2, 14
Mackenzie (of Canadian National
  Railway) 66
Mackenzie Lyall (company) 16
Mackinnon, Duncan 16, 25, 50, 53,
  57–8, 61, 108, 154

Mackinnon, John 26, 62
Mackinnon, Peter 14, 25
Mackinnon, Sir William 32, 47, 53, 60, 92
  appoints M 12
  founds Gray Dawes 12
  profits and investment, 14, 25, 27–8, 35
  and government subsidies 23
  and weights and measures system 39
  ill-health and death 30, 50, 67
Mackinnon, William (son of Duncan Mackinnon) 89–90, 108
Mackinnon Eastern 11
Mackinnon (William) & Co. 60
Mackinnon/Inchcape group 25, 62, 186, 188–9
  1914–1918 89, 92, 99, 101, 113
  1918–1932 121, 122, 151, 153, 190–1, 195, 199–201
  see also Inchcape PLC
Mackinnon Mackenzie (company) 186, 188–9, 190–2, 199–200, 204
  1874–1894 11–14, 16–22, 24–9, 33–4, 38–41, 47
  1894–1914 49–56, 60–1, 67, 70–7 *passim*
  1914–1918 90, 94, 98–9, 103, 106–7, 113
  1918–1932 121, 124–6, 133, 135, 137, 141, 151, 153, 181
Maclay, Sir Joseph 110, 158–61, 169, 173
MacMichael, Neil 25
Macneill, Duncan 26, 30, 62–3, 68–9, 135
Macneill & Barry (company) 113
Macneill & Co. 12, 16, 26, 61, 62, 204
Madras 23, 41
  1874–1894 23, 35, 41
  1894–1914 51, 60–1
  1918–1932 131
Madras Chamber of Commerce 35

Manchester Chamber of Commerce 44–5
Mantola (ship) 99
Mantua (ship) 138
marriage
  child 41
  market, India as 29
  see also wife
Mashobra (ship) 141
Mata Hari (ship) 92
Mataura (ship) 96
Matiana (ship) 133
Mercantile Shipping Co. Ltd 101, 105
Merchant Shipping Act (Britain) 75
Mesopotamia 154
  1894–1914 54, 66, 81, 84–5, 87
  1918–1932 180–2
Mesopotamia Persia Corporation 153
Mesopotamian River Fleet 180
Messageries Maritimes (company) 92
Middle East 45, 49, 92, 95
  1918–1932 126, 132–3, 139, 144, 155, 177
  see also Mesopotamia; Persian Gulf
Midland Bank 165
Mills, Sir James 59, 103
Milner, Viscount 115
Minto Viceroy 86
Mizen, Wilfrid 72, 113, 114, 148–9, 153, 199
Mogul Steamship Co. 10
Mombasa (ship) 109
Money Wigram (company) 96
Monson, Lady Anne 13
Montagu (Secretary of State) 171, 177
Montagu Norman (company) 168
Monteath, A. M. 50
Mookerjee, Sir Rajendra 178
Morley (Secretary of State) 73, 86–7
Muir, James 6, 7, 8, 9
Muir, Sir John 62
Muir (Finlay) & Co. 16, 18, 62

Munro, J. 1, 27
Murray, Sir Alexander Robertson
    178

Naldera (ship) 138, 141
Narkunda (ship) 138
National Bank of India 93
National Maritime Board 145
National Provincial Bank 62, 115,
    131, 163, 165–7, 190, 203
nationalisation 99, 114, 195
nationalism 137–8, 151–2
Navigation Act (Australia) 130
Nerbudda (ship) 22
Netherlands 128
Neuralia (ship) 63
Nevasa (ship) 63
New Oriental Bank 42
New Zealand *see* Union Co.; New
    Zealand Shipping
New Zealand Shipping Co. Ltd
    1914–1918 95–8, 100, 102, 103,
        109–11, 119
    1918–1932 123, 125, 140, 147, 191
News Chronicle 187
Newsham (of AUSN) 58
Nichol (of Mackinnon Mackenzie)
    30
Nichol and Co. 20
Nippon Yusen Kaisha (company) 55
Norddeutscher Lloyd (company)
    118
Northcote 58
Northern Dooars Tea Co. 25, 26
Norway 50, 150
Nott, Major General 13
Nourse, Captain James 105
Nourse Line 101, 104–5, 147, 150

Ocean and China Mutual 114
oil-burning ships 131, 136, 143, 146,
    150
opium trade 21, 34, 36, 46
Orient Steamship Co. 111–12, 140,
    146, 182
Oriental Banking Co. 26
Ottoman Co. 84
Overseas Trade, department of 172

Pachumba (ship) 23
Pacific Islands 102, 105, 111
Pacific and Orient *see* P & O
Panama canal 111
Parry & Co. 51
Pates, Sir Percy 182
Pease, Sir Joseph 36
Peat (W. B.) & Co. 157
Persia (ship) 91
Persian Gulf/Persia 181, 203
    1874–1894 18, 21–2
    1894–1914 53, 54, 66
    1914–1918 100, 108
    1918–1932 132, 133, 139, 148,
        154
Philipps, Sir Owen 114, 132
pilferage 22
Pioneer, The 141
Plender, Lord 127
P & O (Pacific and Orient) 9, 204
    1874–1894 17, 19, 21, 24, 29
    1894–1914 51, 54, 59, 87
    merger with BI 49, 67–72, 90,
        188
    1914–1918 89–115, 118–20
    1918–1932 121–54, 167, 169, 177,
        183, 186—96 *passim*,
        199–201
P & O Banking Corporation 123–4,
    131, 144, 152, 163, 165,
    167, 204
Port Commissioners 16
Port and Transport Committee
    118
Post Office 175, 176
profit-sharing scheme 124, 141–2,
    145
profits/remittances/earnings 189,
    190–1, 200–2
    1874–1894 14, 19, 20, 25–8
    1894–1914 51–3, 54, 70, 72, 75–6
    1914–1918 89–91, 93–113 *passim*,
        119–20
    1918–1932 121–2, 125–6, 128,
        130, 134, 137–43, 145, 152–3
    see also investment
protection 18, 41, 194–5
public expenditure cuts *see* Geddes

public life of M
   in India (1874–1894) 31–48
  as plenipotentiary and
    government
  watchdog (1894–1914) 73–88
  during First World War 89–120
  post-war retrenchment and
    disillusionment (1918–1932)
    155–85
Punch 156

railways 95, 151
  1874–1894 15, 24, 33, 34
  1894–1914 81, 82, 83–4, 87
Ramchandra, Shivram 23–4
Ranchi (ship) 143
Rawalpindi (ship) 142, 143, 146–7
Razmak (ship) 140
Reading, Lord 196
recreation and sport 20–1, 46
Registration of Ships Bill (India) 40
remittances *see* profits
requisitioned ships in wartime 91,
    118, 119, 133
Rewa (ship) 29
Rise, Captain 29
River Plate Railway Co. 26
Rivers Steam Navigation Co. 25,
    26, 27–8, 61, 203
Rohilla (ship) 90
Rothschild family 83, 201
Rover (M's yacht) 149, 186, 198,
    199, 201
Royal Air Force 156, 174–5
Royal Bank of Scotland 62, 203
Royal Mail Group 95, 114, 132,
    142, 149, 160, 191
Russell, T. M. 16, 19, 25
Russell/Lithgow (company) 63
Russia 41, 45, 78, 194, 195

sale of ex-enemy shipping 158–9
Salisbury, Lord 76
Salsette (ship) 68, 140
Sanderson, Harold 114
Satow, Ernest 80
Scandinavia 50, 128, 150
Scindia Line 133, 144

Scoble, Sir A. 39–40
Scotland 1–2, 5–8, 32, 197–9
Scott, Sir Walter 5
Seafield (ship) 7
Selfridge, Gordon 165
Shanks, James 26, 32
Shanks, Jane Paterson *see* Mackay,
    Jeannie
Shanks (Alexander) & Sons 5–6
shareholding *see* investment
Shaw, Alexander 101, 121, 126–8,
    134–5, 146, 148–9, 186, 191–
    2, 200
Shaw, Savill & Albion 97, 114, 160
Sheng-Ta-jen 77, 78–80
Shepherd Shuster (company) 51
shipbuilding
  1894–1914 63–5
  1914–1918 93, 100, 112, 114
  1918–1932 127, 128, 129–30, 132,
    133, 135
Shipowners' Parliamentary
    Committee 128
shipping *see* preliminary note to
    index
Shipping, Ministry of 106, 132, 133,
    135, 158, 159–60, 169, 184,
    194
Silley Weir (company) 110–11
silver standard 18, 41–6
Sim, John 7
Sim, William Mackay 133
Simon, Sir John and son 200
Smith Mackenzie (company) 133
Smith's (Bank) 165–6
Smiths (Howard) (company) 58
Snowden, Lord 196
son-in-law *see* Shaw, Alexander
South Africa, 9, 129, 142, 144, 164,
    174
South America 92
Sovereign of the Seas (ship) 4
Soviet Union *see* Russia
special funds 122–3
Spectator, The 169, 179
sport 20–1, 46
Standard Shipbuilding &
    Engineering Co. Ltd 100

Stanley, Venetia 86
Steel-Maitland, A. H. 106
Stephen, Frederic John 63–, 100
Stephen (Alexander) & Sons Ltd.
     63–4, 111
Stock Exchange 166, 186
Strathaird (ship) 150
Strathnaver (ship) 148, 150
Strick Line 124, 139, 152, 190
strikes and labour unrest 51–3, 54,
     57, 134, 136, 142–3
Sturmey, S. G. 150
Suez Canal 16, 37–8, 48, 67, 92,
     118, 142, 148, 153, 159, 190,
     203
Suez Canal Co. 37, 118, 142, 153,
     190, 203
super tax 167–8
Supply, Ministry of 156, 184
Sutherland, Sir Thomas 67–72, 90–
     2, 94, 101
Swann & Kennedy (Messrs)
     (company) 39

Takada (ship) 144
Tallack, Sir Hugh Mackay 199
Tasmanian Steamship Co. 102
Tata, Sir Jamsedji and family 187,
     192
taxation *see* income tax
Taylor, A. J. P. 169
tea 25, 26, 61–2
telegraphs 34
telephone 47
textile industry in India 34, 48
   see also Binny
Thames Iron Works Co. 38
Thomas, J. H. 145
Tibet 34
Tigris and Euphrates 81, 84–5, 87,
     153, 181–2, 203
Tillett, Ben 161
Times, The 130, 136, 167, 174, 187
trade *see* preliminary note to index
Trade Facilities Acts 142, 191
tramway 38
Transport, Ministry of 172
turboelectric ships 144, 150

Turkey 84–5
Turner, Sir Montague 132
Turner (of Mackinnon Mackenzie)
     39–40, 55
Turner Morrison (company) 54
typewriter 47

Umeta (ship) 91
Union Bank 115, 165–6
Union Castle Line 9, 92, 129, 160
Union Company of New Zealand
     59
   1914–1918 96, 98, 101–3, 109, 119
   1918–1932 123, 125, 140, 147, 191
United States 44, 92, 111, 129, 136,
     150
   1918–1932 162, 168, 177, 187, 191
Upper Assam Team Company 25,
     26, 61–2
Usines du Rhône 157

Vasna (ship) 100
Velocity (ship) 3, 6
Verney, Sir Harry 115, 116–17
Viceroy of India (ship) 144–5, 147,
     150
viceroyalty of India
   M almost offered 86–7, 197
   see also Lansdowne
Viceroy's Legislative Council 11, 31,
     39–41, 45, 177, 188

Waltons (company) 71
War, First World 89–120, 158–9,
     175, 189, 193, 195, 196–7
Wartime Shipping Committee
     158–9
Washington conference 172
Webb Sidney, 165
Webster, Francis 8–9
weights and measures, Indian 39
Weir of Eastwood, Lord 174
Weir (Silley) (company) 110–11
West Cumberland Iron and Steel
     Co. 38
West Indies 104, 111
Westminster Gazette 129
White Star Line 114, 129, 160

wife of M *see* Mackay, Jeannie
Wilcox (P & O founder) 123
Wills family 201
Wilson (Thomas), Sons & Co. 9
Witch of the Wave (ship) 7
Wonkhaus (company) 53
Workshops, Government

Committee on 81, 82–3, 87, 193
Wyandra (ship) 64–5
Wylie, E. D. 16, 19
Wyreema (ship) 65

Yokohama Specie Bank 152
York, Duke and Duchess of 141